Music and Altered States

of related interest

Music Therapy and Neurological Rehabilitation
Performing Health
Edited by David Aldridge
ISBN 1 84310 302 8

Case Study Designs in Music Therapy
Edited by David Aldridge
ISBN 1 84310 140 8

Music Therapy Research and Practice in Medicine
From Out of the Silence
David Aldridge
ISBN 1 85302 296 9

Music Therapy in Dementia Care
Edited by David Aldridge
ISBN 1 85302 776 6

Music Therapy in Palliative Care
New Voices
Edited by David Aldridge
ISBN 1 85302 739 1

Spirituality, Healing and Medicine
Return to the Silence
David Aldridge
ISBN 1 85302 554 2

Health, the Individual, and Integrated Medicine
Revisiting an Aesthetic of Health Care
David Aldridge
ISBN 1 84310 232 3

Music Therapy in Context
Music, Meaning and Relationship
Mercédès Pavlicevic
Preface by Colwyn Trevarthen
ISBN 1 85302 434 1

Music and Altered States
Consciousness, Transcendence, Therapy and Addiction

Edited by David Aldridge and Jörg Fachner

Jessica Kingsley Publishers
London and Philadelphia

Figure 2.1 on p.18 from Fischer, R. (1971) 'A Cartography of the ecstatic and meditative states.' *Science* 174, p.898. Copyright © 1971 AAAS. Reprinted with permission.

Table 2.1 on p.20 from Rouget, G. (1985) *Music and Trance: A Theory of the Relations Between Music and Possession*. Chicago, IL: University of Chicago Press. Copyright © University of Chicago 1985. Reproduced with permission.

Figures 6.2, 6.3, 6.4, 6.5 and 6.6 on pp.76–80 from Shu, S. (1997) *Musical Folklore of Adyghs in Notation of G. Mkontsevich, Maikop*. Reproduced with kind permission from Schumaf Schabanowitsch Shu.

Figure 7.1 on p.84 from Keidel, W.D. (1975) *Kurzgefaßtes Lehrbuch der Physiologie*. Reprinted with permission from Georg Thieme Verlag.

First published in 2006
by Jessica Kingsley Publishers
116 Pentonville Road
London N1 9JB, UK
and
400 Market Street, Suite 400
Philadelphia, PA 19106, USA

www.jkp.com

Library of Congress Cataloging in Publication Data
A CIP catalog record for this book is available from the Library of Congress

British Library Cataloguing in Publication Data
A CIP catalogue record for this book is available from the British Library

ISBN-13: 978 1 84310 373 8
ISBN-10: 1 84310 373 7

Printed and bound in Great Britain by
Athenaeum Press, Gateshead, Tyne and Wear

Contents

List of Figures

List of Tables

List of Sounds

The sound files cited in this book can be downloaded from the 'Music Therapy World' website – www.musictherapyworld.net/ASC – or from the publishers's website – www.jkp.com/catalogue/book.php/isbn/1-84310-373-7.

4.1   Monotonous drumming; 210 BPM; recorded from synthesizer
8.1   Sound example from Ayahuasca healing session
8.2   Sound example from Ayahuasca healing session
9.1   Polyrhythmic harp music with polyrhythmic clapping
9.2   Polyrhythmic harp music with horizontal and vertical mirroring
9.3   Mouth-bow music
9.4   Bamboo canes music 1
9.5   Bamboo canes music 2
9.6   Bamboo canes music 3
9.7   Bake music
9.8   Balafon music 1
9.9   Balafon music 2
14.1 Meditation from David Aldridge and Lucanne Magill recorded during a therapy session in New York

Chapter 1

Music, Consciousness and Altered States

David Aldridge

Music and consciousness are things we do. And we can do these things together.

Music is what we do together when we play together as musicians, or partake as listening audiences or when we engage in that sublime activity of dancing. When I write of music here, and as we will see in the rest of the book, I should maybe be referring to *musics*. The notion of one universal music, or some high concept of Music, is not applicable here. Being a passionate traditional folk-singer, an unrepentant addict of early rock and roll, having spent my formative years immersed in rhythm and blues and many adult years ensconced in dark places with juke boxes, then my taste can only be described as low, rather than high, and eclectic, rather than discerning. Throughout the chapters we will be returning to music but each will present its own variety of music, and each be located in its own setting.

While we read about personal responses to music, we will also see that musics are also communal activities that bring people together. While being personally expressive, they may also be socially expressive. These forms of expression are achieved in performance; in some cultures those forms will be fixed as conventions; in many cultures the actual making of music is something that challenges convention. My earliest recollections are of my grandfather teaching cornet or rehearsing with his brass quartet round the fire at home. Music was something we did like eating and drinking. It was social in its rehearsal and on the bandstand in the park on

Sunday afternoon, it was communal in its manifestation. For those not having the privilege of knowing British brass band music, it was strongly connected to identifiable working communities and some of its venues were municipal parks where a bandstand was provided for community enjoyment and musicians were recruited from the working communities.[1]

Achieving con-sciousness, from the Latin *con* (with) and *scire* (to know), is the central activity of human knowledge. At the heart of the word is a concept of mutuality, knowing with others. Our consciousness is a mutual activity; it is performed. Consciousness is also a means of personal knowing, our self-consciousness. We have interior understandings that are privatized but we also have experiences that are external and socialized. Balancing our internal lives with our social performance is a necessary activity of everyday living.

Performing both music and consciousness are potent ways of achieving this balance of unity of the external and the internal. Music itself has been used in varying forms to achieve changes in consciousness.

While we talk in this book of altered states of consciousness, it is important to state that this position of states to be altered assumes a steady stable state of everyday consciousness, a normative description. Personally, I challenge this normative account, just as the notion of one music is questionable. Maybe we have to consider that our states of consciousness are constantly shifting, sometimes steadily and sometimes abruptly. We are in a steady stream of influences both internal and external from which we filter a state that to most of us appears to be steady. A normative understanding of consciousness is perhaps a cultural sop to keep us stable and compliant. Practically, it offers an everyday reality as a consensual state: consensual, in terms of relating our activities and senses to those of another person, voluntarily, with choice in a legal sense, yet involuntarily in a physiological sense. Learning to alter our states of consciousness at will can promote our voluntary consensuality. A better understanding of those transient states of consciousness, and the ability to rise above them in terms of transcendence has been the central feature of many Eastern religions.

---

1   Tia DeNora writes also that music was originally designed to be heard in social contexts when she discusses music in everyday life (DeNora 2000).

Sense is made, it is an activity. In the terms of both my previous work and this book, sensing, too, is performance. We literally make sense of our world in an active way. When we perform music we are making and listening; this is a dynamic cycle of activity. We are not passive organisms but constantly in creation. Culture, too, is a performance and an extension of our biology. New developments in neurophysiology show that exposure to language develops mirror motor neurons when an active sound is perceived (Westermann and Reck Miranda 2004), and language evolves from gestures (Corballis 2003). It is possible for us to know what is happening in the other person, as intersubjectivity, when we resonate with them. The activity of neurons is referred to as firing, and it is this mutual firing that we find in performance. And on the basis of this we can reflect on what is happening to the other person when we perform together. The significance of this understanding is that when we talk about consciousness we are essentially talking about intersubjectivity. Making music together is an active way of changing consciousness that is embodied, which is why dance has been such a powerful medium for cultural and personal expression.

We also see that human activity is a performance. Consciousness, or 'knowing-with', is a dialogical activity. We can speak of the ecology of dialogic communication as a mutual dynamic performance. Rhythm is a substrate of this ecology, not fixed but dynamic and flowing, and is the basis of music in changing states of consciousness.

Performative development

I use the performative metaphor in my writings to get away from the mechanical concept of chronological time and a body that can be repaired like a mechanism. We are more like works of art in progress, or better expressed as *working art* in progress. This has implications for the performance of our development. Development is not simply a process that takes place in babies and small children. We develop throughout our lives, as do our states of consciousness.

When we think about development, we often consider this in linear progress like climbing a ladder upwards for most of our lives with a rapid decline at the end. However, maybe our lives are not so simply performed in a linear progression. Sometimes we regress, to make leaps forward. If we release ourselves from the idea of a developmental ladder of progress, then we can open ourselves to a constellation of stages through which we move during our life course. And stages are those places where performances can take place. Each stage will be accompanied by an altered state of consciousness.

Participative performance

Participative performances are traditionally the basis for healing rituals that include music. Changed states of consciousness are necessary for the healing endeavour. Music as an agent in healing, music in healing rituals and music therapy in cultures of care are all vibrant activities that we can be involved in. We have resources of knowledge that can be shared and pooled. There is no one singular way of understanding this multiplicity of knowledge. Fortunately we are developing research cultures of tolerance that see human knowledge as being many-sided. Together we can orchestrate our knowings into a symphony of wisdom. In this sense, health is a performance that can be achieved. Health is not simply a singular performance; it is performed with others. When we perform together we can begin to understand each other, even without speaking.

An altered state of consciousness differs from baseline or normal consciousness and is often identified with a brain state that differs significantly from the brain state at baseline or normal consciousness. However, it is not the brain state itself that constitutes an altered state. The brain state is an objective matter, but it should not be equated with an electroencephalogram (EEG) reading or a magnetic resonance image (MRI). If that were so then sneezing, coughing or sleeping would be altered states. Such images, or traces, reveal brain activity or inactivity, not consciousness. We can easily see that changes in the brain occur through modern technology, but this technology does not tell us what the person is thinking about or why.

Our baseline brain states are defined by the presence of two subjective characteristics: a psychological sense of a self at the centre of my perception and a sense that this self is identified with my body. States of consciousness where we lose our sense of identity with the body or with our perceptions are altered states of consciousness. Such states may be spontaneous and brought about by a variety of means: trauma, sleep disturbance, sensory challenges, neurochemical imbalance, epileptic seizure, or fever. They may also be induced by social behaviour, such as frenzied dancing or chanting. Finally, they may be induced by ingesting psychotropic drugs, as we will see later.

However, these states are representative of a personal self-consciousness. What we may need is to go beyond this, as all mystical traditions encourage us, to altered states of consciousness where we lose our sense of self and attain that sense of unity with others. This is a difficult message in cultures where we look only to develop ourselves and attain personal states of knowledge. But we have to ask ourselves, for what purpose is consciousness (Ornstein 1996)? Simply for our own benefit? Although a key element of our survival has been to develop a personal consciousness that separates the self from others and has been critical in the development of modern technological culture, we need a holistic consciousness that complements the personal and analytic approach when we consider the situations that affect humanity as a whole. Ornstein (1996) argues for a mode of consciousness that considers relationship rather than the egocentric self.

Religion, spirituality and states

Many religions identify the ideal state as an altered state of consciousness: losing one's body and one's self, uniting with some sort of Divine Being. The Eastern traditions also encourage a sense of mastery in that we can go beyond fluctuations of consciousness and change states of consciousness. The means of achieving these changes are sometimes meditation but often include activities like music, dance, specialized movements and postures that break the train of sequential verbal thinking. The emphasis here is not on one mode of consciousness or another, but a mastery of varying modes that brings us to a unity of knowledge. This is in effect an extended consciousness where we unite the analytic and the intuitive and has been at the heart of varying spiritual traditions. Spiritual traditions, when made manifest in religious forms located in their varying localized cultural contexts, are simply ways for us to understand the purpose of our lives. Those forms need to be constantly revised in performance and informed through intuition if they are to maintain any present-day reality. That is why many religious forms feel redundant or restrictive because they have achieved a verbal dogma that fails to encourage the intuitive wisdom of current performances. Once religions, or sciences, begin to say that this is the only way of gaining knowledge, then the way to personal experiential knowledge is obstructed.

The same thing goes for understanding music and how it works in performance. We need to play different music in differing contexts with different people to understand what remains in performing and what is culturally specific.

Change

One of the difficulties of a self-centred consciousness is that all attention becomes directed to the self, when what we may need is to direct attention away from ourselves. In the esoteric traditions, the everyday self is set aside as unreliable. Humility and service are emphasized to divert us away from ourselves. Attempts at expanding our own consciousness for our own sake is, from the perspectives of such traditions, merely an extension of self-indulgence.

We hear how people achieve a catalogue of altered states or a range of exotic yoga postures, but so what? We may achieve various forms of getting high through drugs or music, strenuous activities of breathing or fantastic feats of imagery. But what is the purpose of these posturings if they are simply an extended form of self-indulgence? What we may need is to develop an awareness of a social consciousness for the development of humankind.

Differing forms of consciousness serve the extension and integration of knowledge. We do not achieve this 'by an instant cultural transplant, by a sentimental journey to other cultures, by adopting the habits of an ancient tradition, or the dress of the Indian holy man' (Ornstein 1996, p.81). In the end, we have to ask what an extended consciousness brings for all its talk of states and musics. Our everyday lives go on. We live, we die. How we actively align ourselves in the world in performing our lives with others is what will distinguish us as having changed. This is a simple reflection of the saying 'By their fruits, you will know them.' Those fruits are carried by the tree of knowledge.

Chapter 2

Music and Altered States
of Consciousness: An Overview

Jörg Fachner

Altered states of consciousness

> Our normal waking consciousness, rational consciousness as we call it,
> is but one special type of consciousness, whilst all about it, parted from
> the filmiest of screens, there lies potential forms of consciousness
> entirely different. (James 1902, p.228)

The term 'altered states of consciousness' implies that there is a consciousness that is unchanged, or 'normal'. Tart, as well Dittrich (1996) or James
(1902) discuss consciousness as a complex psycho-physiological system of
states whereby our so-called 'normal' consciousness is only a specific construction in the sense of a 'specialized tool' for everyday purposes (see Tart
1975, p.3). With this tool, we find orientation in our social and physical
environment but consciousness may be intentionally changed and altered
by various influencing factors. According to the 'Thomas Theorem', there
are no altered states of consciousness: 'If men define situations as real, they
are real in their consequences' (Thomas 1927). There is a continuous flow
of changing situations and situative definitions of persons in various
contexts where intensities of conscious states take changing forms dependent on the individual's attention, intention and situation, as well as his
cultural background.

Nevertheless, everybody experiences altered states of consciousness;
that is, in a waking but altered state, we are aware of changes that may be

observed by others as well (Roth 1994). Tassi, from a neuropsychological stance, differentiates between, on one hand, 'physiological states of consciousness' depending on spontaneously changing levels of vigilance, arousal and biological rhythms, and on the other, intended and therefore 'evoked states of consciousness' induced by psychotropic drugs, meditation, sensory deprivation, etc. (Tassi and Muzet 2001, p.185). This notion of a personal intention to evoke altered states of consciousness positively stresses the voluntary character of an induced change, but disregards states that are changed because of pathology or traumatic events. Dittrich further differentiates between sleeping and waking consciousness and coins the term 'altered states of waking consciousness' to distinguish 'states of consciousness in sleep as e.g. REM dreams or related psychic activities' (Dittrich 1996, p.1). To distinguish a normal waking state from an altered state of consciousness Glicksohn (1993) discusses personal modes of meaning during altered state cognition and stresses that altered states of consciousness are primary cognitive events. He denies a definition that reduces altered states of consciousness to vigilance changes only. An altered state of consciousness is 'any mental state...recognized...as representing a sufficient deviation in subjective experience...from certain general norms... during alert, waking consciousness' (Ludwig in Glicksohn 1993, p.2).

Ludwig (1966) describes the following 'general characteristics of altered states of consciousness': alterations in thinking, disturbed time sense, loss of control, change in emotional expression and body image, perceptual distortions, change in meaning or significance, a sense of the ineffable, feelings of rejuvenation and hypersuggestibility.

Dittrich (1998), in his international comparison of altered states of consciousness, finds that independent of the stimulus, there are five core experiences of altered states of consciousness: Oceanic Boundlessness (OSE), Dread of Ego Dissolution (AIA), Visionary Restructuralization (VUS), Auditive Alteration (AVE) and Vigilance Reduction (VIR).

Measuring instruments and cartography of altered states of consciousness

Cartographies of the variety of human experiences (Fischer 1971; Fischer 1976; Scharfetter 1995) and topographies (Grof 1993) of altered states of consciousness have also been suggested for scientific and therapeutic purposes. Fischer maps deviations from 'normal' conscious states and divides them into a continuum of ergotropic (exciting) and trophotropic (damping) states.

> Varieties of conscious states mapped on a perception–hallucination continuum of increasing ergotropic arousal (left) and a perception–meditation continuum of increasing trophotropic arousal (right). These levels of hyper- and hypoarousal are interpreted by man as normal, creative, psychotic and ecstatic states (left), and Zazen and samadhi (right). The loop connecting ecstasy and samadhi represents the rebound from ecstasy to samadhi, which is observed in response to intense ergotrophic excitation. The numbers 35 to 7 on the perception–hallucination continuum are Goldstein *et al.*'s (1963) coefficient of variation, specifying the decrease in variability of the EEG amplitude with increasing ergotropic arousal. The numbers 26 to 4 on the perception–meditation continuum, on the other hand, refer to those beta, alpha, and theta EEG waves (measured in hertz) that predominate during, but are not specific to, these states. (Green, Green and Walters, cited in Fischer 1971, p.898)

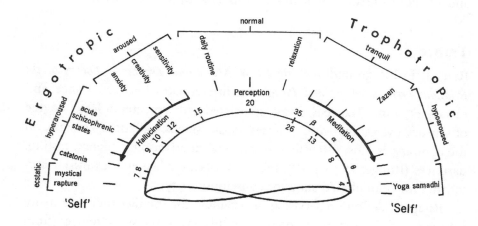

Figure 2.1 Varieties of consciousness states according to Fischer (1971). Reprinted with permission from Fischer, R. (1971) 'A Cartography of the ecstatic and meditative states.' Science 174, p.898. Copyright © 1971 AAAS.

Fischer writes[1]: 'The mapping follows along two continua: the perceptive–hallucinatory continuum of increasing central nervous (ergotropic)
excitement, and the perceptive–meditative continuum of increasing
(trophotropic) damping' (Fischer 1998, p.48). 'Along the two continua, the
sensory/motoric ratio increases. This means: the further you go along one
continuum, the less will it be possible to verify the sensory element through
random motoricity.' (Fischer 1998, p.51)

Psychometrics

Interview manuals and tests have also been designed for a psychometric
evaluation of the experience of altered states of consciousness: Phenomen-
ology of Consciousness Inventory (PCI) by Pekala (1991); 5D-APZ (ques-
tionnaire on abnormal psychic states) by Dittrich (Dittrich 1996; Dittrich,
Lamparter and Maurer 2002); Stanford Hypnotic Susceptibility Scale: form
A+B+C (SHSS: A–C) by Weitzenhoffer and Hilgard (1959; 1963);
Harvard Group Scale of Hypnotic Susceptibility (HGSHS) by Shor and
Orne (1962; 1963); and during some drug investigations the Subjective
Drug Effects Questionnaire (SDEQ) by Katz, Waskow and Olsson (1968)
and Waskow, Olsson, Salzman and Katz (1970) has been used.

Trance

Rouget, in his groundbreaking book *Music and Trance: A Theory of the
Relations between Music and Possession*, differentiates between trance and
ecstasy. For him, 'Trance is always associated with a greater or lesser degree
of sensory over-stimulation – noises, music, smells, agitation – ecstasy, on
the contrary, is most often tied to sensorial deprivation – silence, fasting,
darkness' (Rouget 1985, p.10). Table 2.1 lists the subcategories and characteristics for both altered states of consciousness types.

Rouget's definition serves as an example for the fact there are many
different and, in part, contradictory definitions of the term 'trance' (from
the Latin *transire* for 'passing through') or 'ecstasy' (from the Latin *exstasis*
for 'to be out of one's head') in the literature (Meszaros, Szabó and Csako

---

1   Author's translation from German

Table 2.1 Differentiation of ecstasy and trance according to Rouget 1985, p.11

Ecstasy	Trance
Immobility	Movement
Silence	Noise
Solitude	In company
No crisis	Crisis
Sensory deprivation	Sensory over-stimulation
Recollection	Amnesia
Hallucination	No hallucination

Reproduced with permission from Rouget, G. (1985) Music and Trance: A Theory of the Relations Between Music and Possession. *Chicago, IL: University of Chicago Press.* Copyright © University of Chicago 1985

2002; Pekala and Kumar 2000; Rouget 1985; Winkelman 1986). This reflects the difficulties in defining distinct topics of altered states of consciousness, especially when facing altered states of consciousness in the field of music. Trance seems to have a more direct relationship to the body, its functions and vigilance states, while ecstasy seems to be more concerned with mental activity like meditation and contemplation.

Various depths of trance can be observed associated with many motor components: for example, the 'Mevlevi Sema' in Sufi dervishes, which can be distinguished from passive trance (or *enstasis* as defined by Fischer 1971), or trance with few motor elements, as in classical hypnosis (Hess and Rittner 1996a). This passive–active spectrum is reflected in Fischer's cartography of ergotrophic and trophotropic states as outlined above. The trance spectrum reaches from everyday and mini trances, e.g. daydreaming, over-hypnoid trance in autogenous training, or the religious trance of a Tibetan oracle, to obsession trance where for a short period human bodies are obsessed, or possessed, by other beings like spirits or gods (Oohashi *et al.* 2002; Rouget 1977; Rouget 1985). A characteristic of intensive trance and obsession trance in particular is subsequent amnesia, which means the 'obsessed' do not remember anything, and experience deep psycho-physiological personality changes for the duration of the trance. The same phenomenon occurs in hypnotic amnesia.

Various inductive techniques like relaxation, imagination, or motor activities produce an increasing focus of attention on inner processes and narrow down the field of perception aiming at a more intensive introversion with a simultaneous exclusion of external factors.

Trance, music and ritual

Trance during rituals in ethnic ceremonies has been often associated with music. In the late 1960s, Rouget (1985) analysed ethnographies on the use of music and trance and concluded that there is no universal law that determines the relationship of music and trance. Trance is a context-dependent phenomenon relating to the cultural meaning of symbols and action during ceremonies. Every trance occurs in a ritual context and receives its power from the particular music used during the different progressions of such ceremonies. The function of music is to provide atmosphere, to evoke identification processes in ceremony groups and to induce a trance (invocation) or to accompany or to lead a trance. This happens according to cultural beliefs, and therefore music and trance are connected in as many ways as there are cultural beliefs. There are no common features of music causing trance. All trance music varies culturally, no matter whether it is melody (see Rouget 1985, pp.94–9), analysis of invocation songs for certain spirits, or rhythm. 'No rhythmic system is specifically related to trance' (Rouget 1985, p.317).

Rouget differentiates emotional, communal and shamanic trance (Rouget 1985, p.315ff). Emotional trance has the most direct relation to music, because it draws its power out of a high degree of correspondence between words and music, a sophisticated art of poetry and music. To create such a relationship in perfect harmony overwhelms the listener (Rouget 1985, p.25).

In communal trance, music induces or maintains trance through the use of increasing and decreasing rhythms and volume: further, specifically sung religious hymns, songs, spells and formula. 'Music – singing and dancing combined – seems to have the function of creating excitation' (Rouget 1985, p.317).

Shamanism uses specific body techniques as a repertoire of biological methods to establish communication with gods or spirits.

> To shamanize, in other words to sing and dance, is as much a corporeal technique as a spiritual exercise. Insofar as he is at the same time singer, instrumentalist, and dancer, the shaman, among all practitioners of trance, should be seen as the one who by far makes the most complete use of music. (Rouget 1985, p.319)

In shamanic trance the function of music is similar to that in theatre, loaded with symbolic and emotional qualities. Singing as a communication with the audience and as an invocation of spirits transcends the imaginary world of the shaman. It is mostly songs, ceremonial or mundane, which induce trance. As Eliade (1954) points out, the shaman's voice imitates animal, ancestor or nature sounds with an attitude of incantation or is symbolized in the use of falsetto. The shaman goes on his trip to the spirits and gains control over them, incorporating such procedures during the shamanic trance in front of those present at the ritual. Music creates the context, which fosters the onset of trance, regulates the form and process of trance and makes it more foreseeable and controllable. As it is not possible to produce an automatic onset of trance with the use of music and dance, some shamans tune in by taking drugs at the beginning of their trip into the other worlds. This happens both in order to remember their shamanic crisis more intensively and to be more sensitive to any encounters and experiences with spirits, and to maintain control over such processes (Rouget 1985, p.319).

Emotional trance develops out of listening to poems and music, whereby the invocatory character of a guided communal trance and the incantatory music of a shamanic trance act via the corporeal techniques of theatre, music and dance.

In obsession, playing music for the obsessed induces trance. The obsessed has to identify with the culturally mediated, different form of God, to represent this identification during dance and, possibly, to entice the invoked spirit through characteristic movement. During obsession, the spirit incorporates in the body of the obsessed person and reveals itself to other participants, in a ceremonial theatricality, through figurative or mimic dances. Here – much more than in other trance forms – music and dance serve as means of communication between the obsessed, the attendees of the ceremony and the gods. During obsession it is believed that gods or spirits might sing or play through the obsessed (Rouget 1985, pp.35, 103, 105–108).

The most common musical features (see Brandl 1993) during such ceremonies are: continuous accelerations, mostly in tempo and volume; a focused use of accelerando and crescendo (see Rouget 1985, pp.82–86), but also extreme constancy and monotony during ecstasy; long duration (over hours); simple forms with minimal variations and many repetitions; bordun or ostinati; no exact motives but step-by-step progressions; a play around tones often with slow glissandi and a narrow tonal range. Occasionally, there are complex parts and crossings of voices, which do not allow a unifying resolution. A constant timbre, low, pulsating structures, but also sharp high-pitched modulations (suspension, acoustic 'roughness') seem to be appropriate and support trance induction. Acoustic triggers of trance are mostly certain transitory processes and accentuations, as well as slow, constantly increasing and decreasing amplitude curves.

> There is no mystery to it at all…if we must seek for an explanation of this, it might be found in the overriding power of a certain conjunction of emotion and imagination. This is the source from which trance springs. Music does nothing more than socialize it and enable it to attain its full development. (Rouget 1985, p.326)

Hypnosis, suggestibility and trance

The literature on hypnosis frequently uses altered states of consciousness synonymously with trance or hypnosis. But it should be noted that hypnosis in this context is the way into a state of trance while trance defines the altered states of consciousness.

In the discussion of hypnosis, Meszaros *et al.* (2002, p.502) distinguish between 1) hypnotic susceptibility, 2) the hypnotic context and 3) changes in subjective experience. Hypnotic susceptibility appears to be an individual trait and may be determined quantitatively and qualitatively through psychometric tests. The question of whether trance is a state or a personal quality, whether hypnotic susceptibility is accompanied by individual suggestibility or depends on attitudes or factors of state or context, reflects the state–trait discussion in psychology and is addressed in the discussion and research on hypnosis (Brady and Stevens 2000; Kirsch 1997; Meszaros *et al.* 2002; Pekala and Kumar 2000; Pekala and Pekala 2000).

Context influences subjective experience in altered states of consciousness and in connection with these is discussed as influences of set (psychosocial context, personal memories, moods and attitudes) and setting (temporal–spatial, symbolic and physical context) (Eisner 1997; Rätsch 1992b; Zinberg 1984).

Altered subjective experiences may be explored through tests, narrative inquiry, standardized interviews and correlated neurophysiologic changes as accessible through electroencephalograms (EEGs) (see Fachner 2004a). Available EEG studies on hypnosis do not directly address music and trance but analyse individual differences in the trance experience (Brady and Stevens 2000; Crawford 1994; Guttmann 1990; Jaffe and Toon 1980; Sabourin et al. 1990). Persons with high hypnotic susceptibility show increased theta activity in frontal brain regions even in rest EEGs (Brady and Stevens 2000; Graffin, Ray, and Lundy 1995), which suggests a cognitive mechanism of selective suppression (inhibition) of certain cognitive functions during trance (Park et al. 2002). This is accompanied by a focusing of attention and increased hypnagogic imaginations (Schacter 1977). Hypnagogic states refer to dream states beginning before sleep, while hypnopompic states define the transition from sleep to wakefulness.

Hypnosis and music

Mesmer used music (mostly a glass harp) to stage his demonstrations of hypnosis and therapy sessions (Bowers, 1983). For our purposes of therapy and research here:

1   music in hypnosis may serve as a context factor of limited effect (see above) to support induction and maintenance and influence hypnotic susceptibility (Biasutti 1990; Maurer et al. 1997; Meszaros et al. 2002)

2   in the debate on susceptibility to hypnosis, music is discussed as an important factor for the ability of absorption (exclusion of surrounding factors and more intensive concentration on imaginative stimuli, e.g. music) in highly hypnotizable persons in hypnosis (Hilgard 1974; Nagy and Szabó 2003; Snodgrass and Lynn 1989; Tellegen and Atkinson 1974);

3   music and post-hypnotic suggestions may be used for
     therapeutic suggestions, to enhance mood, creativity and artistic
     performance (Biasutti 1990; Kelly 1993; Mellgren 1979).

Hypnotic susceptibility, context and monotonous drumming

As repetition of simple and monotonous sound and rhythm to induce
trance has been discussed, monotonous drumming has become the focus of
various experiments. A test group of 29 people without previous hypnotic
experience were to be sent on a 'shaman trip' through the underworld,
according to Harner (1990), in a dark room for 15 minutes while listening
to synthesized monotonous drumming (210 bpm). A comparison of the
hypnotic scores (SHSS/B) between verbal induction and monotonous
drumming revealed that drums make subjects as suggestible ($r=0.89$;
$p<0.001$) as verbal induction (see Meszaros *et al.* 2002, p.506).[1]

   In a study based on these findings, Szabó (see Chapter 4 in this book)
tested participants' subjective experience with a computer-based content
analysis of verbal reports after sessions. He found direct or indirect links to
rhythmic activity in the experienced imaginations using drums. In comparison with the same setting without drums, however, the experience had a
different quality and rhythm played a noticeably smaller role.

   Maurer *et al.* (1997) used Pekala's Phenomenology of Consciousness
Inventory (PCI) to test 206 persons who listened to monotonous live
drumming prior to or after hypnosis induction for 15 minutes. They were
asked to reflect their experience of the last four minutes of drumming with
the PCI. These last four minutes are considered as particularly important
for trance induction (see Maxfield 1992). An analysis of the Harvard Group
Scale of Hypnotic Susceptibility (HGSHS) showed that drumming prior to
or after hypnosis induction did not influence objective depth of trance. The
subjective depth, however, as measurable with the PCI was more pronounced when drumming preceded hypnosis. Those persons with high

---

1   'r' is the multiple correlations coefficient, and measures the degree of
     correlation, here between drums and suggestibility. 'p' is the probability
     value, here the degree of probability that change of consciousness state is
     induced by drumming.

scores on both scales (PCI and HGSHS) reported in narrative interviews on their subjective experience of relaxation states and shaman impressions while listening to the drums (Maurer *et al.* 1997).

In a subsequent experiment with 47 inexperienced subjects, Meszaros *et al.* (2002) first determined their susceptibility to hypnosis, and then attempted to influence students' fear of examination with suggestions and relaxing music. He compared the scores of hypnotic susceptibility (HGSHS: A) and the depth of relaxation with a test (Relaxation Experience Questionnaire). He found that persons of high, medium, and low susceptibility to hypnosis had the same experience of relaxation, focused attention, altered consciousness and depth of experience while listening to relaxing music, subsequent suggestions and again relaxing music. However, significant differences ($p < 0.05$) between the three groups (particularly between high and medium degree of susceptibility) were found for the factors of imagination/hallucination (see Meszaros *et al.* 2002, p.510). A difference was found between the three groups in their preferences for the hypnotic setting. Highly susceptible persons preferred verbally induced hypnotic suggestion to reduce examination anxiety, whereas persons with low susceptibility tended to opt for relaxation through music. Consequently, context factors appear to be not significant for persons with high or medium susceptibility to hypnosis. In general, however, Meszaros concludes that the context of experiences in altered conscious states deserves particular attention.

Absorption

Snodgrass and Lynn (1989) looked for correlations between persons with high, medium and low susceptibility to hypnosis and their degree of imaginative absorption while listening to highly and less imaginative music. The imaginative quality of music considered important for hypnosis and imagination was first polarized with a rating procedure. A test group of 49 people categorized a total of 12 pieces of classical music as 'highly' or 'less imaginative'. They rated as highly imaginative Stravinsky's 'Danse Infernale' from *Firebird* and Mussorgsky's 'The hut of Baba Yaga' and 'Great Gate of Kiev'; and as less imaginative Handel's 'Sarabande' from the eleventh suite, and J. S. Bach's 'Kleine Fuge für die Orgel in G-moll'. They were also interviewed about their musical preferences and attitude to classical music. Irrespective of imaginative qualities, highly hypnotisable persons reported markedly more absorption than people with low susceptibility to hypnosis. In written reports of imaginative experiences, however, all the respondents revealed clearly higher imaginative performance with highly imaginative pieces compared to less imaginative music. Differences in imaginative performance were found between people with high hypnotic susceptibility while listening to highly imaginative music, but not with less imaginative music. Highly hypnotizable 'fans' of classical music showed significant (p<0.01) correlations between absorption and hypnotisability. Absorption scores correlated (r=0.57) with attitudes towards classical music. The qualities may also be interpreted as subjective identification performance in the course of the research process. 'It is possible that hypnotizable subjects, relative to low hypnotizables, may see themselves as hypnotically talented and possessing seemingly related abilities such as creativity, imaginative abilities and so forth' (Snodgrass and Lynn 1989, p.51).

Nagy and Szabó (2003) addressed the question of whether personal interest and involvement in music is a characteristic of individuals and determines their musical experience. The test group listened to classical music by Holst ('Venus','Mars'), easy listening by Kitaro, and techno music. Highly involved persons had more trance and altered states of consciousness experience compared to less involved persons who mainly reported memories and relaxation. Following Gabrielsson's (2001) classification scheme of categorizing emotional experience, Kitaro's music produced the most positive emotional statements and Holst produced regression, negative and conflicting emotions, while techno music evoked visual perceptions and movement. Intensity of involvement and musical style has a measurable influence on musical experience in this experiment.

Suggestions and improved musical performance

Kelly (1993) used individually preferred music with positive emotional attributes to couple desired emotional states in hypnosis. As a result of therapeutic suggestions, patients were able to hallucinate certain pieces of music. As a post-hypnotic effect, those pieces were intended to evoke the desired emotional states through an inner hallucination of the pieces of music coupled via suggestion; in the six case studies presented she appeared to have succeeded.

The physician Mellgren (1979) demonstrated in his hypnotherapy research that post-hypnotic suggestions may improve a musician's performance. He suggested to musicians in a light to medium trance that after waking up they would feel lighter and more secure and would play with confidence and inspiration. Prior to and after hypnosis a piece of music was recorded on tape and played to three independent critics without indication of the phase in which the piece was recorded. In 30 out of 36 cases, expert opinion concurred with that of the musician in regard to improved performance after post-hypnotic suggestions.

In 1900, Rachmaninoff was treated with hypnosis because he had a 'creative block'. After suggestions, in light trance, that indicated change and improvement, there followed, after a short period, an extremely creative phase. His piano concerto in C minor is dedicated to the hypnotherapist Nikolai Dahl (Walker 1979). Rhodes appears convinced that hypnosis gives singers, instrumentalists and actors a new personal perspective and better voice control.

Therapy, music and altered states of consciousness

Altered states of consciousness are also used within therapy. Applications of therapy-intended altered states of consciousness with music in single and group sessions are: 1) guided imagery while listening to music, 2) trance inductions with voice and instruments in receptive and/or active form, and 3) combinations of hypnotic techniques and music.

The unconscious, dreams and music

Walker (1979) reports compositions by Schumann, Stravinsky and Tartini that were heard by those composers in dreams and written down after waking up. Some compositions, however, were created after more or less chance events in the lives of Schoenberg, Haydn, Mahler and Manuel de Falla. Such occurrences caused a 'subconscious motivation' to process them creatively (Walker 1979). Diaz de Chumaceiro (1996) discusses the sudden and unintentional emergence of melodies with or without memories of texts on the background of Freud's 'Psychopathologie des Alltagslebens' (Freud 1904). Musical memories appear to emerge out of the subconscious in certain contexts and may be useful starting points for psychoanalysis or even keys to repressed complexes. For processes of transference and counter-transference in particular, the subconscious of both people involved in a therapeutic relationship may trigger memories, so that for example the therapist, in talking to the client, feels reminded of a song and realizes that this song is of specific relevance to the dialogue situation or the patient's state (Diaz de Chumaceiro 1996).

Coma, music and consciousness

Music also appears to be a successful way of entering into contact with patients with brain injuries or in coma. A characteristic of coma is unconsciousness. Nevertheless, the ability to feel and perceive and to distinguish – although to a smaller degree – (see Jones *et al.* 1994) acoustic stimuli remains possible; but the cognitive powers of the waking state are almost eliminated. Coma patients experience sounds on an intensive ward like a dream, but in a differentiated, psycho-emotional way, as may be seen from the following description: 'The sounds of the computer were ship sirens, the noises of hemofiltration were marching soldiers' (Gustorff and Hannich 2000, p.29).

Aldridge, Gustorff and Hannich (1990) describe music therapy with a comatose patient on an intensive care ward. For the duration of music therapy all unnecessary sounds of the ward were reduced. Soft, empathic, wordlessly phrased singing in the rhythm of a patient's pulse and breathing sought access to him and succeeded in guiding him out of the comatose state. The therapists observed changes in heart frequency (slower at the beginning, then accelerating), deeper and slower breathing frequency, and an acceleration (desynchronization) of EEG waves from slower to quicker frequencies, in addition to small hand and head movements after the onset of therapy.

The comatose state is possibly also a changed state of consciousness that represents an adaptation of the organism to its environment after trauma. Music therapy permits the evaluation of the remaining perceptive abilities of patients with serious brain injuries (Herkenrath 2002). Traditional oriental forms of music therapy consider trance as an important aspect of the healing process (Tucek, Auer-Pekarsky, and Stepansky 2001).

Music, relaxation and imagination: Guided Imagery in Music (GIM)

Helen L. Bonny (1975; Bonny and Savary 1973) developed a concept that uses music and guided altered states of consciousness for therapy purposes. Working at the Maryland Psychiatric Research Center in Baltimore, US (with Stanislav Grof, among others), she combined a music programme – empirically developed from the Baltimore research project of psychotherapy ('psychedelic therapy') based on hallucinogens (e.g. LSD) (Bonny and Pahnke 1972; Grof 1994) – with the technique Guided Affective Imagery ('Katathymes Bilderleben') in the sense of a guided imaginary trip designed by H. C. Leuner (1974; Leuner and Richards 1984). The programme consists of introductory deep relaxation, concentration exercises to focus attention, and a subsequent client-specific music programme – mostly classical music on tape – intended to produce free or guided associations, images or daydreams; the client reports these either immediately or subsequently in discussion with the therapist who then asks pertinent questions. Such 'self' encounters and imaginings by patients are interpreted on the basis of Freud's concept of the mental apparatus, individual maps of experience, or Fischer's cartography. While Grof developed a concept of ergotropic trance induction, the access proposed by Bonny was more in the nature of a trophotropic trance (see Bonde 1999).

A further important reference was Jung's theory of archetypes for the interpretation of induced imaginings (Short 1997). Music is used to find access to subconscious or repressed emotional complexes of the psyche or to transpersonal experiences that give the client a new perspective on his problems. Music serves here as a projection technique that stimulates the inner world of images (see Bush 1988, p.219). Although the music is selected specifically for each client, GIM therapists use a standardized catalogue of classical music with individual works that in the course and empirical development of this approach generate characteristic imaginings to be used almost as tools in practice (for further details see Grocke 2005)

Sound trance

At the beginning of the 1980s some experienced music therapists in Germany perceived a growing interest in the effects of music from outside Europe and started experimenting with trance-inducing effects of monochromatic sounds of the monochord, gong, didjeridoo and sound bowl

(Bossinger and Hess 1993; Hess and Rittner 1996a; Strobel 1988; Timmermann 1996).

The function of music in therapy from this perspective is to induce, control and withdraw the sound trance as an altered state of consciousness (Hess and Rittner 1996b). Music serves not only to induce altered states of consciousness but also to 'maintain and structure them in order to open the healing potential of trance states for the therapy process' (Bossinger and Hess 1993, p.239).

> In musical psychotherapy with sound trance, music…is effective in two directions: (i) physiologically stirring (ergotropic) towards ecstasy by intensified rhythm in the field of perception…or (ii) physically calming and internalizing (trophotropic) towards enstasis with reduced field of perception and focusing via monochromatic sounds. (Hess and Rittner 1996a, p.401)

Altered states of consciousness may be induced by live or recorded music, but also by free improvisation in a corresponding ritual context (Bossinger and Hess 1993). Rituals provide a structure to the suggestive context of set and setting and 'open the biological door' (Hess and Rittner 1996b). A perspective of the self that has possibly been changed through such an experience may enhance consciousness beyond the horizon of everyday consciousness and trigger healing processes. The experience of (partial) loss of control or reduction of affective control during sound trance may stimulate effective therapeutic experiences and creative resolution processes with a long-term pain-reducing effect (Risch, Scherg and Verres 2001). 'The tremendous trance experience then has the function of a deposit or implant, with a marked and structure-giving effect' (Haerlin 1998, p.233). Haerlin sees sound as an inductive background for the spontaneous productions of the subconscious. For interpreting imagery and experiences, mostly psychoanalytical explanations are used, particularly those by Jung, concepts of Grof's perinatal matrix and also Wilber's transpersonal psychology (Haerlin 1998).

The therapist strives for a 'non-conventional, healing state of consciousness' (Haerlin 1998, p.238) in single or group sessions with sound instruments (sound bowls, gongs, monochord, etc.) and pulsation instruments (drums, rattles, etc.). Timmermann (1996) underlines the significance of a monotonous repetition of sounds as a core element of trance induction. The duration of sounds, taking their effect on a client, appears to be important for trance induction. According to Arrien, 'most individuals need 13 to 15 minutes in order to be influenced or carried away by drums' (Haerlin 1998, p.239). Haerlin writes that the main effect of trance-inducing instruments is the 'induction of an empty trance matrix that reduces the noise of thought and more or less suspends the normal and pathological frame of beliefs and references' (Haerlin 1998, p.240).

Efforts to base trance on the sounds of instruments alone deny the influence of set and setting, i.e. the uniqueness of situation and context, of the personality and history of the receiving client and also the specific social situation of the persons involved in the therapeutic process and their attitudes. 'Instruments are useful only if they constitute musicalized and rhythmicized relation, or if they prepare contact' (Haerlin 1998, p.223). From a psychodynamic perspective, Strobel (1988, p.121) writes: 'Strictly speaking, it is not only the sound, but the therapist via the sound who affects the client, and the client re-influences the therapist with his responses.' In the patient–therapist relationship, the 'unspecific trance effect' (p.134) of the sound has a bridging effect. Dependent on the type of instrument, the 'sound archetype…without sharply delineated significance area' (p.122) as guiding 'analogy between the themes of the experiencing subject and the physical sound phenomena' (p.124) in the 'sound-guided imagination' (p.121) causes the altered state of consciousness of an 'inner attention' (p.127), a 'meditation accompanied by the therapist'. Not only instruments but also the voice as the primary expressive form in humans may induce trance, and may enchant a client – as of Odysseus by the sirens (Rittner 1994; Rittner 1996; Timmermann 1996).

Fachner and Rittner (2004) made an explorative attempt to represent such interdependencies of set and setting, sound and trance through electrophysiological correlation in the topographic spontaneous EEG. They opted for a trance induction with a body monochord in the context of a group ritual. In comparison with uninfluenced rest, they found individual, but not necessarily induction-specific, changes in spontaneous EEG. Trance reactions to sound were seemingly more determined by the person's different hypnotizability as measured with Pekala's PCI than by sound alone. The low hypnotizable participants exhibited an ergotropic reaction with an overall desynchronization of the EEG marked with right fronto-central increase of beta-II waves. The high hypnotizable participants exhibited a trophotropic reaction, marked with a synchronization of EEG in left parietal-occipital brain regions.

Electrophysiological studies of music-related altered states of consciousness

EEG has become established as a measuring instrument in neurology, psychiatry and consciousness research. In neurology, it serves as an indicator of epilepsy, brain cancer and damage of cerebral lobes (Niedermeyer and Lopes de Silva 1993). In psychophysiology, it is sensitive to personality factors, linkable to psychological test batteries and is interpreted as a somatic indicator of psychological processes (Becker-Carus 1971; Empson 1986; Hagemann, Naumann et al. 1999). Because of the time-locked occurrence of EEG, it has been used to show cerebral changes of music perception and experience compared to rest. Therefore, we have a dynamic indicator that is sensitive to personality, situation and cognitive cerebral strategies and also shows inter- and intra-individual differences to music perception (Petsche 1994).

Results of an EEG experiment are mostly shown in a distinct brainwave pattern exhibiting wave ranges like alpha (α), beta (β), theta (ϕ) or delta (δ). Such topographic activation patterns differ on frequency ranges. This is an important feature of the EEG, because dominant brainwave frequency ranges represent arousal and vigilance states, that represent different consciousness aspects of the measured experience (see Fachner 2004a).

Slow delta waves dominate in dreamless deep sleep; theta and slower alpha waves increase in changed consciousness states like meditation (Kohlmetz, Kopiez, and Altenmüller 2003; West 1980), music and dance-induced trance (Oohashi et al. 2002; Park et al. 2002), or with various psychedelic drugs like LSD, mescaline and cannabis, but are also present in falling asleep or waking-up states (Schacter 1977). The quicker alpha and beta waves are dominant in waking consciousness. Hans Berger, who discovered EEG, identified coffee as a beta wave booster (Berger 1991). It is hoped that by understanding fast waves, we will begin to answer the question of how processes of consciousness are constituted physiologically (Lehmann et al. 2001; Tassi and Muzet 2001).

Hypnotizability, laterality and music

Wackermann *et al.* (2002) studied the differences between states of beginning sleep, a monotonous visual and acoustic 'Ganzfeld' stimulation (waterfall rushing on both ears and red light stimulation on both eyes without other visual percepts), closed eyes and sleep itself. The 'Ganzfeld' stimulation produced a slight acceleration of alpha frequencies. In beginning sleep, time intervals were assumed to be longer, compared to waking state and 'Ganzfeld' stimulation. Asked for subjective experience and imaginations, the test group reported mostly visualizations connected with water or similar liquids (Wackermann *et al.* 2002, p.132).

Meszaros differentiated according to hypnotizability and interpreted the test group's EEGs for differences in hemispheres; he described a primarily right-hemispheric, parieto-temporal EEG reaction of the alpha and beta band in highly hypnotizable persons. He concluded that right-hemispheric changes were to be expected in the 'mainly emotion-focused hypnotherapies' (Meszaros *et al.* 2002, p.511).

Brady and Stevens (2000) tested the variability of individual suggestibility in persons with high, medium and little susceptibility to hypnosis with a presentation of two slightly different notes and frequency-modulated 'pink noise' ('binaural beats'). Both notes – heard via earphones – make a rhythmic pulsation perceivable. Depending on the frequency combination, these rhythmic sounds have a relaxing or stimulating effect on a listener and consequently are experienced as an altered state of consciousness. The inventors of this Hemi-Sync technology aim at a synchronization of both hemispheres and use it for therapeutic purposes (Atwater 1995). In five of the six examined subjects, the EEG shows an increase of frontal theta waves in the brain while they listen to music. The sound-induced altered states of consciousness produce increased hypnotizability in persons with medium and low suggestibility.

Trance and obsession

Park *et al.* (2002) discovered changes in the EEG of a Korean Salpuri dancer during rest, listening to music, and trance memory. They found EEG differences between a remembered trance state of dance and music perception. The memory of an ecstatic trance passage in dance produced – in comparison with rest – significant frontal increases of deep alpha frequencies (8–10

Hz) and frontal–occipital theta increase. In comparison with rest and listening to a piece of pop music (Celine Dion's 'The Power of Love'), the frequency and amplitude of high alpha frequencies rose significantly (10–12.5 Hz) over the entire cortex, while 9.5 Hz was identified as the global top frequency in rest and dance memory, with an increase in amplitude energy during the dance memory. While the subject listened to music, the main frequency rose to 10 Hz and high beta frequencies increased. The lower alpha band (8–10 Hz) is related to the continuity of attention processes, while the upper alpha band represents differentiation powers and memory processes (Klimesch 1999; Krause *et al.* 1999). While the dancer recalls his state, he directs attention to this experience, whereas in music he differentiates and compares structurally. Park assumes that the Salpuri dancer 'reaches the altered state of ecstatic trance via suppression of frontal cortex functions and activation of sub cortical functions' (compare Park *et al.* 2002, p.961); accordingly, trance is characterized by theta frequencies (the dominance of which in the EEG suggests such activation).

Neher (1962) claims that Obsession Trance and its phenomena resembling those of epilepsy in ceremonial drumming are causally evoked by drumming mainly with bass frequencies and certain frequency patterns. He calculates the number of drumbeats and their frequency per second as analogous to the EEG frequency (oscillations per second). Neher hopes to prove an 'auditory driving' in his laboratory experiments with the same frequency range as the epilepsy-producing effect of 'photic driving' (through rhythmic light emissions). But his findings show (which he hasn't acknowledged) that the possible drum frequencies are in the theta range (4–8 Hz), while the 'photic driving' is in the alpha range (8–13 Hz) and for technical reasons this is almost impossible to achieve with drums (compare Neher, 1962, pp.153–4). Rouget (1985, pp.167–183) considers such explanations of a 'trance mechanism' as incomplete since the experimental laboratory situation for trance cannot be compared with the real situation.

Oohashi *et al.* (2002) was the first to produce a naturalistic EEG image of an Obsession Trance ('Kerauhan') in a ceremony in Bali with a radio system, specific software and attached electrodes. At the culmination of the ceremony, one test participant fell into trance (see Oohashi *et al.* 2002, p.438). In the trance phase analysis they found a distinct increase of theta and alpha frequencies.

In summary, theta increases – specifically in frontal brain regions – and alpha changes may be physiological indicators of a trance state.

Trance in music performance

Kopiez et al. (Kopiez et al. 2003) analysed a piano performance of Erik Satie's *Vexations*, which has a duration of almost 29 hours, for tempo and loudness. The entire performance was observed and recorded. Parallel to the music, an EEG was taken at the back of the pianist's head (P3+P4), and he was interviewed in the short intervals and after the performance.

The pianist reported that he was rather alert at the beginning but went into trance, and towards the end, a tired state. After fourteen hours, at the beginning of the trance, the pianist experienced a confusing reality comparable to a dream; he lost control of his body, had extra-physical experiences, the musical piece dissociated into single tonal groups, errors occurred more frequently, sections were mixed up, and improvisations sprang up. For about a two-hour period (19–21 hrs), he felt very tired. After 25 hours of performance, in a permanent slight trance, time seemed to pass more slowly, he varied themes and sequences of the piece freely and forgot what he wanted to play. Ultimately, he believed that he underwent a Buddhist rite, thinking that he might have been given a new name at the end of the performance, and ended the music as if obeying an inner command (Kohlmetz et al. 2003).

An analysis of performance data revealed that these states influence the parameter's volume and tempo. They were stable for the first 14 hours; in trance, the tempo was increasingly accelerated, and uncontrolled changes in volume were noticeable at the end of the trance, after approximately 19 hours. However, acceleration was not equivalent with volume changes, and faster play did not necessarily mean higher volume. Volume was reduced gradually over the first 18 hours and became more dynamic at the end of the trance. Accordingly, the fluctuating de-synchronization and disintegration of tempo and volume increased continuously, and the pianist's exhausted state was marked by consistent instability and reduced control (Kopiez et al. 2003). A comparison of waking and trance phases, however, did not show any significant change in the medium duration of a chosen sequence. Sensory-motor performance remained astonishingly stable in trance. Probable explanations for this are free neural oscillators that, in interaction with the circadian rhythm, permit reliable timing for motor functions but themselves are influenced by altered states of consciousness. As known from studies on meditation, the trance phase in EEG is marked by synchronization and a significant increase in the frequency of low alpha waves (8–10 Hz) and also an increase of lower beta waves (13–15 Hz). Delta waves increased continuously over the entire performance. Increases of alpha and delta waves were observed mainly in the left posterior hemisphere around the EEG measurement point P3, which suggests a reduction of left hemispheric in favour of right-hemispheric brain functions (Kohlmetz *et al.* 2003).

Summary

Music and altered states are connected in various ways concerning context, personal set and socio-ecological setting, and cultural beliefs. Altered states of consciousness are induced or evoked for various purposes. We might divide these into two broad categories of socio-cultural and individual reasons for altered states of consciousness. There are ritualistic, therapeutic and hedonistic meanings but a clear distinction is not possible because altered states of consciousness depend on the depth of involvement, experience, meaning and purpose according to specific contexts.

Individually differing degrees of hypnotizability seem to be a factor determining personal onset time, quality and depth of altered states of consciousness. In hypnosis and suggestion, music may serve as a contextualizing factor, helping focus on the music-related induction that absorbs and denies external objects. Induction-specific vigilance changes, combined with the intensified, narrowed or broadened focus of attention, may result in a different emotional profile of meaning experienced with music and its symbolic, metaphoric and physical content.

Still the question remains open as to whether there is a 'trance mechanism' directly related to music. Cognitive processing of music changes its modes of awareness of musical elements during altered states of consciousness. Rhythm, pitch, loudness and timbre and their sound staging in the perceptive field of a person seem to culminate in a certain sound that – corresponding to the cultural cognitive matrix – induces altered states of consciousness. Repetition, long duration, monotony, increase and decrease of patterns, volume and density, high pitch and frequency ranges, rescaling of intensity units are observed with some trance phenomena but there is no clear causal explanation for the induction of trance. The connection of time and space perception alterations and the resulting changes of music perception are important. Therefore, rhythm remains the target of discussion for altered states of consciousness induction.

Music might be visualized in certain imagery systems, which become more vivid when focused intensively or might become experienced 'as if' it happens in the real world, mediated and evoked via an increased amount of cross-modality. Intensification of emotional qualities and meaning, change of cognitive processing (frame of reference) and enhanced cross-modal perception promotes a 'unity of the senses' experience, which is dependent upon cultural context. It might be a psycho-physiologic mode of uncensored sensual processing, a broadened attention span for intensively focused objects of the mind and through enhanced imagination and visualization experienced in a form of synaesthesia.

The holistic experience of music can only be a personal event and is by itself ineffable. To adapt all the necessary ingredients for the individual to transcend his or her own being demands the art, knowledge and experience of a guide. Some reported experiences, as in obsession trance, alter internal perception of loudness or acoustic relations and do not fall readily into the categories of natural science explanations.

Chemically induced altered states of consciousness (see Chapters 7 to 11) together with music, can be studied as psycho-physiological models of altered states of consciousness and might help us to understand altered states of consciousness processes *in vivo*. Electrophysiological studies have revealed theta changes as indicative for altered states of consciousness. Music and drug action are processed in the same limbic brain areas, a region associated with low-frequency generations. The question of whether gamma frequencies might indicate altered cognitive modes needs more research.

Chapter 3

Music and Trance

John J. Pilch

In order to stimulate a satisfying and rewarding discussion of the topic 'music and trance', it is important to begin with a definition of terms. In *Music and Trance*, Rouget (1985, p.63) offers this definition of music as:

> any sonic event that is linked with this state [trance], that cannot be reduced to language – since we would then have to speak of words, not music – and that displays a certain degree of rhythmic or melodic organization.

This rather broad definition encompasses sounds as diverse as rustling leaves, drums, tinkling bells, chanting *recto tono* (i.e. on a single note), and even most complex vocal polyphonies. The key elements to consider here are rhythm and melody.

Trance, on the other hand, is one of a large group of altered states of consciousness of which human beings are capable (Goodman 1990, p.9). According to Ludwig, an altered state of consciousness is:

> any mental state(s) induced by various physiological, psychological, or pharmacological manoeuvres or agents, which can be recognized subjectively by the individual himself (or by an objective observer of the individual) as representing a sufficient deviation in subject experiences or psychological functioning from certain general norms for that individual during alert, waking consciousness. (Ludwig 1969, pp.9–10)

In relation to music, Rouget uses the word 'trance' to mean simply that kind of altered states of consciousness, which is obtained by means of noise (sonic events), agitation, and in the presence of others (in contrast to 'ecstasy' which is attained in silence, immobility, and solitude. Rouget 1985, p.7). At the same time, though he examines in great detail the complex relationship between music and trance, Rouget denies that music 'directly' causes trance states. Music is rather only one of many components causing trance states (Gregory 1997). Often it is an essential element, but other cultural factors enter the picture, too. These factors vary from society to society. Moreover even the same factor, like music, will function differently in different societies, so that it is very difficult to generalize about music and trance. In one society, the trigger for trance may be soft music, in another it may be loud sound. In one society quick rhythms may induce trance, while in another slow rhythms are preferred.

The neuroscience of trance music

On a biological or neurological level, the relationship of music and trance is easily explained. The one thing that human beings have always had in common is biology, namely, the human body. Contemporary cognitive neuroscience has helped us to understand not only the potential for the human nervous system to enter altered states of consciousness but also that this potential is of great antiquity.

> It seems likely that Australopithecines (1.4 million years ago) hallucinated [that is, went into trance], highly probable that Neanderthals (100,000–35,000 years ago) hallucinated, and certain that at least some of the anatomically modern human beings of the Upper Palaeolithic (35,000–8,000 years ago) also hallucinated. (Clottes and Lewis-Williams 1998, p.81)

In general, ecstatic trance can be induced neurologically in one of two ways: 'from the bottom up' (primarily by means of the nervous system) or 'from the top down' (primarily by means of the brain: d'Aquili and Newberg 1999, pp.23–27, 99–102). Inducing a trance 'from the bottom up' involves the brain and the autonomic nervous system, which has two components: the sympathetic or arousal subsystem and the parasympathetic or quiescent subsystem. The autonomic nervous system connects the brain with the rest of the body and plays a key role in generating basic emotions like fear, joy, and shame. The sympathetic or arousal subsystem helps human beings adapt to beneficial and harmful stimuli in the environment principally through the 'fight or flight' response. This subsystem can halt digestion, increase the heart rate and blood pressure, increase respiration, decrease salivation, and the like. The parasympathetic or quiescent subsystem maintains homeostasis and conserves the body's resources and energy. This subsystem controls such things as cell growth, digestion, relaxation, sleep. In other words, it deals with vegetative functions and maintenance activities. By stimulating (hand-clapping, drumming, rattling, and the like) or quieting (as happens in normal sleep, chanting, reciting a mantra, and the like) the senses, it is possible to produce a brief but intense ecstatic trance experience.

In a simplified presentation of their research published after d'Aquili's death, Andrew Newberg (Newberg, d'Aquili and Rause 2001) offered some specific reflections on music and trance from the context of neuroscience. In a New York City church, a concert combining music with the recorded howling of wolves eventually stirred one audience member (who was soon joined by others) to stand up and howl along with the wolves.

> The stimulation of autonomic and limbic responses, triggered by the rhythms of the wolf music, is the force that called Bill and his fellow audience members to rise out of themselves and into a larger and more exhilarating state of being. (Newberg *et al.* 2001, p.79)

The repetitive rhythmic stimulation of the howling of the wolves stirred a trance in these audience members 'from the bottom up'.

In another example, Newberg presents the hypothetical case of a person returning home tired on a Friday night from a hard day at work (Newberg *et al.* 2001, pp.114–115). The worker draws water for a leisurely bath, lights a few candles, pours a glass of wine, and tunes the radio to a favourite station. As the worker relaxes in the tub, a soft romantic ballad plays on the radio. The slow rhythms eventually stimulate a trance 'from the top down,' that is, the rhythms stimulate the body's quiescent system, which in turn prompts the hippocampus to cause a slight deafferentation of the orientation area of the brain and brings on a mild trance. The type of music may very well differ for different people, but the music's effect will be the same. This in a very simplified form is the basic neuroscience behind a trance to which music has contributed as one element.

Music across cultures

There are a number of sound features that are fundamental to music across cultures. Among these are pitch, tempo, repetition, rhythmic patterning, rhyme and alliteration (Trehub 2003, from whom I draw the following observations). Research on the musical interests and abilities of pre-linguistic infants has demonstrated that they are as sensitive to these sound features as adults who have had years of informal exposure. In general, infants and adults are capable of discerning the smallest pitch and tempo differences that are musically meaningful in any culture.

Adults have observed that toddlers routinely invent songs before they can reproduce the conventional songs of their culture. School-age children also create songs and chants that share features across cultures such as repetition, rhythmic patterning, rhyme and alliteration. Trehub believes it is reasonable to conclude 'that the rudiments of music listening are gifts of nature rather than product of culture'.

Music, however, parts with language when it comes to meaning. Musical pieces are not meaningful in the same way that verbal utterances are. Music communicates emotion and feelings but not meaning. According to Trehub, music lacks semanticity. Sensitivity to culture-specific details of tone and harmony structure seems to emerge between 5 and 7 years of age. Though musical training can aid in this learning, incidental exposure suffices to generate perceptions similar to those of trained musicians. But experiments also show that in this matter, culture specific exposure is relevant to adults but not to infants! Much has been learned from infants and much more remains to be learned.

Investigations of mother–infant interactions have provided intriguing insights into the social and musical beginnings of human beings. All over the world, mothers contribute various kinds of music information to their pre-linguistic infants (Fernald 1991). They speak in a melodic tone of voice to infants who cannot understand what they are saying. (One can sometimes witness such tonal communication between mothers and infants in the baby food aisle of grocery stores). Mothers also sing a great deal to children. They utilize a special genre of music like lullabies or game songs with features that are common across cultures: simple pitch contours, repetition and narrow melodic range (Trehub and Trainor 1998). Lullabies are performed in a very expressive and highly ritualized manner (see the Supplementary Video 1 in Trehub's 2003 article online). Already from the neonatal period, infants prefer renditions sung in a maternal style (that is, from mothers of other infants) to non-maternal renditions of the same song. Further, infants are entranced when they can see and hear the singer. They enter an altered state of consciousness, a trance, as reflected either in extended periods of focused attention or reduced body movement (e.g. they may go to sleep).

Liam Muhammad al Hindi (Omaha, NE) was 18 months old when the picture in Figure 3.1 was taken. It marks an emotional transition. You could see his pleasure or excitement building until he would close his eyes, cross his arms over his chest in a struggle to hold inside, to contain intense pleasure or high spirits. He was never able to contain the emotion. His eyes would open, his arms would fly out and he would do some little dance with his feet as joy flowed throughout his entire being.

Figure 3.1 Liam Muhammad al Hindi

Infants are much more interested in maternal singing than in speech. In fact, experts believe that it is the music in speech that underlies its appeal to pre-linguistic infants.

Music and trance

We have already noted Rouget's denial that music directly induces trance states (see above). The research on infants and music just reviewed may help us to understand his position. More, it may help us to understand a broader picture regarding trance in general. In 1968, Erika Bourguignon (1973) conducted a foundational anthropological study of altered states of consciousness. She compiled a sample of 488 societies (57 per cent) from Murdock's *Ethnographic Atlas* and made a fresh investigation of the data in the *Human Relations Area Files*, an exhaustive collection of ethnographic reports available in many libraries on microfiche and CD-ROM. Her sample included all parts of the world and traditional societies at various levels of technological complexity. Altered states of consciousness were found to exist in 90 per cent of the 488 societies. By region, altered states of consciousness exist in 80 per cent of Circum-Mediterranean societies (the low), and in 97 per cent of the 121 North American societies in the sample (the high).

In the light of this evidence, anthropologists agree that altered states of consciousness are universal human phenomena, experienced in at least one of a wide variety of forms by all human beings. 'Societies which do not utilize these states clearly are historical exceptions which need to be explained, rather than the vast majority of societies that do use these states' (Bourguignon 1976, p.51).

The physician-anthropologist Arthur Kleinman (1988) offers an explanation for the West's deficiency in this matter as one society that not only does not use altered states of consciousness but frequently vehemently denies that they are of any value. 'Only the modern, secular West seems to have blocked individuals' access to these otherwise pan-human dimensions of the self' (Kleinman 1988, p.50). What is the Western problem? The advent of modern science in about the seventeenth century disrupted the bio-psycho-spiritual unity of human consciousness that had existed until then (Price-Williams 1975, p.87). According to Kleinman, we have developed an 'acquired consciousness', whereby we dissociate self and look at self 'objectively'. Western culture socializes individuals to develop a metaself, a critical observer who monitors and comments on experience. The metaself does not allow the total absorption in lived experience, which is the very essence of highly focused altered states of consciousness. The metaself stands in the way of unreflected, unmediated experience, which now becomes distanced. This distancing renders the Western self vulnerable to pathology such as borderline or narcissistic personality disorders which appear to be culture-bound to the West (on culture-bound syndromes, see Pilch 2000, p.152).

Thus, infants bear witness to this human potential prior to the emergence of the superego, the metaself, in the process of development. Infants and young children still possess the ability to become totally absorbed in every aspect of their lived experience. The photograph of Liam Muhammad al Hindi in Figure 3.1 is a perfect illustration. Dr Goodman describes the experience of what she lost around the age of twelve in her own life eloquently, if with understandable sadness (Goodman 1990, pp.3–4). In her later years and subsequently in her career, Dr Goodman rediscovered through research and experimentation how to reclaim and rejuvenate that gift for entering trance, the 'magic' of her youth as she called it, a pan-human potential. The Cuyamungue Institute, which she founded continues her work and research, and it is as part of this ongoing research that I offer these reflections on this topic of music and trance.

Inducing trance with music

In the ritual used by members of the Cuyamungue Institute, members use either a rattle or a drum to induce trance. Dr Goodman's research discovered that shaking a rattle (or beating a drum) approximately 220 times a minute for a 15-minute period provides the optimal sensory stimulus to the nervous system for inducing a trance 'from the bottom up' to use the phrase of d'Aquili and Newberg. Two personal friends with whom I attempted to share the gift that I learned from Dr Goodman and the Institute found this mode of sensory stimulation jarring and disturbing. It would and could not induce an altered state of consciousness in them. The one, LH, is a trained musician (a pianist) and says such rattling quickly gets on her nerves. The other, AB, has a long-standing and well grounded personal practice of contemplative prayer most often performed alone and in silence. When I played the rattling tape for her during a communal prayer session, she quickly asked me to shut it off. That sound was disturbing, agitating, grisly to her ears. She requested a different sound.

My alternate suggestion was the sound track from the 1980 film *Somewhere in Time* starring Christopher Reeve, Jane Seymour and Christopher Plummer. Composed by John Barry (the 'James Bond' score is among his other hits), the nine cuts on the CD from the soundtrack also include 'Rhapsody on a Theme of Paganini' by Rachmaninoff. This music is Barry's all-time best selling score. AB found it very helpful in enhancing her prayer session. She said that this quiet sensual music was more in tune with her body. Her prayer sessions tend to have a moderate kinesthetic quality. In fact, they are characterized by deep emotion felt and expressed in her body.

Why is this score so helpful in AB's practice of prayer? I propose these possible explanations. From a neurological perspective, AB induces trance 'from the top down.' Among other strategies, she often selects an image from the Christian scriptures (e.g., 'the bent woman' described in Luke 13:11–17) and reflects upon it intently. Thus AB's prayer in trance begins in the brain and then travels through the rest of her body. From the perspective of the music that AB uses, John Barry composed his score shortly after the death of his parents. Since music has no semanticity, the emotion Barry appears to have instilled into his music is calming, soothing and peaceful. It can easily trigger the quiescent dimension of the nervous system coinciding with AB's preferred mode of entering prayerful trance. In other words, there is a good match between AB's strategies and the music that appeals to her, both of which stimulated trance 'from the top down'.

This music has served me personally in a similar way, even before I learned about altered states of consciousness and ways of inducing them. Some time after viewing the film, I had made audiotape copies of this score, one of which I kept in my car to calm me during any rush-hour traffic in which I might have had the misfortune of getting caught. The music helps me to manage and maintain a healthy level of blood pressure and pleasant mood in very stressful conditions. The music is in a romantic musical style, pleasant, performed mainly by the strings, and creates a soothing and calming mood. I also made a copy for use in personal prayer or reflection sessions, which was the copy I shared with AB. Though I have viewed the film more than once, I would say that the music works its effect apart from anything that I remember about the film's story line. (AB never saw the film.) As the research indicates, the music communicates emotion rather than a message.

Ethnomusicology and trance

Two ethnomusicological studies confirmed some information gained from other sources and also contributed additional insights to my reflections: Kartomi's report on 'Music and Trance in Central Java' (Kartomi 1973) and Baklanoff's study of the Black Baptist Footwashing Ritual (Baklanoff 1987). Kartomi observed and analysed five types of Central Javanese village music used most often in association with dance: Ebeg (an enacted folk drama); Tiowongan (a rain dance by females to the rice goddess); Pentjak (a dance of self-defence); Pradjuritan (a military trance dance); and Kotekan (rice-block stamping music, very popular but no longer associated with trance).

The investigation concluded that subjects of trance behavior in Central Java perform in a culturally conditioned way. 'Even in trance, the individual holds strictly to the rules and expectations of his culture and his experience is as locally patterned as a marriage rite or an economic exchange' (Benedict 1934, p.77). The music used in Central Java is similar to other music in their culture, yet it does have some differences. In general, however, 'The trance dancer abandons himself to the despotism of the regular metre, the magic-motto-like repetitiveness of the melodic phrases and, in the case of instrumental ensemble, to the strange dissonant sound of the musical combinations' (Kartomi 1973, p.166). The notion of 'abandon' has already been highlighted by Kleinman. The person who wants to enter a trance state must suspend restrictions and plunge without reserve into the totality of lived experience at a given moment. This is aided by the trait of music known as 'absorption', a trait recognized by some hypnotherapists as naturally facilitating the connection between music and trance which good hypnotic subjects are capable of making (Kelly 1993, p.84). In selecting music with a strong potential for assisting in inducing trance, a subject should pay special attention to its 'absorption' character. Some music, like rattling to some ears, is jarring and repulsive and does not seem capable of absorbing the listener into its tones or melodies. Indeed, Trehub's research with infants discovered that 'infants are more precise in perceiving diatonic melodies – those conforming to keys of major or minor scales – than melodies that violate the conventions of known musics.' Infant perception of intervals is more precise when these intervals are consonant or pleasant sounding, like the perfect fourth, or the perfect fifth.

To assist in inducing a trance state, music must be mesmeric in effect (Kartomi 1973, p.167). Music that best assists in inducing trance has regular pulsation and repetitive tonal patterns based on a restricted number of pitch levels. At the same time, it must not sink to musical boredom. Since 1940, The Ecumenical Community at Taizé has committed itself to prayer and reflection. In the 1970s as youths became interested in and attracted to the Community, the members decide to open the group to work among many people in many places while maintaining the central location in Taizé. In the 1980s, because of the international membership in the Community, members sought simple music and prayer forms that would facilitate rather than impede prayer. Beginning with Chorales and Psalms from the sixteenth century, the Community then added psalmody created by Joseph Gelineau (1962). Eventually, Jacques Berthier (1978) experimented still further and decided upon repetitive structures, short musical phrases with singable melodic parts that could be readily memorized by anyone. Latin was the original language, but others were added later.

The music of Taizé is simple and absorbing. The lyrics, whether in Latin (e.g., 'Veni Sancte Spiritus') or in English ('Jesus remember me, when you come into your Kingdom') or any other language are brief and mantric in character. The congregation or Community repeats these brief refrains while a cantor (or choir) sing verses. Sometimes the congregation or Community might begin to harmonize the refrain. Of the sacred music familiar to me, the songs of Taizé seem best suited to assisting in inducing trance and promoting richly rewarding prayer experiences. Just as the Javanese in trance believe that they are in contact with their deities and spirits, such as the goddess of rice, their ancestors and spirits of the dead, and animals, so too do modern devotees of Taizé prayer (or similar methods) believe this music is most capable of bringing a person into the presence of the Deity.

Kartomi makes another important observation:

The music serves primarily as a communication of mood (from musician to trance dancer) through the music's associativeness and mesmeric continuity; not only does it assist a subject into a trance state but it lends colour to and is part of the traumatic experience itself. It builds up and sustains a state of undifferentiated emotional excitement. Music has become one with ritual and is not a separate aesthetic category. For its purpose, Central Javanese trance music is highly potent and effective. (Kartomi 1973, p.166)

Researchers are agreed that music communicates emotion rather than a message. Kartomi notes that resulting emotional excitement is 'undifferentiated'. This would seem to be a logical conclusion from music's ability to absorb a listener. However, a tone poem, such as Smetana's 'The Moldau' (The Vltava) from *Ma Vlast* for which the composer wrote explanatory notes does seem to have been intended to convey images, but perhaps secondarily the images would stir emotions.

Kartomi raises another issue of importance for our reflection. 'It is probable,' she writes, 'that, in practice, aesthetic value judgments are to some extent culturally determined, or at least culturally coloured' (Kartomi 1973, p.166). She has in mind the question of whether someone who has heard the music but not witnessed the folk trance dance would be able to render an adequate appraisal of the music's aesthetic value. This is certainly true of the Javanese trance events she has studied. One would have to know the social connotations and the mood of the actual performances.

On the other hand, given the subjective interpretations that are possible in listening to music alone (i.e., without a dance performance, or perhaps even just a live instrumental or vocal performance), it would seem that all kinds of music could accompany trance or serve to assist in inducing it depending upon the listener. Meyer (1967, p.126) offers this observation: 'What we 'know' and 'believe' has a profound effect upon what we perceive and how we respond.' During a nine-year period (1954 to 1963), I was an organist in a Roman Catholic community of religious men (Franciscans). My major assignment was to play 'background' music in the keys of F and G to help the Friars sustain pitch during their *recto tono* choral chanting of Latin prayers (the Divine Office). Initially, I tried to read and recite the prayers along with the choir but could not concentrate on that and playing at the same time. So I began to listen attentively to what was recited while I concentrated on playing the organ. As the prayers became more familiar and in fact memorized, one or another would trigger a thought, which would in turn induce a reverie, a small trance that was further enhanced by the music. On many occasions a strong emotion would also emerge: 'O quam bonum et quam jucundum habitare fratres in unum' – 'How Good, how delightful it is to live as brothers all together!' (Psalm 133:1). The process actually became a feedback loop. What began for me as a distasteful assignment eventually became transformed into a very satisfying occasion of prayer. Since we recited these prayers at four different times during the day, with the longest stretch of time extending for about an hour at 5pm, the practice became a habit and left its imprint on personal life.

Conclusion

This brief reflection on music and trance was inspired by the pioneering research of Dr Felicitas Daniels Goodman and stimulated by the on-going research of the Cuyamungue Institute. The Annapolis (MD) Group in which I am a regular participant is hosted by Judy Lazarus and Joan Scott. Both of these pioneer members of the Institute are warmly encouraging and supportive of ongoing research in trance and comparative religion. In a recently published book, I designed a ceremonial rite for experiencing the realm of God in altered states of consciousness (Pilch 2004, pp.181–187; for a different model, see Weir 1991). This rite is based on the ritual developed by Dr Goodman and used by the Annapolis Group at its weekly session.

I have also discussed the relationship between rite and trance in this book (Appendix Two). Here, I focused particularly on the Roman Catholic Liturgy as designed and intended already in antiquity to facilitate worshippers' entry into trance. The 'Holy, Holy, Holy' sung or recited by the congregation are the very words reported by the prophet Isaiah as what he heard the angels singing, which he received in the smoke and incense-filled temple, during his call by God to be a prophet. It was a pleasant surprise in my research for this chapter to discover a study of the Sipsey River Association of the Primitive Baptist Church (founded in 1872) who celebrate three times a year a feast known as 'Footwashing' rooted in the story of Jesus washing his disciples' feet at the Last Supper (see John 13:14–15). The aim of this celebration is to achieve an altered state of consciousness induced by rhythmic sensory stimulation initiated by music, body movements, sermons and alcohol consumption (Baklanoff 1987, p.381). This group further reinforces the observation of Kartomi that trance-inducing music becomes one with the ritual and no longer remains a discrete aesthetic category.

Music might not directly induce trance, but it is recognized as key among the cluster of elements that contribute to inducing trance. For the most part, music works a neurological effect on the listener. Cultural associations that accompany the music also play an important role in stimulating a trance experience. The ultimate choice of music, however, will rest with the individual, or better yet, the community, since most of the reports reviewed about music and trance are communal experiences.

Chapter 4

The Effects of Listening
to Monotonous Drumming
on Subjective Experiences

Csaba Szabó

Background

We experience daily in listening to music what a strong effect its rhythm has on us. We see frequently that adolescents, listening to rock music, experience a trancelike state of consciousness. As we have seen in previous chapters, drumming has an important role in inducing a shaman's trance. In our times there are popular exercises of neo-shamanism, during which participants listen to monotonous drumming, have peculiar experiences and make imaginary journeys into other worlds.

Although anthropologists claim that monotonous drumming has very strong effects on our subjective experiences, there are few studies into the quality and quantity of these changes, nor are the mechanisms clear as to how drumming affects our experiences. Our present research addressed these questions.

Our hypotheses were:

1   Drumming has a significant effect on subjective experiences.

2   These experiences are similar to the altered state of
     consciousness induced by hypnosis.

3   Drumming has an effect on the content of the experiences.

Methods

Subjects

A test group of 118 university students volunteered to participate in the experiments. None of them had any previous experience in hypnosis. They were divided into the following groups:

1   listening to drumming during imagery (28 students)

2   imagery (24 students)

3   hypnosis (22 students)

4   alert control (44 students).

Experimental setting

The experiments were carried out in a quiet, dimly-lit laboratory. The students participated individually in the experiment. During the experiments participants sat in comfortable armchairs. The drumming was played from audiotape (Sound 4.1).

Participants were asked to close their eyes and listen to the drumming and to make an imaginary journey into the underworld. The instruction and the rhythm of drumming corresponded to Harner (1990). Participants were asked to close their eyes and imagine a hole leading down into the earth. They were told:

> When the drumming begins imagine this hole, enter and begin your journey in that imaginary world. Through this entrance go downwards into the tunnel. You must not make too much effort during your journey, just relax and follow your imagination. At the end of the tunnel you'll reach the somewhere. Observe the sight, make a tour and notice all its characteristics. When the drumming fades, come back the way you went down.

The pulse of the drumming was 210 beats per minute. The duration of the experiment was 30 minutes.

Control groups

'Imagery'   They were given the same imagery task, but without drumming.

'Hypnosis'   They were hypnotized with the induction procedure of the Stanford Hypnotic Susceptibility Scale (Weitzenhoffer and Hilgard, 1959). An imagery task was given to them after the hypnosis induction.

'Alert'   They spent three minutes in silence, with eyes closed.

Interviews

After the experiment the subjects reported their experiences. This was tape-recorded for content analysis. The experimenter listened to them without interruption. The Phenomenology of Consciousness Inventory (PCI, Pekala 1985) was also administered. This is a Likert-type questionnaire, with several subscales, and is used in research of the altered state of consciousness.

Results

Drumming vs. alert

The subjective experiences during drumming and the alert state, measured with the PCI, were compared. There were significant differences between the experiences of the two groups (MANOVA, Hotelling's Trace $F=1.97$ $df=17$ $p<0.05$). Drumming had a significant effect on subjective experiences. These differences can be measured with the PCI (Table 4.1).

Table 4.1 PCI scales during drumming and alert state

PCI Scale	Drumming	Alert	Sign
Body image	3.09	2.27	*
Time	3.06	2.03	*
Perception	2.83	1.77	**
Meaning	2.67	1.47	***
Self-consciousness	3.57	4.74	***
State of consciousness	3.45	1.77	***

*p< 0.05; ** p< 0.01; *** p< 0.001

Unpaired 't'-test was counted to identify the PCI scales where the differences are. The drumming caused significant differences on the next scales.

Body image

Participants, while they were listening to drumming, felt their body image change. They felt as if their body had expanded beyond the usual and this is a feeling common to many people in trance states.

Perception

They felt changed in their perception of the surrounding world and of themselves.

Time

They felt changes in the passing of time. They felt that time was passing more slowly or quickly than usual. This is also a common experience in hypnosis or meditation.

Meaning

The meaning of things had been changed. Participants sometimes report after trance experiences that they understood or revalued something suddenly.

Self-consciousness

They felt that their self-consciousness was less distinct. The border between the self and the world became fuzzy.

State of consciousness

They felt that their state of consciousness differed from the normal, alert state.

Imagery vs. Alert

The PCI scores in the two situations were compared and there were no significant differences. If participants were involved in the same imagery task, but without drumming, their state of consciousness had not been changed.

Drumming vs. Hypnosis

The PCI scores Inventory during drumming and hypnosis were compared and there were no significant differences between these. This means that participants who were listening to the drumming experienced the same strong alteration of their subjective experiences as subjects who were in hypnosis.

Content analysis

During the content analysis of the interviews we found some mentioning of rhythmic activities that are probably due to the effects of drumming (Table 4.2).

Table 4.2 Rhythmic categories in the content of the interviews

Category	Frequency
Dance	19
Other rhythm	15
Heart beat	3

Dancing

This activity frequently appeared in the reports. Generally the participants were dancing; sometimes they saw other people dancing. For example:

> I remember when I was very young, in the first class, my mother sewed me a little skirt from the leaves of corn. I wore this and I felt that I was dancing, to the rhythm of the drumming.

> I felt the rhythm and I was dancing.

Rhythm

There were reports without drumming or dancing, but with other kinds of rhythmic activities. For example:

> I was falling in a mining truck, in which the coal is transported, and that truck was clicking very loudly.

It was as if the underground is running in the darkness, and on the wall of the tunnel lights are flashing, repeatedly.

Somebody hammered swords.

Heart beat

Sometimes subjects felt their heart beat or their mother's heart beat. For example;

The rhythm of drumming was living within myself, I felt it in my chest, and this helped me to relax.

I heard a heart beat, as if I were in the womb of my mother.

Birth

The very fast rhythm may have induced near-birth experiences, which were associated with very great effort and heart rate. For example:

I reached a place where I had to break through a wall or a rock, and after that I was in a horizontal funnel, and I was not able to follow the way.

Control

There were reports without any kind of rhythm activities but in many cases participants felt as if they were directed by the drumming. Sometimes they wanted to stop in a place of their imaginary world but the drumming drove them away. Others wanted to move but they felt that the drumming did not let them do so. For example:

I became more and more tense. This was caused by the music. This music did not let me see. It didn't let me wander over the area I imagined.

There was a passage, downwards. It was of stones and there was darkness. I felt that there were ways to the right and left, and I wanted to see them, but the music did not let me do so. In these cavities there were colours and fragrances. The music didn't let me go there.

The music drove me further. It was like when you are passing by a shop-window, you could see that but you had to continue, and you were driven further. The drumming had a definitive role in the experiences.

It was the drumming that controlled the process and not me, everything was ruled by the drum.

These statements indicate also that the drumming had a very strong effect on subjective experiences. There were none of these phenomena in the reports of the 'imagery' group (see Table 4.3).

Table 4.3 Categories in the content of the interviews associated with drumming

	Drumming	Imagery
Dance	19	2
Other rhythm	15	2
Control	12	1
Sum	46	5

Regression

It was a common occurrence that participants, after reporting their experiences, could speak only with difficulty. They were looking for the right word and formed sentences which were incorrect grammatically. This uncertainty dissolved only by the end of the reports. This is also an indication of the deep regression. The regression appeared in the content of the reports as well.

I saw my grandfather, who took me by my hand. I was a young boy.

I saw my grandmother. I was very young when she died. I saw her grey hair.

Transcendence

In some cases subjects reported important, transcendent feelings.

I felt the freedom, I saw the ocean below and the sky was beautiful.

I tasted that essence and I felt the power coming into myself.

Sometimes they reported ecstatic feelings such as 'I was totally involved in the whirling.'

There were other experiences they could not communicate in words.

Conclusions

If participant subjects listen to drumming, subjective experiences change significantly compared with experiences in the usual alert state. There are changes in the perception of body-image and the passing of time. A perception of self and the world changes, as does the meaning of things. Self-consciousness becomes less accurate and the border between the self and the outside world becomes fuzzy. Participants felt that during drumming their state of consciousness had changed very strongly. All these changes indicate that drumming can induce an altered state of consciousness.

Listening to drumming has a definitive role in the process, because if participants were given the same imagery task without the drumming, there were no significant changes in subjective experiences.

The alterations of consciousness during listening to drumming are very similar to the alterations in hypnosis.

Listening to drumming influences the content of the imagery process, too. In some cases participants imagined that they were dancing or they imagined someone else dancing. In other cases there were other rhythmic activities, a train clattering along, or hammering. In some cases there were heartbeats and near-birth experiences.

Participants frequently felt that the direction and speed of their imaginary journey was controlled and guided totally by the drumming. They felt that the drumming was driving them or making them fly, and they could not stop, or the drumming concealed something they would like to see.

The effect of listening to drumming was very strong. Sometimes subjects cried, because they met important persons and relived very deep emotions from childhood. They relived important events and sometimes talked to relatives who had died a long time ago.

We conclude that listening to drumming influences subjective experiences very strongly and effectively because the experimental situation was unstructured. Participants were sitting with eyes closed while involved in their imagery. In this situation the associations evoked by listening to continuous drumming can influence the content of the subjects' imaginary processes. It may be that all the rhythmic experiences are somehow connected with heartbeat or near-birth experiences and this is the reason for the effectiveness of drumming.

Acknowledgement

This research was supported by the National Scientific Foundation (OTKA) No. T. 043394.

Chapter 5

Perception and Responses to Schemata in Different Cultures

Western and Arab Music

Dalia Cohen

Introduction

The basic variables of rules of organization, form and cognitive activity (including memory) are, as we know (Tversky 1977), *difference* and *similarity*. But what is difference? What is similarity or even identicality? And how are these perceptions influenced?

   In this chapter we attempt to answer these questions by experimenting with responses to selected patterns of music representing different cultures, Western and Arab. We will focus on characteristics of the schemata that form the basis of musical tradition, the listeners' cultural background and knowledge base, and cognitive constraints. Our purpose is to gain a better understanding of the significance of the various schemata, perception of them, and responses to them. Various aspects of each of these subtopics have been researched before but they have not all been studied together as they are here.

   This chapter has ramifications for both music therapy and music education, because in both of these fields the subject's cultural and musical background are extremely important. The work presented here is based in part on my experience in teaching Western and Arab music to students from two cultures at the Jerusalem Academy of Music and Dance where the results of the study have had an impact on my teaching method.

Assumptions

1   Every style (of a culture, period, or even composer) is characterized by the selection of schemata manifested in the various stages of musical activity: 'raw material' (for example – intervals, scales, metres, and rhythmic patterns); rules of composition; and rules of performance. The schemata link events and elicit expectations.

2   The specific (unconscious) selection of schemata reflects the aesthetic ideal of a period or culture, subject to psychoacoustic and cognitive constraints (Cohen and Granot 1995).

3   One of the characteristics of the aesthetic ideal is the type of complexity and directionality (Cohen 1994).

4   Listening to music, both perceiving and responding, and memory of music, like other cognitive activities, take place with constant reference to schemata that are formulated unconsciously in our minds at an extremely young age (Donchin and Coles 1988; Leman 1995). Listeners do not respond to details of music based on schemata that are unfamiliar to them. An event that is considered salient, due to deviation from expectations regarding schemata specific to a particular culture, will not be perceived as salient by listeners who are not familiar, even unconsciously, with the schemata. This will affect the perception of difference or similarity (Tversky 1977).

5   Part of the ability to respond to music, like mathematical aptitude, is expressed in the form of skill at uncovering the schemata, which may be extremely well hidden. This ability, which is very useful to memory (Bertz 1995; Boltz 1991; Chaffin and Imreh 1997), is influenced by learning (Gardner 1982), which increases awareness of the schemata, and by mathematical aptitude.

6   Musical schemata may be either 'learned' or 'natural'.

    a)   The 'learned' schemata (e.g. scales and rhythmic patterns) are hardly known outside the realm of music and are culture-dependent – although not necessarily arbitrary (e.g. Agmon 1989; Balzano 1980).

b)   The 'natural' schemata are rules of organization that are meaningful and familiar to us from outside the realm of music. The ones that are relevant to the present study are those that affect the type of directionality: contours (e.g. Dowling 1978; Huron 1997), degree of definability (Cohen and Wagner 2000), and kinds of operations (Cohen and Dubnov 1997).

Hypothesis

The influences on the way we distinguish between the basic variables of organization – 'difference', 'similarity' and 'identity' – stem from the types of directionality and complexity of the musical material, culture, learning, and even mathematical aptitude (we are not looking at the effect of age and musical talent here).

The selected cultures

The focus here is on the responses of Arabs and Westerners in Israel to Arab and Western musical patterns that represent very different ideals. Some of the differences between the two selected cultures are as follows. Western music has overall directionality with complexity, whereas Arab music has a strong focus on the moment. Western music has maximum separation of all kinds (between metre and rhythm, scales and other characteristics, composition and performance), whereas Arab music has numerous predetermined relationships, as manifested in the *maqam* framework or predetermined rhythmic patterns.

Western music has an interval system with maximum coherence (Agmon 1989; Balzano 1980), including clear categories, and many types of harmonic realization, whereas Arab music has more intervals with less coherence, and most of the large intervals in Arab music are meaningless. Western music has many binary aspects and kinds of contrast on various levels (e.g. two kinds of metre, duple and triple, and two kinds of scales, major and minor), which allow for multiple complex superstructures. Arab music has fewer contrasts, binary aspects are rare, and the large number of rhythmic patterns (there are approximately one hundred in theory) increases momentary complexity and prevents a hierarchical superstructure. In Western music a variety of operations are used in complex ways at various levels, whereas in Arab music only a few operations are used in a simple manner.

Method

We carried out an experiment on the responses of Arabs and Westerners to Arab and Western musical patterns and to series of numbers.

Subjects

Fifty-five participants, aged 20–30 (38 Westerners and 18 Arabs), with various amounts of music education were chosen. The Arabs have not studied music formally and have not been exposed to Western music, but most of them (14) sing regularly in a choir and some (4) play an instrument, meaning that they have greater awareness of musical material. The Westerners are students either in a general college or in a music academy, where the level of music education is higher.

The material examined

In addition to the musical material, mathematical material was examined. The musical material included some patterns characteristic of Western tonal music and some characteristic of Arab music. They were all used for identification and comparison by all of the subjects; some of the patterns were also sung, with each group singing only its own material.

The Western musical material included 33 patterns that related only to the pitch factor, with constant duration. The patterns were played from a computer in the timbre of a piano. Most of them were monophonic and had between five and seven events (only seven of the patterns were long, with 12 or 19 notes). The patterns were based on some learned schemata (scales and harmonic patterns) and natural schemata, which could be simple or complex, long or short. These were divided into six categories, differentiated by directionality.

Thirty pairs of these patterns were selected for comparison, and 20 patterns were selected to be sung. Most of the pairs consisted of patterns from the same category. The simplest category of pairs consists of patterns based on a simple, standard schema – a broken chord followed by a series of seconds going in the opposite direction (Example 5 in Figure 5.1). The

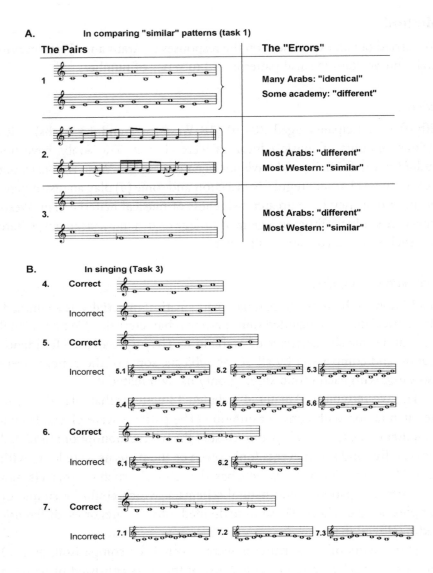

Figure 5.1 Example of some errors

operation may be shift (chord inversion, register change) or contrast (convex/concave; major/minor).

The relationship between the schemata in the pair may be 'different' (from different categories), 'identical' or 'similar' (the difference comes from various operations).

The Arab material included 15 patterns belonging to 4 categories; 16 pairs were used for comparison and 7 patterns were selected for singing. The patterns were played on the *oud* – living phrases with rhythm and clear beats but no clear metre. The categories were differentiated by *maqam* motifs and length. The operations in 'similar' patterns were shifts, addition of ornamentation, and changes in rhythm. 'Identical' patterns were not performed exactly the same way.

The mathematical material included numerical patterns – 20 series of numbers (6–9 in each) in five categories of schemata, including randomness.

The task

In the mathematical section, subjects were told to repeat the entire pattern (a series of numbers) in writing after viewing it for 25 seconds. In the musical section there were three tasks:

1   to compare the patterns in each pair and note whether they were very different, similar, or identical

2   to explain in writing how they were similar or different and to specify the strategy used

3   to repeat a selection of 20 patterns by singing them. In both music and mathematics subjects had to specify the strategy used.

Results

In general, the 'errors' caused by flaws in musical memory and perception (in the three experimental tasks) were found to be influenced to varying degrees by all of the factors investigated: types of schemata and realizations thereof; types of relationships between patterns (in the pairs); culture; degree of learning; and mathematical aptitude. Note that the concept of an error depends in part on our definitions.

Below is a selection of the findings:

- a general summary of principles governing the effects of the musical patterns and the influence of culture and knowledge
- selected details from Figures 5.1–5.7 and Table 5.1.

General findings

Characterizations of the patterns that influence memory of them

Certain natural principles in the patterns were found to facilitate musical memory among all the subjects in all the tasks: short length, convexity (as opposed to concavity), ascent (as opposed to descent), clear differences, clear structure, a small number of simple operations (e.g., shift is simpler than contrast), and little 'competition' (non-concurrence) between parameters or schemata (for example, a pair of chord patterns with identical harmony and different melody or vice versa). In singing, most of the errors were 'corrective' – in the direction of simpler directional or symmetrical schemata.

Culture and knowledge

The general effect of musical culture and knowledge, as expressed by the number of errors in the three tasks (Figures 5.2–5.7). Among Westerners: the academy students erred less than the college students (especially in Figure 5.1.3); among Arabs: the instrumentalists erred less than the singers; for Western music: the Westerners erred less than the Arabs; for Arab music: Arabs erred less than Westerners. (In many cases in Arab music, however, the academy students did better than the Arab singers.)

Answers to Task 2: a verbal explanation of the difference or similarity between the patterns in the pair

Responses to patterns from the two cultures (Figure 5.2a)

Altogether, the percentage of 'no answers' in Task 2 is greater for the Arab material than for the Western material and is greatest for the Arabs (40 per cent for the Western material and 51 per cent for the Arab material). As for the quantity of errors, but not necessarily their quality, fewer errors were made on the Arab material, and the fewest of all were made by academy students (on either kind of material).

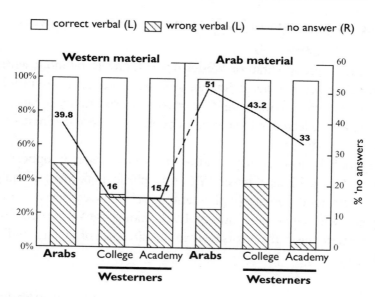

Figure 5.2a Proportion of correct and mistaken verbal explanations and percentage of 'no answer' from Task 2

Western culture (Figure 5.2b)

The difference between academy and college students is salient when there is a contradiction between the answers in the two tasks (1 and 2) for the same patterns, i.e. when the description of the relationship between the two patterns in a pair (in Task 1) – different, similar or identical – was correct but the verbal explanation of the differences and similarities (Task 2) was wrong.

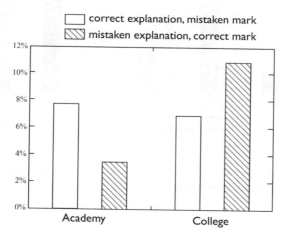

Figure 5.2b The effect of musical knowledge on explanation from Task 2 (Western patterns)

Direction of errors in Task 1: more similar or more different (Figure 5.3)

Each cultural group (Arab or Western) was found to be more sensitive to differences in *its own* music. Studying music makes us aware of what our minds unconsciously know and heightens our sensitivity to small differences. This is reflected in the direction of errors towards difference or similarity.

Figure 5.3 shows clearly that the Arabs' errors were in opposite directions for the two kinds of music. With Arab music there was a salient preference for greater difference (with a ratio of 7:1 between the two directions, compared with an average ratio of 1:7:1 among the Westerners), whereas with Western music, the errors were in the direction of greater similarity or identity.

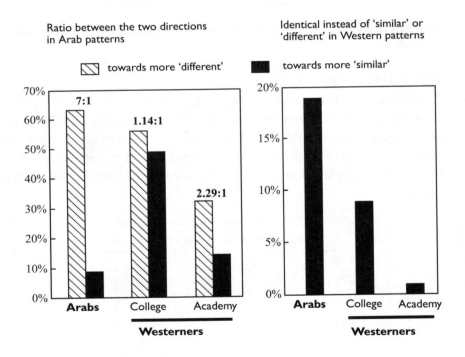

Figure 5.3 Directions of errors: 'identical–similar–different' from Task 1 (each cultural group is more sensitive to differences in its own music)

Selected details about the findings: responses to Western patterns (Task 1)

Responses to harmonic schemata (Figure 5.4)

As we see in Figure 5.4, for all the patterns (in the 12 pairs) the Arabs made about twice as many errors as the Westerners. The most salient difference between the two cultures was in the responses to one pair (I–IV–V–I I–V–IV–I). Although they are similar according to our terms, some of the academy students marked them as 'different', while most of the Arabs marked them as 'identical'.

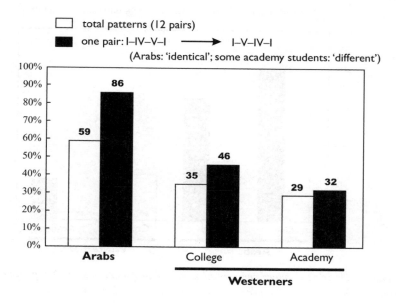

Figure 5.4 The effect of learned schemata and culture from Task 1: percentage of errors in comparison of Western patterns based on harmony

Responses to the operation of contrast, which is not common in Arab music

Patterns related by 'retrograde' and even by 'inversion' were considered by Arabs to be very different, not similar (Figures 5.1, 5.3).

Responses to Arab patterns (Task 1)

The principle of separation between components of a musical unit, which is common in Western but not Arab music (Figure 5.5)

Figure 5.5 shows the errors (different, rather than similar) for two pairs in which separation does exist with respect to Arab patterns. In one of the pairs, the patterns are identical in terms of the notes in the melody and different in terms of rhythm. In the other, the patterns differ only in terms of the *maqam* scale. Thus, even though this is Arab music, the Arabs made more 'errors' (compared, of course, to our definitions).

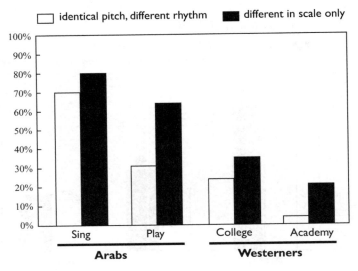

Figure 5.5 The effect of culture and separation between components from Task 1: percentage of errors ('different' instead of 'similar') in comparison of two kinds of Arab pairs.

Responses to minuscule events typical of Arab music that focuses on the moment but not of Western music (Figure 5.6)

We see in the figure that Westerners made more errors than the Arabs did, while in both groups the degree of musical knowledge was important.

Errors in singing Western music (Figure 5.7): The effect of knowledge and the nature of the pattern

In Figure 5.7, we see a high correlation between the number of errors in singing Western patterns and the degree of learning (the academy students versus the college students). A correlation was also found among the six categories, arranged hierarchically by the number of errors.

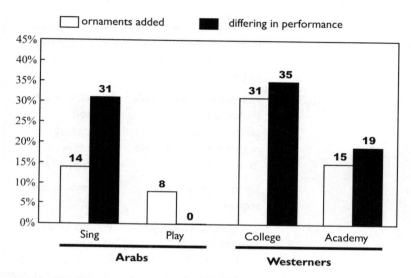

Figure 5.6 *The effect of minuscule momentary events, culture and knowledge from Task 1: percentage of errors in comparison of Arab patterns.*

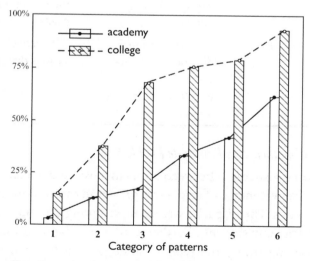

Figure 5.7 *The effect of category of patterns and knowledge from Task 3: percentage of errors in singing Western patterns.*

Table 5.1 The six categories arranged hierarchically by errors and degrees of directionality

Category	No. of notes per pattern	Characterization of the pattern	Remarks about errors
1	5–6	Broken chord followed by seconds in the opposite direction	Concave > convex
2	7	Harmonic patterns with broken chords, ascending or descending, in different inversions	Inversion > basic position Descending > ascending 'Corrective' error
3	6	Internal splits with sequence	Non-salient note > salient
4	12, 19	Long and divided: (a) into six links of trichords with sequence; (b) into two convex curves for a chord and for seconds	Various kinds of reduction 'Corrections' in the direction of symmetry
5	7	No directionality, zigzag with large intervals	Shifts of seconds, not of the opening notes and peaks
6	12–14	Deviations from a directional schema a: I–IV–V–I b: I–V–I and leading tones	'Corrective' errors in various directions

The effect of mathematical aptitude (Table 5.2)

A correlation is also found between errors in music and in mathematics. For all groups, the percentage of errors was greater in the random series than in the logical series. The disparity was smallest among the Arabs and greatest among the academy students. Furthermore, a correlation is found between the responses regarding the type of strategy used to remember musical patterns and the strategy used to remember series of numbers. The significant correlation may attest either to the effect of mathematical aptitude on analytical activity in music, or to the effect of musical activity on mathematical ability, or both. In any case, it bolsters the arguments regarding the importance of the analytical aspect of musical activity.

Table 5.2 The effect of mathematical aptitude and negative correlation between success in identifying numerical series and errors in music (the higher the score the smaller the number of errors)

Target in music	Participants	Pearson correlation coefficient
A) Identification of patterns Arab music Western music	All participants (Arabs and Westerners)	-0.47 (p=0.04) -0.15 (p=0.38)
B) Singing of Western patterns	Western (Academy and college) College only	-0.72 (p=0.04) -0.58 (p=0.03)

Note: For all of the groups, the percentages of errors was greater in the random series than in the logical series. The disparity was smallest among the Arabs and greatest among the Academy students. Furthermore, a correlation was found between the responses regarding the type of strategy used to remember musical patterns and the strategy used to remember series of numbers.

Conclusion

Further research is required, but these findings tentatively support the hypothesis that there are cultural influences on musical perception and memory and on responses to music. We show that the differences between responses to different patterns depend on the subjects' degree of music education; the degree of directionality and complexity of the patterns, which is itself influenced by the kind of schemata; types of relationships between the patterns in the pairs, that depend mainly on the kind of operation; relationships between musical and mathematical activity; and culture-dependent differences that reflect the aesthetic ideal. This sheds additional light on the meanings of the natural and learned schemata, the ways in which they are realized, and possible competition between them, and reinforces the assumption that the relationship between types of directionality and complexity (which represent an important characteristic of the aesthetic ideal) and the 'selected' schemata of a particular style is more than mere convention.

Chapter 6

Music as Medicine: The Adyghs' Case

Alla N. Sokolova

Background

The Adyghs (Circassians) are natives of the North Caucasus. They speak a language that belongs to the Iberian-Caucasian family. The Adyghs have their own culture preserved in numerous ancient rites and rituals, as well as traditional views on the magical force of music. In the course of history these views have remained virtually unchanged.

The Adygh musical culture is essentially unknown to European ethnomusicologists. The purpose of this chapter is to present information about music as a therapeutic agent for the Adyghs throughout their history and to analyse the reasons for preserving ethnic views on music as a magic power.

Medical properties of music and the universe

Many peoples have regarded music as a special divine agent that has healing effects allotted by a supernatural force . Directly or indirectly, music has been used as medicine in many traditional cultures. Illness, in archaic and traditional societies, has been accepted as evidence of disequilibrium, where there is a disharmony between the person and nature. In the perspective taken here, music is considered as part of both nature and space, and capable of acting as a healing agent by reconciling the person with nature. Secondly, music – like a liquid remedy, or decoction taken by sick people – deeply penetrates the organism of the person and acts as a medicine.

74

Medicine is being used in a wide sense of the word: as a drug or remedy used for treating illness and as a ritual practice or sacred object believed to control supernatural powers or work as a preventive or remedy of illness.

Correlation between Caucasian nature and music

The basic elements of music include pitch, rhythm, timbre, tune, harmony, tempo and dynamic. These agents of musical expressivity do not carry any special divine purpose. In the music healing perspective suggested, these expressive means of a culture correlate with the geographical landscape and the ethno-social conditions, rather than with divine ideas.

Figure 6.1 Topography of the mountains of the North Caucasus

Thus, there is a distinct correspondence between pitch, rhythm and timbre of the ethnic music and climatic conditions of the region where a given ethnic group lives. For example, Russian ethnic groups, traditionally living along the wide and open plains, have also an extensive tuneful development of musical material and wide melodic forms. The Adyghs, in contrast, are mountain people; therefore, Adygh ethnic music is characterized by rather short melodic forms and a special type of performance which combines two components, namely a high man's voice (of the leading singer) and the low attending voices (for supporting vocal parts). The high voice carries on the meaningful part whereas the low male voices intone senseless syllables – e–rai–da, o–ri, o–ri–ra, etc. The timbre colouring of a high voice is bright, ringing, while supporting voices appear muffled and dull, like a mountain echo.

For the Adyghs, such singing offers the highest aesthetic pleasure. The Adyghs have a special form of polyphonic choral singing, the so-called solo-drone. The scheme of traditional Adygh songs resembles a mountain topography where the foothills of the mountains are a drone sustained by a supporting voice, and the pitch phrases of a leading singer resemble the pointed peaks of mountains at different altitudes (Figure 6.2). Conditions of the mountain landscape and the sound environment (mountain rivers, stones rolling down the hill, screams of birds and animals) seem to have an effect on the Adygh language which contains two or three times as many sounds as, for instance, the Romance languages, the majority of which are composed of consonants. Verbal language finds its expression in musical language. Thus the original sounds and structures of the Adygh form their conventional music.

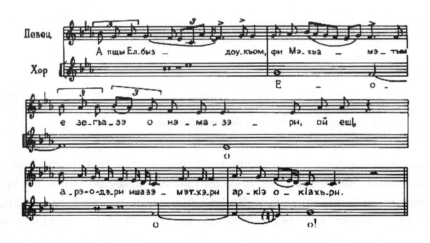

Figure 6.2 Melody for the Chapsh ritual (from Shu 1997, p.31)

Medical properties of music in its perception

Ethnomusicologists investigating ceremonial tunes and their related 'medical' rituals, do not see anything 'supernatural' in them and prefer to speak of their 'salutary properties' (Zemtsovsky 1986). Nevertheless, the immanent properties of the music allow us 'to see' something that distinguishes this music from other kinds of art. Music is a distinctly organized system of rhythm, pitch, composition, structure, and coherence of verbal

Figure 6.3 The rites at the bed of injured or traumatized people, the North Caucasus, settlement of Khakurinokhabl, 1927. Adygh National Museum, photographer unknown

and musical text. In music perception that coherence is holistic, arising from the interplay between physiology, psychology and the music itself. Music then has the potential of bringing out positive changes in a person's psychological and physical well-being. The more elevated and refined the music is, and more integrated as an overall system of music, then the greater are its therapeutic properties.

Similarly, music is also considered as influencing not only people, but also animals, insects, birds and plants. Since antiquity, the Adyghs' shepherds remarked that rams grazing under the sound of a horn become healthier, fatter and, even, more obedient (Chashba 1998).

Adygh rites and rituals in which music is used for therapeutic purposes

Rites at the bed of injured or traumatized people

The Adyghs did not know of any opiates or any other drug widely used in other ethnomedicines. Their traditional medical culture developed different methods.

From ancient times to the middle of the twentieth century, Adyghs performed a rite called 'Chapsh' for people with bullet wounds, snakebites or bone trauma (see Figure 6.3).

Figure 6.4 Music used in the Chapsh ritual (from Shu 1997, p.30)

The idea of this rite is that a sick person is not left alone during the night or in the dark and participants of this rite do not allow the patient to fall asleep, but entertain him with games, songs (see Figure 6.4), jokes and humorous performances. Girls and boys are invited to dance and sing to the accompaniment of a violin. The performer on the violin is always a man who knows the ritual and how it is to be performed well. Cheerful games are replaced by dances, followed by a sequence of songs. These songs, with heroic texts, help the sick person tolerate pain, where he can identify himself with the heroic images. Cheerful dance tunes distract a sick person from pain, while the young onlookers have a good time (see Figure 6.5).

The performance of a ceremonial tune during the period of recovery is obligatory. Legend assigns the tune to a musician who was invited to this rite by Kodgeberduko, hero of the Caucasian war. According to legend, a doctor removed a bullet from Kodgeberduko's leg while listening to a certain folk tune. Surgery was performed without an anaesthetic, only an optimistic tune. Since then, this special tune has been used traditionally for this rite as an obligatory ceremonial musical text (see Figure 6.6).

Figure 6.5 Melody for distraction from pain (from Shu 1997, p.32)

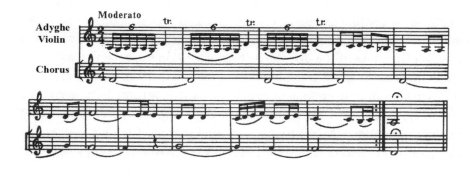

Figure 6.6 Melody for the operation of removing a bullet (from Shu 1997, p.33)

Music performed in this rite is considered to have magic properties and a beneficent influence on a sick person. One song is by nature severe and heroic; other tunes have a quiet, narrative content; others sustain a playful, dancing atmosphere. Almost all of the tunes (except for a tune special to this rite only) can also be performed outside the rite. The tunes have achieved their healing function precisely because they occur in the context of this salutary rite where the function of the magical impact on a sick person has raised them above mere domestic songs or folk tunes. A simple song has then been turned into a ceremonial song. A common dancing melody has been turned into a magic dancing melody. Formerly separate tunes, by becoming integrated within the context of a rite, became the acoustic symbols of the rite. Thus, these specific tunes gained medical power because they were performed during special rites. These tunes then became salutary because people perceived them as salutary.

Impact on the state of mind and the treatment of somatic diseases

Adyghs consider that music treats body and soul. It has a special influence on a person before the beginning of a battle, invoking bravery. In Abkhaz-Adygh fairy tales, there are scenes where the musician heals the wounds of warriors and the warriors are ready then to fight again. Even in the twentieth century, people wishing to praise a good harmonica player would say that he played so well that the paralysed rose from their beds and began to dance.

Adyghs and Abkhazes are known to have songs for the treatment of smallpox. According to legend, each disease had a special god, whose anger invokes the disease. A female researcher was invited to visit a sick person to discover the cause of the disease. At her instigation a special rite was held, involving a night spent at the bedside of the sick person, accompanied by songs in honour of the god who visited the patient. A song dedicated to the god of smallpox, Achi Zoschan (Golden Zoschan), was performed during this rite. Sometimes Achi Zoschan's marital partner, Chaniya White, was also glorified in a song (Chashba 1998, p.33). Chashba (1998) also points to the special significance of music in the treatment of burns. According to another folk legend, a song about a burn caused the wounds to heal more quickly.

When children become ill with contagious diseases, the Abkhazes sing lullabies, in which they express a wish of death for the child. Probably, they contain a magic by contradiction (Chashba 1998, p.34). Lullabies are performed at a difficult birth in the woman's room and cases of successful birth have been affirmed (Chashba 1998, p.34). Most of all, music influences the emotional state of a person, allowing the expression of mutual feelings of pleasure or pain together. We have recorded many testimonies of how sick people recovered much faster after surgery while listening to their native music and how their desire to live and to work, to care about relatives, is stimulated.

A therapeutic interpretation of the functions of music in the traditional culture of the Adyghs shows at least four 'facets' of research: a magic-salutary force, specific texts, musical instruments and dance as a kinetic act. Each of these facets has its own action and outcome. Contagious diseases are traditionally 'treated' by songs in which the verbal part plays the pre-dominant role and the musical text plays a supporting role.

Both songs and instrumental folk tunes are important for uplifting the spirit and in creating a militant heroic state. Musical instruments and the music performed retain the formal conventional elements through the special qualities of the instruments themselves and the influence of masterly performance. The authority of the instrumental music conventions offers a situation that encourages faith in healing (Sokolova 1999, p.177).

Aerophones, by virtue of their own morphological characteristics, are capable of connecting the earth and the unearthly worlds through breathing. Therefore, they are used in rites of searching for a drowned man and for those trapped under snow or rock falls (Kharaeva-Gvasheva 1999, p.43).

Ceremonial dances are also related to public prayer. The dance 'Sandrak' is performed in the naming of a child (Sokolova 1998) and dance is also used as a means of driving away a malicious spirit that has caused a person's illness.

Conclusion

Historic and ethnographic data show that music is used for medical purposes in the Adygh and Abkhaz traditional cultures. The salutary prop-erties of the music lie in the attitude of people toward them rather than in the melodies, intonations and rhythms.

In the contemporary music of Adygh culture, as in the past, there is a public health function, that preserves mental equilibrium and harmoniza-tion in society. Music still dominates family rituals, especially weddings, childbirth and a child's first entering school.

Chapter 7

Music and Drug-Induced Altered States of Consciousness

Jörg Fachner

Introduction

Drugs have different action profiles that may be theoretically categorized according to Julien (1997) as mainly euphoric, sedative, or psychedelic. Euphoric drugs, like cocaine and amphetamines, and sedative drugs, like heroin and tranquilizers, primarily alter the quality of emotional states. Psychedelic (from Greek *psyche delos* – enhancing consciousness or soul) drugs (e.g. LSD, Mescaline, psilocybin) produce qualitative changes in the conceptual–cognitive evaluation of sensory input data. Sedative drugs may help to keep sensory reality in its emotional relation to the perceiving individual at a distance, whereas euphoric drugs eliminate distance almost completely. Psychedelic drugs flood the brain with sensory data and weaken sensory brain functions through contradictory associations of sensory reality (see Emrich 1990). A common quality of all psychoactive drugs is that they alter the evaluation of sensory input, its conceptual comparison with known contents and the assessment parameters of (not) relevant information. This happens through drug-specific individual activation and inhibition of the interaction between midbrain, cerebrum and cerebellum. The limbic system of the midbrain that changes the evaluation parameters through the emotional colouring of sensory data plays a specific role in this context.

Altered states of consciousness, drugs and apperception

Roth (1994) underlines a brain functionality independent of culture as the physiological precondition to grasp the content and meaning of what we perceive through our senses. The selection of contents in sensory awareness (perception) depends on the individual and his situation, his history of learning and the ego of a person who deliberately or unconsciously differentiates in selection and meaning (apperception) (Eckel 1982; Spintge 1991). Emrich (1990) defines three components of differentiations: (1) sensory data, which are (2) conceptualized and (3) useless concepts are censored by experience and memory.

From an information theory stance, Keidel (1975) describes apperception as a personal situation dependent on reduction and selection of in- and output information units as an important function of the central nervous system in sensory and motor processes.

As shown in Figure 7.1, 10^9 sensory information bits per second reach sensory receptor units from the environment and are reduced for consciously perceived information in the proportion of 1:10 million. During motor behaviour and speech, about 10^7 bits of information per second will be transmitted to the environment. The rest of information processing happens unconsciously. Thus the notion of 'expansion or heightening of consciousness' (see Nixon 1999) may be functionally understood as an evoked altered state of consciousness (see Tassi and Muzet 2001, p.185) resulting in a flooding of sensory data.

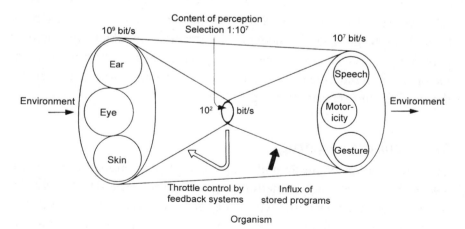

Figure 7.1 Apperception, functionality of perceptual reduction from Keidel (1975).
Reproduced from Keidel, W.D. (1975) Kurzgefaßtes Lehrbuch der Physiologie, *Chapter 16, p.1. Reprinted with permission from Georg Thieme Verlag*

Emotion, music reception and intoxication

Music and intoxication appear to have common forms of emotional processing, at least in regard to processing in the limbic system. Everyone has a particular musical style or styles he prefers to others. Some very special pieces of music may even send shivers down the spine. It is exactly these shivers or chills felt in listening to favourite music that were used by Blood and Zatorre (2001) to demonstrate that musical information reaches those brain structures involved in conveying emotion. Listening to our favourite melody, we register changes in the activity of the autonomous nerve system, changes in heart beat, muscle tension, skin resistance and depth of breathing and also in the blood flow in brain structures that are also involved in processing emotional stimuli. The activation pattern of brain regions show a surprising similarity to activity patterns induced by drugs with a primarily euphoric effect like cocaine. Our favourite music interacts directly with structures associated with emotions (Blood and Zatorre 2001).

This finding mentioned above may help to explain why music has the power to 'intoxicate' individuals who love a particular type of music and to transport them to an altered state (Brandl 1993; Mayr-Kern 1985; Rösing 1991b). It depends on the listener whether in contemplation this becomes an inner spiritual experience, whereby the music 'lends wings to the soul', as admirers of classical music like to point out, or whether the rhythm 'gets into your legs' stimulating movement and thereby triggering an experience of the entire body (David, Berlin and Klement 1983) such as ecstatic dance at a rave party (Mitterlehner 1996). Rösing writes, music 'can only be of limited importance in the network of receptive variables compared to personal and social factors. Consequently, music seems to be only what the recipient, as an individual marked by his social environment, makes of it in the moment of listening' (Rösing 1991b, p.8).

Music culture and drugs

The combination of music and drugs as a phenomenon specific to the 1960s is certainly not something new. Walther von der Vogelweide described drunken festivities with wine, women and song in castles during the Middle Ages, and the Greeks even added psychedelic substances (ergot) to the wine for their bacchanalia (Rätsch 1995a). Drugs were discovered in nature and cultivated for use by experienced shamans in initiation rites or for tribal festivities (Metzner 1992). These drugs could be found by the wayside and used to promote rest or contemplation, cause thoughts to wander or dive into inner worlds, pose questions about the nature of reality and help the brain to mature (McKenna 1992) or create an awareness of a hunger for knowledge. There are situations of revelation that 'tell' intoxicated individuals something and mark an altered state of consciousness (Rätsch 1992a). Whether this happens in dance, in love-making, or in contemplation depends on individual lifestyle and preferences (Taeger 1988). 'The ritual of drugs' (Szasz 2003) has often created mood, led to ecstasy, produced a primary experience (Laing 1967) or opened up new worlds of imagination (Masters and Houston 1968), ideas, visions, or even spirits (Rätsch 1992a).

Walter Freeman (2000) discusses connections between music and dance and the cultural evolution of human behaviour and relationships. He assumes that the knowledge of the induction of altered states of consciousness is connected with chemical and behavioural forms of induction. The trance states produced this way serve to break through traditional customs and concepts of reality but also to heighten susceptibility to new information. Such intended changes lead to the formation of 'initiated' groups and confidentiality in passing on significant findings. Musical skills in particular appeared to be important for an efficient trading of knowledge.

Ideas of a more bodily world of experience were postulated in the arts, literature, movies and music in the 1960s, and psychoactive substances served to accompany and intensify individual and social processes (Leary 1990). The 'Sputnik shock' in the 1950s triggered a search for means to promote creativity and talent in the West, specifically the United States (Barber-Kersovan 1991). Research into consciousness-enhancing, psychedelic substances was also funded in this context (Lee and Shalin 1992). Cultural changes in the 1960s made drugs very popular and highly publicized creations by artists, music and movie stars (Taqi 1969; Taqi 1972) and provided a fertile social ground for ideas about heightened, expanded consciousness, altered perceptions and de-conditioning of behaviour (Carey 1968; Kupfer 1996a; Kupfer 1996b; Leary 1990; Nixon 1999).

Drug influences on creativity, spirituality and lyrics?

Various authors explored the cultural aspects of drug use among artists and its influence on artistic creativity and performance (Aldrich, 1946; Böhm 1999; Boyd 1992; Fachner 2000a; Fachner 2002a; Fachner 2002b; Kimmens 1977; Krippner 1977; Krippner 1985; Kupfer 1996a; Kupfer 1996b; Markert 2001; Masters and Houston 1968; Plant 1999; Plucker and Dana 1998; Taeger 1988; TenBerge 1999). Barbara Kerr (1992) interviewed artists on drug habits and found a significantly higher tendency to consume cannabis in musicians compared to other artists. In answer to the question as to what inspired the Beatles' music, or what it expressed, at the time when the album *Sgt. Pepper's Lonely Hearts Club Band* was published, Paul McCartney said:

> Experience with drugs, mostly. But remember that in 1967 our drug habits followed a long-established tradition among musicians. We knew about Louis Armstrong, Duke Ellington, and Count Basie that they had always taken drugs. Now it was time for our musical scene to make the experience. Drugs found their way into everything we did. They coloured our perspective of things. I believe we realized that there were fewer limitations than we had expected. And we understood that we were able to break through barriers. (Davis and Pieper 1993, p.7)

Masters and Houston (1968) as well as Krippner (1977) described effects of psychedelic drugs on the creativity of visual artists. Psychedelics produced an inner flood of images that the artists wanted to project onto their works. The authors also mentioned musicians who expressed their experience in a combination of text and music. Taeger (1988) proposed that the combination of music and drugs in the pop culture was not just born from a wish to make cash, but that the music and texts of pop artists revealed a spiritual search or longing. Taeger explored interpersonal correlations between psychedelics and religious-mystical aspects in the counterculture of the 1970s. He found many indications of spiritual experience and attitudes of musicians and artists on the covers of albums and in texts by pop artists of the 1960s and 1970s. Psychedelics provided access to the collective subconscious. Many images and symbols described in texts revealed a mystical experience produced by psychedelics, as already described by Jung in his theory of archetypes (Taeger 1988, p.131ff).

Explicit hints of drug habits in the song texts by rock and jazz musicians were regarded as an invitation to take drugs, and radio stations banned certain titles on the basis of more or less arbitrary criteria (Markert 2001; Shapiro 1998). Schwartz analysed song texts and, like other researchers (Douse 1973; Robinson, Pilskaln, and Hirsch 1976), concluded that the texts were no explicit invitation to take drugs but rather reported the experience involved in drug consumption (Schwartz and Feinglass 1973). A more recent media study of drug consumption in movies and music found clear indications of a high acceptance and presence of legal drugs like alcohol, coffee and nicotine. US hip-hop texts with political motivation contained the most allusions to the ban on cannabis and the effects of the substance (Roberts, Henriksen and Christenson 1999).

In a study on subliminal messages in popular music, Rösing reported just one (Queen: 'Another one bites the dust', that was recorded backwards) which has a clearly understandable invitation to consume cannabis. Various social groups with a religious or conservative background claimed that song texts contained subliminal messages that were explicitly clear, but this was not confirmed. Respondents in test groups recognized any subliminal messages only after a transcription of attributions of such text passages (Rösing 1991a).

Böhm (1997, 1999) gives a musicological insight into the effects of psychedelics on the composition process with the Beatles record *Sgt. Pepper's Lonely Hearts Club Band* as an example. Baumeister (1984) reflects the acid rock of the 1960s and 1970s, reggae music and the culture of Rastafarians in Jamaica (see Blätter 1990, 1992, 1995; Rubin and Comitas 1975; Shapiro 1998), and also the cannabis-inspired Rembetiko music in Greece in the 1930s (see Behr 1982, p.208). More recent developments in punk, hip-hop, techno or Goa trance (Cousto 1995; Lyttle and Montagne 1992; Rätsch 1995b) will only be mentioned in passing in this context.

Sheila Whiteley analysed music by Pink Floyd, the Beatles and other groups of the 1960s and 1970s and developed the concept of 'psychedelic coding' that described symbolic and semiotic codings of elements of 'psychedelic culture' in composition. On the basis of text and material analysis she discusses links between cultural semantics and drug effects in music and socio-cultural environments of the groups analysed (Whiteley 1992) who distinguished themselves in the production of a specific sound from other groups (Whiteley 1997).

Shapiro suggests that every popular musical style was the expression of a lifestyle that should also be seen in relation to the habits of the artists and the artistic scene marking that style (Shapiro 1998). From a socio-pharmacological perspective, the predilection of a sub-cultural scene for a certain drug always was a kind of fashion to get 'turned on', that is, to enter certain physiological states in order to experience normal and unusual events and moods more intensively and from a new perspective (Lyttle and Montagne 1992).

'Sex & Drugs & Rock'n'Roll, that's all my brain and body needs': with this lyric, Ian Dury paraphrased the feeling and lifestyle of the 'party culture'. As discussed by Harry Shapiro, almost every popular musical style had its own (party) drugs. Among jazz musicians (see Becker 1963; Behrendt 1956; Cambor, Lisowitz, and Miller 1962; Curry 1968; Czadek 1986; Jonnes 1999; Mezzrow 1946; Sloman 1998; Webster 2001; Winick 1959; Winick 1961; Winick and Nyswander 1961) in the 1920s and 1930s it was marihuana, in the 1940s and 1950s even heroin, whereas the Rock'n'Rollers of the 1950s mainly tended towards the various 'uppers' and 'downers' like amphetamines and barbiturates. The hippies of the 1960s preferred psychedelics (see Leary 1990; Martin and Pearson 1995; Whiteley 1992), the punks of the 1970s experimented with chemical solvents, the 'fashionable set' of the 1980s used cocaine as a euphoriant, and the 1990s saw an increased consumption of synthetic drugs, in particular MDMA (ecstasy) among party goers (Abdelkader 1994; Adlaf and Smart 1997; Fachner 2004b; Lenton, Boys and Norcross 1997).

Alcohol, tobacco, psychotropic drugs and coffee are examples of legal drugs that have been loyally consumed specifically by classical musicians until today (Bessler and Opgenoorth 2000). Berlioz' 'Symphonie Phantastique' hints at opium and music, and Richard Wagner's musical description of the 'consciousness-enhancing qualities of Isolde's love potion' (Rätsch 1986, p.313) suggests that the currently fashionable drugs were not unknown to the representatives of so-called 'serious' music.

Drugs in music and therapy

In the last century, the physician Moreau de Tours (1845) described the effects of cannabis on renowned authors like Baudelaire (1966) or Gautier (1877) in the Paris 'Club de Haschischin' and hoped for insights into potential processes and states of consciousness. Such induced alienation from the normal states could serve as a model whereby we can understand psychotic structures. He sought contact with artists because he expected writers to convey a detailed and appropriate description of drug effects on a creative spirit (Kupfer 1996a). The setting of those hashish studies also involved music, as may be seen from a pen-and-ink drawing that was made during sessions, and shows Moreau de Tours at the piano (Behr 1982). The attendant musicians enjoyed freely improvised fantasies (Baudelaire 1966).

Music perception altered by drugs was addressed in music therapy research in the early 1970s when Charles T. Eagle and Helen Bonny published several explicit articles on research into music and psychedelic substances in the American Journal of Music Therapy. Most studies were performed with stronger psychedelics like LSD or psilocybin (Bonny and Pahnke 1972; Eagle 1972; Hess 1992; Weber 1974). Hess (1973) and Koukkou and Lehmann (1976, 1978) explored cannabis and music as means for model psychosis research and psychotherapy treatment.

Guided Imagery in Music (GIM) emerged from the psychedelic therapies of Leary, Grof and Sandison, where subjects took LSD or psilocybin under supervision by a psychotherapist (Eisner 1997; Grof 1994; Melechi 1997; Weil, Metzner and Leary 1965). The idea was to weaken resistance and selective mechanisms of the psyche for therapy purposes and thus to produce an unhampered flow of associations for issues to be addressed by psychotherapy. Pieces of classical music and jazz were selected specifically and individually for therapy sessions and were presented in a particular sequence. Emerging associations, emotions and imagined stories were analysed together with the client in subsequent sessions in order to process his experience and problems. Medical aid and an antidote to the substances were available in the 'drug phase' of this 'psychedelic' therapy.

Revers, Harrer and Simon describe a further attempt to use drug effects on music perception as a psychological model for purposes of music therapy in their book *Neue Wege der Musiktherapie* (Weber 1974). Weber used the psychedelic drug psilocybin to understand the perceptual processes in an individual who develops a lively imagination in a psychotic episode.

Weber assumed that musical perception in an adult is reduced to childlike forms of perception and cognition in the sense of a functional regression. The altered perception of time and body schemata found its correlate in an alteration of the form, movement and gestalt heard in the music. Weber concluded that a deliberate and undivided attention to music constitutes the highest cognitive form of music perception and that drug-induced perception prefers a regression-oriented experience.

Studies on drugs and music

What happens when people under the influence of drugs listen to music? An intensification of the emotional coping processes alone – and they are related anyway – cannot be all. In addition to addiction and pleasure – conveyed by the reward system of the brain through dopamine and opioids – there must be something else, something of significance to listeners or even musicians. Only very few experimental studies have addressed the effects of drugs and music on humans (Fachner 2001; Fachner 2002a; Fachner 2002b; Hess 1995; Waskow et al. 1970; Webster 2001). Music studies on Ayahuasca have been published by de Rios (see Chapter 8 in this book); a study on Ibogaine and music has been published by Maas and Strubelt (see Chapter 9 in this book). These studies also discuss the role of synaesthesia during ritual imagery.

Cannabis and music

Hess (1973; 1995) studied the effects of cannabis on music perception and its correlations in electroencephalography (EEG). For his pre/post-EEG study under 'near-realistic conditions' he created a setting that might be called 'psychedelic', with flickering light, music and a hyperventilation phase. To get the setting right, he tried to accommodate cannabis consumers' habits and cultural preferences. He observed the vigilance during intoxication phases in EEG and described six different effect phases of cannabis in his 25 subjects. In the summary Hess reported significant frontal and parietal increases in EEG alpha activities.

The 'clearest indications of hashish intoxication' (Hess 1995, p.32) were found in subjects while they listened to music, and it was possible to control the altered state of waking consciousness through music. Music was perceived as intensified, details were perceived more clearly and the feeling for time in music changed considerably. Hess rejects an enhancement of consciousness through cannabis. 'We must rather speak of narrowed consciousness in the acute state of cannabis intoxication. However, this limitation is accompanied by a hypersensitization of all senses, not only the optic or acoustic senses. Everyday objects appear in a new light'[1](Hess 1973, p.34).

This description of a hypersensitization resembles descriptions by Curry, who observed drug-consuming musicians and concert goers in the 1960s and 1970s and on this basis assumed a drug-induced 'hyperfocussing of attention on sound' in musicians (Curry 1968). In addition, alpha increases were found in the parietal region of the brain that represents the sensory-receptive functions of perceptual processing. We may assume a proportional increase of alpha activities after cannabis consumption while subjects listened to music, and a decrease of the frequency in correlation to the contemplative state of cannabis effects in a psychedelic test setting.

Waskow (Waskow et al. 1970) attempted a closer look at the influence of music as a setting variable on cannabis effects with a psycho-physiological form of measurement. She compared cannabis under four different conditions with/ without music and placebo with/without music. Test respondents chose their favourite music during test phases. In general, no significant changes in cannabis effects were found in the musical setting; some trends emerged, however. Independent of cannabis, music appeared to have a generally positive effect on increasingly euphoric moods, to produce relaxation and content, and 'tended to endorse items such as "feel like laughing", "feel more free", "wide awake", "more control of feelings"' (Waskow et al. 1970, p.106). But a contrary effect was also found. Cannabis effects were accompanied by unpleasant physical feelings, which were even more pronounced in the cannabis music condition; Waskow illustrated this in higher scores on the scale 'Subjective Drug Effects Questionnaire'. In the placebo music condition, however, the music reduced these feelings of being unwell.

---

1   Author's translation from German

Attention and 'High'

Cannabis intensifies processes of sensory perception, and – like almost all psychedelic drugs – seems to hamper access to the upper brain regions (Cytowic 1993). This is what follows from the literature on EEG and cannabis (Fachner 2001, 2002b, 2004a; Fink *et al.* 1976; Struve and Straumanis 1990) and from Fachner's study on a comparison of the data found in EEG and a pre/post situation. While listening to music without cannabis, higher amplitudes and frequencies were found over almost all regions near the skullcap. With cannabis consumption, however, subjects had weaker amplitudes; an indication that interactions with the cerebrum, the upper brain structures, are inhibited (Fachner 2002b).

Significant change ($p < 0.025$) was to be found with slower frequencies, that is, those that show that more intensive activities take place in the midbrain after consumption. This brain region produces emotions and processes of memory and selection. But the decrease in amplitudes does not occur in all regions near the skullcap; on the contrary, a certain region that coordinates attention and perceptual processes, the parietal lobes, records a distinct increase of amplitudes on the alpha band. The alpha band indicates the various regulations of alertness and the interactions between midbrain and upper brain structures that are supposed to control cognitive functions (Basar *et al.* 1997; Basar and Schürmann 1996). Increased alpha amplitudes are also found in individuals who are assumed to have a high IQ or specific talents and in persons who find it easier to develop complicated cognitive structures (Jausovec 1997).

Might this alpha increase be an indication of the 'high' state (Volavka *et al.* 1973)? A state in which so many complex things appear very easy all of a sudden, when problems just dissolve in front of the inner eye and everything is clear (Baudelaire 1966; Weil 1998)? When we interpret EEG data, then the entire process of listening appears intensified and psychopharmacological substances emerge as supporting individual listening strategies. These findings indicate a temporary intensification of auditory perception that processes acoustic perceptual elements more effectively in a temporarily changed metric frame of reference (Fachner 2000a). This is demonstrated when we look at topographic changes in brain activity.

Acoustic space and altered metric frame of reference

In Fachner's study (2002b), the statistical test revealed, in addition to increased alpha scores, clear and even significant ($p<0.025$) alterations in the right temporal lobe and the left occipital lobe in all respondents. Auditory sound information and visual information are primarily processed in the right temporal lobe, whereas the left occipital lobe is primarily responsible for vision and the processing of spatial information (Kolb and Whishaw 1996). The limited literature available on 'Cannabis and altered auditory perception' (Fachner 2000b) reveals that cannabis induces a preference for higher frequencies. Asked for their preferences of higher or lower notes, respondents reported a dose-dependent preference for higher frequencies (de Souza, Karniol and Ventura 1974). Higher frequencies convey the localization and distribution of sources of sound in spatial listening. Changes in the occipital lobe indicate that acoustic proportions of sound are associated in a different way.

The topographic pattern of music listening remains almost the same compared to rest but is intensified on the alpha band after consumption. On the basis of increased parietal alpha, we may assume that consumption directs specific attention to acoustic perceptual processes. Consequently, cannabis seems to have the same effect as psychoacoustic enhancers, exciters or modulation units as utilized in studio technology that make sound appear more transparent, with clearer contours (Fachner 2002a). Various statements by members of the Beatles or Fleetwood Mac suggest that for some musicians it is part of the critical process to listen to the mix of a freshly recorded piece of music once again under the influence of cannabis (Boyd 1992).

Expanded / intensified musical time-space

Another study shows that the feeling of intensity is significantly changed so that a wider scale appears to emerge for the intensity of sound effects. A perception of volume changed in respondents after cannabis consumption. Globus *et al.* found in their study that a 'moderate volume in altered states of consciousness has a different metric frame of reference from the normal conscious state (Globus *et al.* 1978) like a rubber ruler that is stretched, and in the stretched state still maintains the measuring function but shows 'broader' units.

More questions

Is this then an experimental indication of a 'consciousness enhanced by drugs' and do we observe an altered metric frame of reference (Fachner 2000a)?

In sensory perception, attention serves to curb the complex flood of information (apperception) (Eckel 1982), and what is 'unnecessary' is censored conceptually. Only a specific, individually and situation-relevant excerpt of sensory data is accessible to our consciousness. Emrich discusses psychedelic drug effects as states where all concepts of association of sensory data fail since many new or different modes of association emerge and compete with each other (Emrich *et al.* 1991). Is the psychedelic perceptual process something like an internal neurological dialogue where habitual selection is obstructed and therefore more sensory data are perceived?

The altered perception of time might be responsible. A typical effect of cannabis is that time is expanded. Time seems to pass more quickly than shown by the clock (Jones and Stone 1970; Mathew, Wilson, Turkington *et al.* 1998; Tart 1971). This effect is a possible key to understanding the experience of an unobstructed flow of information. Within the 'broader' measurement units (Fachner 2000a) of the above-mentioned 'auditory rubber ruler', progressively smaller units seem to become possible. The following quote may serve as an allegoric explanation:

> Because the chief effect…is that it lengthens the sense of time, and therefore they could get more grace beats into their music than they could if they simply followed a written copy… In other words, if you are a musician you're going to play the thing the way it is printed on a sheet. But if you're using marihuana, you're going to work in about twice as much music in-between the first note and the second note. That's what made jazz musicians. The idea that they could jazz things up, lighten them up. (Sloman 1998, pp.146–147)

Consequently, cannabis changes the intensity graduation of sensory data (Fachner 2002b). This appears plausible if we look at the distribution of the cannabinoid receptors recently detected in the human brain (Joy, Watson and Benson 1999). In those regions of midbrain and cerebellum that mainly coordinate feelings of intensity, and selective temporal and motor processes, there is a proportionally higher agglomeration of cannabinoid receptors. Cannabis consumption stimulates the activity of such receptors temporarily, and the functional consequence is a changed graduation of musical parameters. Obviously, these processes are far more complex than described here, but a stimulation of cannabinoid receptors may explain the changes discovered above.

Enhancement and experience

It may also explain why 'typical stoner music' always has this resounding or echo-like effect, or why reggae-dub music uses resounding effects and rhythmic echo cascades (Fachner 2002a). According to Böhm (1999), sound, improvisation and ecstasy are stylistic elements of psychedelic rock. Combined with the above-mentioned effects on time perception, intensity and reduced censoring of data, the preference for higher frequencies helps us to understand an increased functional use of sound modulators, resounding and echoing effects in psychedelic rock. The musical time-space of sounds may thus be deliberately changed and we see this in music effect equipment that allows the musician to 'produce music that a person under the influence of psychedelic drugs would like to hear' (Böhm 1999, p.22). Virtual acoustic spaces are overlapped and can be played with if the performer has the musical experience (Becker 1967; Fachner 2000a). Is this perhaps the idea behind the title of Jimi Hendrix's album *Are you Experienced?*

Not only musicians might be attracted by such changes, however. Improved acoustic perception is also interesting for people with hearing impairment, above all for those with significant impairments in higher frequencies. They might profit from cannabis and with a specific auditory training might compensate deficits from weakened acoustic hair cells with memory patterns (Fachner 2002b).

Benzodiazepine

Harrer described a dose-dependent influence of benzodiazepine on musical perception on the basis of several single observations. Vegetative reactions to music like breathing and heartbeat that are normally variable were increasingly obstructed but the respondent did not perceive impairments or changes in musical perception. These experiments demonstrated that psychotropic substances might induce a short-term decoupling from psychic and vegetative processes. No psychic impairments are observed with a medium dose, but normal typical vegetative processes are suppressed. A high dose transforms emotional feeling into an aesthetic-appreciative musical experience, and variable vegetative processes cease almost completely. Very high benzodiazepine doses produce indifference and lack of interest towards music in a subject who experiences dulled affectivity and falls into vegetative rigidity (Harrer 1991).

Summary

Chemically-induced altered states of consciousness together with music can be studied as psycho-physiological models of altered states of consciousness and might help to understand altered states of consciousness processes in vivo. Electrophysiological studies of music and altered states have revealed theta changes as indicative for altered states of consciousness (see Chapter 2). Music and drug action are processed in the same limbic brain areas, a region associated with low-frequency generations. As we will see in the next chapters, drug rituals with music (see Chapters 8 and 9) are used as initiation into a codified legacy of knowledge enabling access to archetype symbols. Artists often use drugs creatively to vary their perspective on conditioned perceptive patterns. Psychedelic drugs act on time and space perception, induce changes of cognitive-emotional valence and therefore induce temporarily changed audiometric scales of psycho-acoustic qualities, melody, rhythm and intensity of acoustic events. Drug-induced cross modal intensification leads to more vivid association and vision correlated to the music in a guided therapeutic context.

Chapter 8

The Role of Music in Healing with Hallucinogens

Tribal and Western Studies

Marlene Dobkin de Rios

Introduction

Over the last 35 years, the author has studied the role of plant hallucinogens in tribal and third world societies (see de Rios 1972, 1984; de Rios and Grob 1994). Several articles have examined the role of music produced by shamanic healers as adjuncts to their healing rituals, particularly with such plant hallucinogens like ayahuasca, as well as other hallucinogens (de Rios and Katz 1975, Katz and de Rios 1971). In the book *Hallucinogens: Cross-cultural Perspectives* (de Rios 1984, p.211), a table was compiled of the then described music that accompanied psychedelic rituals world-wide. They included, among others, tropical rainforest native Indians such as the Chama and Cashinahua of Peru, the Huichol of Mexico, the Jivaro of Ecuador, and the Kiowa and Comanche Indians of North America. It appears that percussion and drumming are the major modalities used.

Peruvian Healing Sessions

Ayahuasca and melody

Fred Katz, a musicologist, and I prepared an article for the American Journal of Folklore (Katz and de Rios 1971) in which we transcribed some of the ayahuasca tapes that de Rios had gathered in urban Mestizo healing sessions in Iquitos, Peru. Healers were adamant about the importance of music in the healing session, and the role that melody played in programming the actual content of the vision in their 'icaros', or chants calling upon familiars to help them to see the cause of illness (often witchcraft hexes) and to allow them to return the evil to the perpetrator so that healing could occur. Katz and I subsequently published a second article on music and drug-induced altered states of consciousness (de Rios and Katz 1971). We argued that the anxiety generated by rapid access to the unconscious may be expressed in such symptoms as nausea, diarrhoea, cramps, tachycardia and increased blood pressure. These components of the 'bad trip' have been reported in all cultures for which adequate data is available. The pervasive presence of music as an integral part of the drug experience constitutes one of the most powerful rituals associated with the social management of altered states of consciousness. For audio examples of the healing sessions, listen to Sounds 8.1 and 8.2.

'Jungle Gym'

The participant in the ritual perceives the structure of music quite differently from the way he would perceive it during normal waking consciousness. We know, of course, of the mathematical precision and structure that all music possesses, whatever the musical tonal system of a given culture or the repetition of musical phrases involved. What Katz and I argued is that once the biochemical effects of the hallucinogenic drug alter the user's perception, the music operates as a 'jungle gym' for the person's consciousness during the drug state. Just like the playground structure that children climb upon, the 'jungle gym' provides a series of pathways and banisters through which the drug user negotiates his way. Here we are using metaphorically the concept of an architectural structure composed of iron bars interlinked in horizontal and vertical planes. In contrast, however, to the child's playtime structure, where the child can choose spontaneous pathways and heights to explore, we suggested that the companionship of music to the hallucinogenic drug experience functions almost like a computer's software. It instructs the machine in a particular course to follow. The cultural patterning of hallucinogenic-induced visions suggest that the mathematical structure of music may serve specific cultural goals – to allow the drug taker to see the guardian spirit of the ayahuasca vine, to achieve contact with a special supernatural deity, and so forth. The shaman, who controls to some degree his client's visual options within this ritualized use of music, imposes the music upon the drug user.

Frequency

The lowest common denominator of the various musics appears to be the frequency of rattling effects, or rapid vibratory sounds, almost always in consort with whistling or singing. Rattles, singing, chanting and vocal productions in general may be a very important part of the hallucinogenic experience in that the 'jungle gym' is built up, torn down and rearranged in a sort of 'block-building' of consciousness to serve specific cultural goals.

Synaesthesia

Synaesthesias are commonly reported by drug users. In most tribal and third world societies where drugs are used, this scrambling of sensory modalities is not only recognized but actually underpins the programming of rituals so as to heighten all sensory modalities. That would include visual, olfactory, tactile, auditory and gustatory senses.

LSD and psychotherapy

In my recent book, *LSD, Spirituality and the Creative Process* (2003), I present work based on LSD research conducted by the psychiatrist Oscar Janiger from 1954 to 1962, when more than 930 people in Los Angeles were given Sandoz LSD experimentally. While the aim of the experiment was not to validate psychotherapeutic benefits of LSD, a large subset of more than 225 people who were then in therapy were given a moderate dose of LSD. Included in the sample were artists and musicians. One world-renowned musician reported the following effects:

> My flesh is charged with emotional responsiveness to the Mozart E-flat symphony. My skin seems microscopically thick and porous so as to admit the music more easily. The inner lines of counterpoint are suddenly so clear. The dissonances are so penetrating and the bass-line is positively alive. It jumps and strides with a kind of cosmic purpose. I am very sensitive but my real emotions still have not been engaged...

My listening is extremely acute. [He listened to Mozart, a Bizet symphony, Mussorgsky's *Pictures at an Exhibition*, the suite from Strauss' *Der Rosenkavalier* and his own incidental music.]

My reaction to these pieces began with the conventional response but gradually took on a new character. It was as though the remaining ecstasy that flowed through me has washed away my patience with the exterior posturing of music. I felt that I saw directly into its heart and was interested only in what the music was really saying, remaining totally indifferent to how I was dressed... The visual hallucinations were one of the more entertaining features of the afternoon...I could not for a time distinguish between sight and sound. Later Mozart's melodic line was filling the room. Later woodwind harmonies released ethereal glowing purples and pinks in shafts of radiant light which streamed out from a picture in precise synchronization with the music. I felt that moment of incredible exaltation. I am, in this very instant, free from every petty negative emotion. I am devoid of anger, of jealousy, of fear.

(de Rios 2003)

Conclusion

If these hallucinogenic substances are to be used psychotherapeutically in the future, the role of music as a primary conditioning agent of the experience will have to be taken into account. Any planning for psychotherapeutic intervention in times to come would necessitate a clear musicological approach to create therapeutic states of consciousness. Not discussed in this article is the work that Grob and I have done on suggestibility and the hallucinogenic substances (see Grob and de Rios 1996, de Rios and Grob 1994), which are also important effects of the hallucinogenic experience. Music can be a major mode of managing the drug-induced altered state of consciousness for therapeutic goals.

Chapter 9

Polyrhythms Supporting a Pharmacotherapy

Music in the Iboga Initiation Ceremony in Gabon

Uwe Maas and Süster Strubelt

Music is used by traditional cultures worldwide to create and accompany trance-states. But the influence of sophisticated compositions and the choice of instruments on the patient's curing has been hardly examined. Rouget (1990) even assumes that the choice of instruments and music is insignificant.

We had the opportunity to assist several Iboga initiation ceremonies in 1999, 2001 and 2003 in Gabon (Central Africa). We could record the music and finally decided to become initiated ourselves. The Iboga healing ceremony induces a near-death experience and is applied to cure serious mental or psychosomatic diseases, but people let themselves also be initiated for reasons of spiritual or personal development.

After analysing the compositions and their function in the ceremonies, we come to the conclusion that neither the musical structures nor the choice of the instruments should be seen as a cultural and incidental quality. There are indications of direct somatic influences apart from the psychological ones. In all probability, the completely constant basic metre, the incessant use of polyrhythms, and also the harmonic organization and the choice of instruments serve to activate the cerebellum and generate theta-frequencies in the electroencephalogram (EEG). These methods seem to be used consciously to create particular reactions like getting into a possessional trance and to facilitate visions.

We suppose that the music increases the effect of the drug Ibogaine, which is used during the initiation rituals, so that the patients may require a smaller amount of the quite risky drug.

In many traditional cultures, young adults experience a meeting with death during their initiation ceremony. For this purpose, Pygmies use the root of the Iboga shrub. Initiation with this drug has been taken over by several other ethnic groups who think that this drug is more effective than their traditional initiation-drugs. In the middle of the twentieth century, Iboga was discovered in Gabon as a remedy for serious mental or psychosomatic diseases. Consequently, the average age of the people being initiated has been increasing. Instead of the traditional initiation rituals on reaching puberty, initiations in the urban sector often serve to solve serious problems or fulfil a desire for self-awareness. The admission to the community of the adults of the Pygmy village has been replaced by admission to the community of initiated people, who continue to meet as a group after initiation, organize ceremonies and offer social protection (Gollnhofer and Sillans 1997; Goutarel 2000; Mary 1983).

As part of a professionally caused stay in Gabon 1999 we got to know traditional healers of the ethnic group Mitsogho in the region of Lambaréné and we examined their work. After having observed several initiation and healing ceremonies and having recorded and analysed the music being played during the ceremony, we decided to be initiated ourselves by the Mitsogho in Mitone in December 2001 (U.M.) and in April 2003 (S.S.).

Our own experience: an initiation report by Uwe Maas

At my initiation in December 2001, with the Mitsogho people in the village Mitone near Lambaréné, six experienced male healers and musicians accompanied the ceremony for two nights. Two female healers and the community of the village also took part. I was fitted out with ritual weapons and protective items for the meetings in the spiritual world. Just before sunset, having taken about 150–200g of the Iboga root's bark in pieces one by one, I responded with nausea, coordination problems and tremor on the left side. I had a typical out-of-body experience in which I experienced myself as a football-sized spiritual being moving through visionary spaces (see Figure 9.1).

Figure 9.1 Iboga visions

Parallel to this I was connected to external reality so that I was able to communicate and to inform others about my experiences. I moved around, floating over tropical steppe and river landscapes, and through long white corridors with a countless number of doors, as well as under water, but without any (physical) resistance. I met several groups of people who seemed to have lived in older times and I also met myself as an independent individual.

My initiated attendants asked me to become active in this world; to move around, to open doors and to get in contact with the people I met. At first I had some problems with the (mental) movement and it was difficult to communicate. It took me about half an hour to learn this. Strangely enough, that mental communication then also worked in the 'worldly' reality. I was able to make out every detail of my companions' faces, although it was nearly completely dark, and I was sure that I could read their thoughts – especially those of the musicians.

At the end of the visions, while the dimensions of space and time changed in a peculiar way, I had a certain vision that was very personal and appeared as divine to me.

The other 15 initiated persons around me – many of them had travelled to Mitone just for the initiation of a person from Germany – had no problems in directing me on my journey and in classifying my experiences. Particularly, my friend and father-of-initiation, Antoine Makondo, who had been looking forward with excitement to my reactions, was apparently pleased that I saw the pictures he expected. The Mitsogho obviously have their secret criteria that also allow the classification of the visions of a foreigner. For example, I was sometimes prevented from speaking because I ran the risk of telling secrets that were only meant for me. This interpretation seems to be independent of the initiate's personal knowledge because the aim of the initiation is not to investigate the initiate's past but a generalized experience: the journey into the hereafter, the meeting with dead people and with God, the experience of dying and rebirthing. The Mitsogho realized that their European friend could also have this experience.

After about six hours the intensity of the visions wore off and I became very tired. I leant against my mother-of-initiation, who sat behind me, and I began to return back to life. This period was accompanied by singing and elements of physical therapy. To loosen up my 'rigor mortis', all my joints were moved – which, surprisingly enough, led to many loud cracks! – and I was asked to stand up and to do some easy movements that at once caused dizziness, vomiting and new visions.

Figure 9.2 On the way to the ritual bath

After a rest I was supposed to dance for the first time in the morning and to take a ritual bath at the river (see Figure 9.2). Afterwards I became partly isolated from the others to introduce the beginning of a new part of my life. I was allowed to talk only to initiated persons and in a ritual way. The ceremony came to an end with a dance celebration at which I was admitted into the community of the initiated and simultaneously released into my real life (see Figure 9.3).

Figure 9.3 Entering the community of initiated men

The Iboga ceremony as a controlled near-death experience

Our visions during the Iboga initiation correspond with the experiences of other Europeans (Samorini 2000), with ethnological descriptions (Fernandez 1982) of Gabonian Bwiti out-of-body-experiences and with the reports of people who were very close to death. Greyson (1984) was able to isolate four aspects of a near-death experience: a cognitive factor (acceleration of time, review of one's life, global understanding), an affective factor (feelings of joy, harmony and peace, a vision of an eternal light), a factor of paranormal experiences (transcendental perceptions, looking into the future, out-of-body-experiences) and a factor of transcendental experience (entering another world, meeting with mystical beings, deceased persons or gods).

It is known from numerous studies that near-death experiences often have significant life-changing consequences. Fear of death diminishes; the persons involved become more spiritual and less governed by material values than previously. They become more tolerant and more open towards their fellow human beings and accept social responsibility, but are at the same time less influenced in their opinions by others than previously (Flynn 1984; Groth-Marnat and Summers 1998; Insinger 1991; Lommel *et al.* 2001).

These changes, also experienced by the authors, correspond exactly to what is expected from a successful initiation in Gabon. According to the traditional healer, Antoine Makondo, the initiation should not be considered as a direct form to heal but as a method to broaden one's self-concept. It allows you to see the world with different eyes, to both see and resolve problems in a new and better way. It should be a step into a new spiritual vision of the world. In conversations with initiated people about the results of the experience we were told that they had become more adult, had given up bad habits like womanizing and lazing around. They had started a serious life, got married and looked for work. Women let themselves be initiated if they have problems in becoming pregnant.

We assume, after our own experience, that these personality changes do not appear directly as a consequence of the vision, but require a reliving through childhood phases. The candidate for initiation is shielded from the outside world in the days following the vision but is caringly looked after by initiates and the village community. According to our experience, he is at this moment in a state of regression. Childhood traumas are re-experienced again. In contrast to psychoanalysis though, not just one single therapist is available for any projections which may occur, but a whole village community. Problems with family members can be dealt with in this way.

Music therapeutic aspects of the ritual

To the Mitsogho, the continuous musical support by musicians playing the mouth bow and the harp, accompanying percussions and singing is essential for the initiation process. The music is the 'safety-rope' reaching from this life to the hereafter and serves as a means of locomotion in the visionary space. And that is exactly our own experience. The reintroducing of musical accompaniment after short interruptions reactivates the faltering visions, facilitating remarkably spiritual communication and improving mental and physical well-being.

Besides our own Missoko – and respectively Mabandji – initiations, we were able to observe two Mabandji initiation ceremonies and three healing-rituals including possessional trance states among the Mitsogho tribe and three Mabundi initiation rituals among the Fang tribe. In total we recorded about 40 hours of ritual music for musical analysis.

Musical structures
CONSTANT PULSE OF 5–6 BEATS PER SECOND

An absolutely constant measure of 5–6 beats per second underlies the poly-rhythmic mouth bow music (in male initiations) and harp music (in female initiations) played during the Iboga healing ceremony. This measure corre-sponds to the elementary beats symbolized by the columns in the following figures.

BIMETRICAL STRUCTURE WITH CONTINUOUSLY CHANGING ACCENTS

The music has the specific structure of a twelve-beat metre with an ambiva-lent division in 6x2 and 4x3 impulses (see Table 9.1).

Table 9.1 Polymetric placing of accents on 12 elementary beats at the time of X

6x2 metre = waltz time	X		X		X		X		X		X	
4x3 metre = marching time	X			X			X			X		

Between these (not always percussively marked) metrics, we have the peri-odically repeated melodic motif; its melorhythmics cannot be clearly asso-ciated with either one of the two, and through continuous minimal varia-tions it emphasizes one and then the other (binary/ternary melorhythm).

In the trance inductional phase there is a striking increase in the number of rhythmic changes resulting from overlapping of different, very fast rhythmic elements.

PERFECT BALANCED ALTERNATING CONCERNING THE BASIS CHORDS, MELODIC MOVES AND RHYTHMIC PATTERNS

Compositions for melodic instruments all show some characteristic symmetries. The harmonic basis is two chords, the roots of which differ by about one tone – minor chords on the harp, major chords on the mouth bow. Following an alternating pattern, these two chords are always well balanced. Melodically, the compositions are contrapuntal, thus giving the same value to baseline and treble voices. Often two rhythmically different melodic motifs are alternating, corresponding to an alternating of solo and choral voices in the singing parts.

PERIODIC REPETITIONS WITH CONTINUOUS MINIMAL CHANGES

The melodic motifs are repeated mostly after 2x12 or 4x12 elementary beats, undergoing minimal melodic or rhythmic variations (as illustrated in Figure 9.4). Here the melodic rhythm frequently slightly gets off the elementary beats, thus suspending between the two fundamental metrics (Sound 9.1). The complexity is further increased through the use of rattles and ankle bells, which systematically appear between or beside the fundamental beat.

Figure 9.4 The art of variation: Raphia cloth of the Kuba tribe, Congo; from author's collection

The repetitions lead to mental anticipations that by these minimal changes are systematically disappointed, thus 'keeping you on the move', as the Mitsogho told us: creating the open attention you need.

Musical instruments in the men's Missoko initiation ritual

THE MOUTH-BOW 'MONGONGO'

The 'male' main instrument in the Missoko initiation ceremony is similar to the Pygmy hunting bow. The 'arrow' strikes the bowstring thus turning it to vibrations. The root is elevated about one tone by pressing a wooden or metallic object against the string. By varying the volume of the oral cavity, the musician is able to produce about eight different overtones corresponding to the root (as on a Jew's harp) (see Figure 9.5). The resulting tonalities are two major chords whose roots differ about one tone.

Figure 9.5 Playing the mouth-bow

Principle of composition

Due to the circumstance of sound production done with the mouth bow a polyrhythmic interlocking of the two voices is not possible. Instead of this, rhythmically, the first six elementary beats are often divided into two, the second into three parts (Sound 9.2).

G'		x	x	x																																												
F'					x	x						x		x	x	x																																
E'																																																
D'							x			x							x	x													x	x	x	x														
C'																			x			x							x	x													x	x	x	x		
H'								x	x																		x	x													x	x						
A'																				x	x																		x	x								
G'																								x																								x
F'																																				x												
G		x	x	x			x	x	x	x							x	x						x			x	x			x	x	x	x							x	x						x
F					x	x						x		x	x	x			x	x	x	x							x	x						x			x	x			x	x	x	x		
RR	x			x			x			x			x			x			x			x			x			x			x			x			x			x			x			x		

Figure 9.6 Mouth-bow music. Lines 1–9 = relative pitch of the overtones at the time of x; Lines 10 and 11 = relative pitch of the roots (bowstrings vibrations) at the time of X; RR = forward movement of rattles at the time of X. From left to right: elementary beats (smallest metrical units)

The root's moves are often mirrored after 12 elementary beats, the predominantly contrapuntal treble (overtones) is either mirrored or shifted vertically as in the following example (see Figure 9.6 and listen to Sound 9.3).

Ritual meaning

The roots (bowstrings vibrations) are considered to derive 'from this world', the variable overtones (corresponding to their 'immaterial' origin) are considered to be the voice of the creator. Symbolically, the counterpoint could reflect the parallels of 'earthly life' and the 'beyond' and the independent vocal leadership could show the different principles of the two worlds.

BAMBOO CANES KNOCKED ON THE GROUND
Differently pitched large bamboo canes accentuate different metres (6x2, 4x3, 3x4, 2x6) (Sound 9.4).

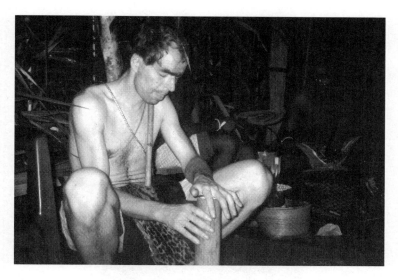

Figure 9.7 Playing the bamboo cane

INSTRUMENTS WITH A LATENCY PERIOD BETWEEN MOVEMENT AND SOUND
In the Missoko initiation ritual several instruments are used whose construction makes exact timing very difficult (Sound 9.5):

- a special bell fixed onto a curved handle (thus moved on the diagonal from behind) producing a clattering sound
- rattles made of seed capsules attached to cords (played right-handedly, in a straight 4x3 metre)
- the 'fly brush' Mognangui (see Figures 9.2, 9.3) (played left-handedly, in an uneven 6x2 metre).

Their delayed, vague accents blur the fundamental beats.

These 'sacred' instruments are only played by initiated persons (and the one who is going to be initiated). The 'fly brush' is almost inaudible, and therefore considered as a really spiritual instrument. The traditional healer Antoine Makondo describes their function as follows: 'It's an education: There are always different paths you can follow.' We understand this as opening the eyes to two alternative ways of coping with problems – adjusting oneself to given facts (the specific latency period between movement and sound – thus learning to move earlier) or calmly awaiting what happens, accepting the timing, free of any value judgements.

Figure 9.8 Antoine Makondo playing the harp

Musical instruments in the women's Mabandji initiation ritual
THE EIGHT-STRING HARP 'NGOMBI'

The eight strings of the harp are tuned on two minor chords whose roots differ about one tone. Using forefinger and thumb only, the four treble strings (fifth and octave) are played right-handedly, the four bass strings (root and minor third) left-handedly (see Figure 9.8).

Principle of composition

Typically, there is a polyrhythmic interlocking, using different metres right-handedly (predominantly the 'other worldly' 6x2) and left-handedly (predominantly the 'worldly' 4x3; e.g. Sound 9.1). These principles should be illustrated by the following piece for harp, basing exceptionally on 16 elementary beats, with its alternating binary and ternary rhythm, its typical 3:2 interlocking of treble and baseline, its inversion of the two minor chords after 16 elementary beats and its continuous mirroring of the melodic movements between root and third on the one hand and fifth and octave on the other (see Figure 9.6 and Sound 9.6).

Ritual meaning

The harp is the 'female' main instrument in the women's Mabandji initiation ritual. Its sound is considered to be the lament of the mythical female ancestor Benzogho who sacrificed herself by bringing Iboga to mankind. The harp also represents the eight-legged spider moving on a thread between heaven and earth and the canoe to cross the river between this life and the hereafter. This 'female' instrument is tuned to two minor chords that use contrapuntal voices, the bass representing this life and the treble representing the hereafter. The Fang attach further meaning in that the eight strings represent the members of the extended family (see Table 9.2):

It is interesting that structural connections within the family have their counterpart in musical harmonies. The changing of the two minor chords reflect the relationship of the two nuclear families, the polyrhythmic play of the two hands represent gender relations (usually attributing the 'spiritual' 6x2 metre to the female part).

Even more interesting is the fact that the 'gender-defined tone' (minor) third is placed in the parents' generation (father and uncle), the 'gender-neutral tone' fifth is placed in the children's generation (sister and niece).

E’	X										X												X									
D’							X										X										X					
H			X		X								X		X										X							
A									X												X								X		X	
G				X										X											X							
F									X											X										X		
E	X										X												X									
D							X										X										X					

Figure 9.9 Polyrhythmic harp music with horizontal and vertical mirroring. Lines 1–8 = relative pitch of the harp strings at the time of X. From left to right: elementary beats (smallest metrical units)

Table 9.2 The meaning of the eight harp strings

Relative pitch	Ritual meaning	Classifying according to			
		Gender Treble/Bass	Nuclear families (two minor chords)	Generations (inversion of chords)	
E'	Mother	X	X	X	
D'	Aunt	X		X	X
H	Sister	X	X		X
A	Niece	X		X	X
G	Father		X	X	X
F	Uncle		X	X	X
E	Brother		X	X		X
D	Nephew		X		X	X

The 'indifference' of the fifth has a practical musical meaning. In the hymn, concerning the lower lying of the two accords, the major third rings out more often than the minor third.

If one interprets the symmetrical construction of the ritual harp compositions on the foundation of this symbolic meaning, one could assume that their task is to (re)produce a balanced relationship between the nuclear families, genders and generations – and this is precisely, according to information from the Gabonese, the task in the (female) healing ritual. The harp is thus the 'family-therapy' instrument.

We suggest this dynamic and continuous alternating between even and uneven reflects and supports the balancing act of the person to be initiated; that is, to be 'ecstatic' instead of 'static'.

THE WOODEN IDIOPHONE 'BAKE'

Consisting of a board, about two metres long and seven centimetres wide, it is played simultaneously by two or three percussionists. While they stress different aspects of the polyrhythm independently, the resulting pattern is fast and permanently changing (Sound 9.7). Like the different rattles, the Bake has a very high pitch.

Ritual meaning

From a cosmological perspective, the primeval egg was broken into two pieces, thus creating the principle of polarization in this world (night and day, birth and death, woman and man...) as well as the three-part division of the spiritual world, as in the Christian Trinity. This 'transition' is identified with the 'cosmic forging' of this very loud and sharp-sounding instrument.

Interestingly enough, during the initiation-trance the considerable difference between the volumes of different instruments, like the quiet harp and the 'bake' beaten with sticks, seems to be insignificant; the musical perception of the person being initiated seems to ignore phonetic laws. For tape-recording, the harp had to be set close to the microphone and the 'bake' some metres away to be recorded at the same volume level; but during the trance – sitting close to harp and 'bake' – both seemed to have the same volume!

THE WOODEN RATTLE 'TSEGHE'

This is a female instrument used before and during states of possessional trance (Sound 9.9) played by spinning the wrist ('diadochokinesis').

Common instruments in the initiation of women and men

THE ORDINARY RATTLE 'SOKE'

Accompanying the mouth-bow, these rattles filled with seeds usually support the 4x3 metre, in the context of harp music, and dance – often the 6x2 metre (Sounds 9.3 and 9.8).

THE DRUM 'BALAFON'

Three or four differently tuned drums are played exclusively during the ecstatic dances that usually start about three o'clock in the morning. The rhythmic patterns are similar to those of the 'Bake' (Sound 9.8).

VOCAL MUSIC

There are no human voices in the spiritual world. That's why the person to be initiated is guided by instrumental music in the spiritual world, but on the long way back to this life is welcomed by singing located between spiritual and earthly communication. The lyrics are only understandable to initiated people, using a lot of symbols – often reinterpreting opposite poles as circular processes – and frequently even a foreign language. Thus, the content is transmitted partly 'spiritually' and serves to hold the balance between this world and the spiritual one (Sounds 9.5, 9.6, 9.8).

Dancing

There are three different styles of dancing:

1 walking in a line in circles or like the mythical python (water spirit), moving rattles often in a complementary metre to the rhythm of the paths; its name 'Mayaya' means at the same time 'rebirth', 'peace', 'release from dependent relationship', 'relieving of segregation' in the Mitsogho language (see Figure 9.10)

2 an individual dance reserved for men whose slow movements seem to express the tension between self-control and liberation

3 the ecstatic dance with high-speed wiggling of the hips. Its performance serves as a proof for a successful initiation process. It symbolizes the vortex of birth and death as transition processes.

Figure 9.10 Mayaya dance

The pharmacological effects of Ibogaine

There are a lot of studies about Ibogaine, the extract from Iboga root, because American scientists have thought of using it for drug therapy (treating heroin, cocaine and alcohol addictions). A single dose of Ibogaine may have spectacular results. Some addicts 'forget' their addiction without any withdrawal effects. Others have deep experiences after the consumption of Ibogaine. For example, they see themselves in a grave during the vision, so that they then decide to continue living without drugs. The effect usually lasts for a few weeks, maybe months, but unfortunately a lot of people then relapse.

Up to now, the fact that Ibogaine creates near-death experiences has been almost completely ignored by the pharmacological literature. But there are parallels between the near-death experiences and the impacts of Ibogaine at the pharmacological level. Studies have shown that Ibogaine in the cerebellum has a similar effect to oxygen deficiency. In very high doses, in rats, it leads to the destruction of definite groups of Purkinje cells. In lower doses, it blocks their influence. These Purkinje cells lack protective mechanisms against an oversupply of glutamate, which leads to them being the first to die through oxygen deficiency – and indeed so fast, that it can be assumed this functions as a safety measure. Purkinje cells normally inhibit the activity of the fastigial nucleus; when these fail and the fastigial nucleus becomes strongly stimulated as a result, the brain undertakes measures for its own protection (Welsh *et al.* 2002). Some authors believe that the near-death experiences belong to these measures (Whinnery 1997).

These protective mechanisms have been well investigated in the hippocampus, an older part of the brain, which forms the whole upper brain in reptiles. In humans, the hippocampus is responsible for spatial orientation and the process of learning. It is assumed that it also plays a large role in the production of near-death experiences.

Hypotheses about neurophysiological effects of ritual Mitsogho music

We experienced during our initiation ceremonies that music had a direct influence on our feelings and the pictures we saw during the visions. This was especially strong in the times we were moving ourselves to the music. Is music a kind of medicine, which provokes special physiological reactions, which promote trance-states? And if this were the case, how do the reactions to music interfere with the effects of Ibogaine?

Augmenting Ibogaine effects

Like Ibogaine, the ceremonial music stimulates the cerebellum and the hippocampus. We assume that it generally augments the Ibogaine effects there.

Induction of theta-waves

Neher (1962) reports laboratory research showing evidence that flashing lights as well as rhythmic drumming of theta frequency (4–7/sec) generate EEG-waves of the same frequency and hallucinations. Goodman (2000) studied the impact of rhythmic stimulation on persons performing ritual body postures known from antiguous Indian cultures. The traditional rhythms of 6 Hz originated theta waves in the EEG. Some of the participants had out-of-body experiences.

Brady and Stevens (2000) augmented theta activity in the neocortex by binaural beat stimulation. This slightly different stimulation for both ears was also used in the initiation ceremony of Uwe Maas at the peak of his visions.

The musical theta rhythm is maintained during the Bwiti ceremonies for days. It corresponds to a spontaneous trembling (or voluntary movement) of the left hand of men and the right hand of women, which is probably caused by Ibogaine effects either on the cerebellum or the hippocampus.

Gabonian ceremonial music is based on the Ibogaine-stimulated theta rhythm and therefore contributes to its augmentation, especially when the person to be initiated moves to the rhythm (dancing, clapping, playing of the rattle). It accelerates the process of overstimulation induced by Ibogaine and the following blockage of hippocampus cells.

Instead cells, which up until then were inactive and in this way escaped being blocked, now relay perhaps quite new thoughts and feelings.

Activation of the cerebellum

Like Ibogaine, music activates the cerebellum. Complex and unknown music is especially stimulating (Khorram-Sefat 1997; Satoh 2001). Even more stimulating is dancing and playing the rattles. The quick hand-movements necessary to play the wooden rattle Tseghe are known by medical students as diadochokinesis. Patients with cerebellar lesions have problems with this kind of movement. The typical Bwiti dance with quick movements of the hips, performed by the initiated at the end of the ceremony, depends also on an activated cerebellum. Gabonian healers see the dance as indicative of the success of the initiation (see Figure 9.9).

We think that activation of the cerebellum by music and movements also augments the effects of Ibogaine.

Figure 9.11 The final dance

Polyrhythms to induce or to go further into a trance

There are few studies about the effects of polyrhythms on the human brain. Neher (1962) reports that optic stimulation by two independent flashing lights induced hallucinations under laboratory conditions. But the effects of acoustic polyrhythmic stimulation have hardly been investigated. So we can only hypothesize on this subject.

We suppose that rhythmic complex structures stimulate the cerebellum, because it is presumed to contain the 'inner clock' of the brain. Studies proved that people with damage to the cerebellum showed poor results when estimating short time intervals compared with people who had suffered damage to the neocortex.

Ivry (1997) presumes after different perception studies that the cerebellum has not only one but various 'inner clocks'. The lateral cerebellum directs tapping a rhythm with one hand. Subjects with cerebellar lateral lesions perform poorly on this task but they show better results if they tap with both hands. The fact that contralateral cerebellum does not influence tapping of the other hand made Ivry presume that the cerebellum has at least two, and probably more, inner clocks.

In consequence, the cerebellum should be able to perform various rhythms at the same time, while it is difficult to think of two parallel rhythms in consciousness. Studies with musicians found performance of polyrhythms based on only one principal 'inner clock'. One rhythm (mostly the faster one) was always more accurate than the second one (Pressing, Magill and Summers 1996). Thinking two rhythms at the same time, as Mitsogho music suggests, and as Gabonian women seem to practise in dancing and playing different rhythms at the same time, requires changes in brain function. This could be the separation of consciousness and cerebellar activity or the unilateral activation of the right brain hemisphere, which can tolerate contradictions better than the left one. Activation of the right hemisphere is presumed to play a role also during

Figure 9.12 Possession trance

near-death experiences, which are frequently experienced during epileptic seizures of the right temporal lobe (Schröter-Kunhardt 1999). The result of polyrhythmic stimulations could be seen in cerebellar activation and/or stimulation of the right hemisphere and is thereby useful in detecting hidden unconscious contents and also for creative thinking.

The induction of a possession trance

We found a special form of over-activation of the cerebellum while observing the possession trance (see Figure 9.12). In the Mitsogo women's initiation, the candidate is led to a state of possession trance exclusively through musical means before the intake of the initiation drug Iboga. This has the purpose of calming the spirits. It happens musically through a certain scheme. The candidate sits on a low stool with a rounded leg of approximately 15 cm diameter, while the initiated women stride-dance and rattle around her to the rhythm of the harp. As the intensity of the music and the stride-dancing increases, the initiate is given a rattle, which she then begins to rattle in an 'even' (marching) rhythm and starts also to sway herself to the rhythm on the unsteady stool. At this precise moment, someone else starts clapping or rattling loudly an 'uneven' rhythm – which, speaking from experience, leads to an immense energy of truly vital character so as not to lose the 'even' rhythm. What then appear to the bystanders are apparently staccato movements and energetic, almost desperate screams, giving the strong impression that the candidate is 'uncontrollable' or 'has lost control'.

In the following example a dominant solo clapping in a 3x4 metre is introduced, overlapping the 4x3 metre of the rattles, thus giving a new rhythmic interpretation to the melodic motif (see Figure 9.13 and listen to Sound 9.9).

It is claimed that uneven metre is used to 'invoke the spirits'; this is also shown in the Mitsogo rituals when, immediately after its occurrence, women whistle on a capsule that hangs on their neck, which is considered as a sign for the appearance of the spirits. The Mitsogo are not alone with this opinion. In the ancient Greek world, uneven rhythms were considered to be intoxicating and were used in the Dionysiac obsessional ceremonies originating from Asia Minor (Rouget 1990, p.166).

D’					X								X		X									
H			X						X		X						X				X		X	
A							X																	
G	X									X									X			X		
F							X						X											
E	X									X									X			X		
D													X											
CC	C						C						C						C					
SC	C				C				C				C				C				C			

Figure 9.13 Polyrhythmic harp music with polymetric clapping. Lines 1–7 = relative pitch of the harp strings at the time of X; CC = common clapping at the time of X; SC = dominant solo clapping at the time of X. From left to right: elementary beats (smallest metrical units)

Concluding personal remarks

There are unfortunately few possibilities to compare African traditional knowledge with Western modern science. Neither the pharmacological, nor the music neurophysiology research has sufficient scientific results to compare both areas. But in all cases, when it was possible to compare Western science and traditional knowledge, we could see that the knowledge of traditional healers was coherent with the findings of modern medicine. Their statements about the effects of Ibogaine lasting about four to five months, the danger for women, the possibility of interactions and complications between Ibogaine and other drugs have been proved by Western medicine. We personally experienced the veracity of Gabonian statements about the effects of the music. We suppose that many procedures in Bwiti are based on neuropsychological knowledge although as yet not investigated by Western scientists. We think it could be useful for pharmacological and musical cognition to formulate hypotheses on the knowledge base of traditional medicine.

Chapter 10

Dangerous Music

Working with the Destructive and Healing Powers of Popular Music in the Treatment of Substance Abusers

Tsvia Horesh

The sirens of ancient Greece sang dangerous music. Nesting on a pile of human bones, on a rocky island off the coast of Sicily, the bizarre creatures, half bird, half woman, sang to the sun and rain; their song had the power to calm or to stoke the winds and to inflame men's loins. Their music was irresistible, the words even more so than the melody. They promised knowledge to every man who came to them, ripe wisdom and a quickening of the spirit. Many a sailor was lured to their shore – where he'd pine away without food or drink, unable to break the sirens' spell. The sirens' music tempted sailors by offering an illusion of power, joy and wisdom. The music was sweet and seductive; the danger of losing one's connection with reality, even losing one's life, was apparent. But for the victims, the attraction was far more powerful than the concept of danger.

(Bulfinch 1959)

Clients

My clients are the modern-day sailors; the sirens can be seen as the drugs they abused for many years, substances whose sweet promises of joy, well-being and transcendental experiences were found to be deceptive, only after addiction overtook the last vestiges of control they had over their habit.

The sirens actually sang 'dangerous music'. Many addicts talk about 'using' music interchangeably with drugs, listening obsessively to music during periods of abstinence. Here, the symbolism of the sirens' music has a dual meaning – not just the deceitful promise of the drugs, but also the powerful attraction of drug-related music.

My clients are chronic substance abusers, undergoing a year-long, inpatient treatment programme in the Ramot-Yehuda-Zoharim therapeutic community in Israel; men and women, aged 19–50, with a history of drug abuse lasting between two and thirty years. The majority have lived lives of crime and spent time in prison, usually as a result of drug abuse, selling drugs, thefts, violence and prostitution. Many come from multi-problem families, with a history of various addictions, life in crime-ridden neighborhoods and easily accessible drugs.

Therapeutic community

The basic ideology of the therapeutic community is one of inclusive, drug-free, therapeutic care for the addict, as an individual and as a member of society. This ideology is based on the assumption that drug dependency is a mix of educational, psycho-social, medical, emotional, spiritual and psychological factors, all of which must be addressed by treatment. It incorporates both psychodynamic and behavior-modification methods in an effort to relate to the complexity of the issues of addiction.

Addiction can be looked upon as a psychological or medical pathology, but it is also a cultural phenomenon and a culture in itself. The aim of treatment is to assist the addicts in leaving this culture and entering the culture of recovery. It is a long and difficult journey.

In his book *Pathways from the Culture of Addiction to the Culture of Recovery*, William White (1996) writes about the role the culture of addiction plays in sustaining addiction, regardless of the aetiology that led to the initiation of the person–drug relationship. And, in the late stages of addiction, the culture of addiction can pose the largest obstacle for clients entering the recovery process.

Culture of addiction

The culture of addiction is a way of life: a way of talking, thinking, behaving and relating to others, that separates substance abusers from those who are not. The culture encompasses values, places, rituals, symbols and music – all of which reinforce one's involvement in excessive drug consumption. A particular client may have initially started to abuse drugs in order to deal with emotional trauma, but it is clear that his addiction has shaped every aspect of his lifestyle, and that all these aspects must be examined in the recovery process. Many addicts have found it easier to break the physiological relationship with their drug than to break their relationship with the culture in which the drug was used. The failure to break the cultural relationship often precedes relapse (White 1996).

Some of our younger clients cannot perceive their social life without pubs, clubs and rave parties – all sites where drugs and alcohol are consumed, all 'danger zones' for the recovering addict. They cannot imagine going to a rock concert without taking – or drinking – something that will enhance their enjoyment of the music and enable them to feel part of the crowd.

Contemporary psychodynamic theories also recognize that much of the psychological dysfunction displayed by addicts is the result of drug abuse rather than the cause. It seems that some aspects of personality disorders apparent in addicts' behaviour have developed secondarily as a consequence of substance abuse, whereas others are primary and stem from the interaction of early developmental wounds and experiences with biological predisposition (Kaufman 1994). The addict is a person with an unstable personality, without inner sources to deal with daily pressures. The drugs enable him or her to deal with frustration, and to become disassociated from an oppressive and demanding reality.

Cues and craving

In making the transition from the culture of addiction to the culture of recovery, the addict has to learn to deal with cues and craving. Exposure to environmental cues associated with drug use can trigger cravings that cause cognitive and physiologic changes – increased thoughts of using and feelings of anxiety.

In the early stages of treatment, each client is encouraged to begin to identify his high-risk relapse factors – the personal cues, the 'people, places and things' (as coined by the Narcotics Anonymous groups) associated with his substance abuse.

High risk factors can include:

- *people*: active addicts, family relationships with elements of co-dependency

- *places*: where drugs are sold or used, personal haunts, neighbourhoods and streets associated with use

- *things*: drugs and the equipment used for consuming them; films, literature and music that either promote drug use or are personally associated with the experience of use.

Most addicts in the early stages of recovery, experience strong emotional and physical pulls back to active addiction, and ambivalence to their commitment to recovery. During such a vulnerable stage, exposure to cues that can trigger craving may start a process that, if not checked in time, can cause them to leave the treatment programme and relapse to drug abuse. Certain types of music can often pose such a threat (White 1996).

The song of the sirens, at times of crises in treatment, can drown out the sound of reason, of the quest for life, and cause our 'sailors' to sacrifice all their gains in the recovery process for the sirens' sweet music.

Music and addiction

Let us put the recovery process to one side for a few minutes, and look at the relationship that people who abuse drugs have with music.

Many of my clients claim that they cannot live without music, saying: 'Music is my whole life.' They tell different stories regarding their experiences with music, the differences relating to divergent ethnic groups, age, musical preferences, drug preferences and personality traits.

There is the music that was listened to together with drugs – different musical genres, each suiting the specific mood brought upon by the various substances ingested (heroin is an exception, its sedative properties usually causing lack of interest in most external, emotional and social activity – music included). Many addicts talk about 'using' music interchangeably with drugs, listening obsessively to music during periods of abstinence.

Music fills the emotional vacuum they feel without drugs, drowns out overwhelming thoughts and emotions, eases their passage into sleep and energizes them on waking up in the morning. Clients also talk about using music to avoid feeling – when faced with emotional conflict. Relying on drugs for these capacities for so many years, they are unable to cope without external help, and music fills that need.

James Lull (1987), in his book *Popular Music and Communication*, discusses similar topics – how listening to music can enable one to escape from personal burdens and tensions, stimulate fantasies and feelings of mental and physical ecstasy, and alleviate loneliness. Music helps to establish, reinforce or change moods. Anger, frustration, depression, restlessness, aimlessness, self-doubt – these emotions lead one to seek music that mirrors the emotions, in an effort to seek validation – which is usually lacking in the addict's social milieu. Certain kinds of music are used to resist authority, assert personalities, develop peer relationships and learn about things parents and schools don't teach. These notions are applicable to adolescent addicts and also to older addicts whose emotional and social development were arrested at the developmental stage in which the addiction began, usually adolescence.

Some clients will listen to any kind of music – whatever is on the radio. Others are experts in specific musical genres and will gladly explain what kind of music goes with each drug they used, and argue with their friends if one can really enjoy music while using heroin, and if so, at what stage of the addiction.

'Dangerous music'

The idea that music can be dangerous came up in a conversation with some of my clients a few years ago. To my (naive) question – what kinds of music do they like to listen to – they each spoke about music-related relapses. They expressed relief that someone was interested in this acute problem, which had never been addressed in therapy programmes they had attended in the past.

The following notes are initial thoughts regarding the concept of 'dangerous music' and of possible therapeutic methods that can be utilized in rehabilitating the complex relationship that addicts have with music. Research is currently being done on the subject, and the results will be published in the future.

The music that was pointed out as potentially dangerous was, basically, of four different genres (note that these findings are specific to addicts belonging to the multi-cultural Israeli society):

1   heavy metal

2   rap

3   Israeli Mediterranean music, a local genre of popular music

4   rave, techno and house.

Interestingly, many of the addicts describe an overlapping between their preferred musical styles, and their 'dangerous music'. They are drawn to listen to music that can, eventually, endanger them.

In interviewing my clients on their preferred choices of music, some generalities arose. People from different ethnic groups prefer different kinds of music:

- Young immigrants from the former Soviet Union, most of whom came to Israel 10 years ago or less, prefer heavy metal and rap.

- Mediterranean music is the choice of addicts who are usually native-born Israelis, whose parents came from Arab countries, such as Morocco, Yemen and Iraq.

- Rave, techno and house are chosen by the majority of the younger clients in their early 20s, regardless of their ethnic background. Much has been written about the 'rave generation' – the mass parties, the 'clubbing' culture, the music and drugs (ecstasy/MDMA and LSD). I have found that the danger such music holds for the recovering addict seems to be in a different category from the other genres. The lack of lyrics, the lack of performing musicians one can identify with, the cultural setting of such music, set it apart from other drug-related music and raise different psycho-social issues. For the purposes of this chapter, I will limit myself to describing the effects of heavy metal and Israeli Mediterranean music.

How are these genres of music connected to drug abuse?
HEAVY METAL

We will start with heavy metal. I recommend listening to Metallica, Iron Maiden, Black Sabbath or Deep Purple. Lean back, close your eyes and allow yourselves to flow with the music. Notice what emotions arise, what your body wants to do.

Whatever emotions were aroused while listening to the music, most of us, we hope, have the capacity to drag ourselves back to reality, and the responsible behaviour expected of us, in the current activity of reading a professional article. Many addicts don't have those capabilities, or they are not easily accessible. After listening to a song of the heavy metal group Metallica, I asked my clients to write down what feelings, memories and thoughts came up. They wrote:

- street fights
- heavy drinking
- I don't give a damn…
- fooling around
- wild behaviour
- hiding behind masks
- it calms me down
- what am I doing here (in treatment)?

The client who wrote that last remark said that while listening to the music, he had felt the impulse to get up and leave – the programme, his gains in therapy, his hope of a new life. He was shaken at how fragile his recovery was.

Research done on the effects of heavy metal music on adolescents reinforces some of my clients' reactions. Jeffrey Arnett (1996) interviewed adolescent boys on their involvement with heavy metal music. He found that some boys tended to listen to such music when they were in a negative mood and that the music had a purgative effect, relieving their anger. The music was 'used', like a tranquillizer, to relieve anger and to gain control. Other boys reported that when listening to the music with friends, it induced greater aggression, and put them into the mood to do violent acts. Arnett sees the popularity of such music as a symptom of alienation, the music being a reflection – and not necessarily the cause – of recklessness and despair.

Much of mainstream society's opposition to heavy metal, punk and rap music is related to the explicit lyrics, which include themes of sex, violence and drugs. It is interesting to point out that the majority of my clients do not know the English language and so can't understand the lyrics, apart from a few repetitive words. They relate, on the whole, to the rhythm, instrumentation, and general atmosphere of the song. I have also noticed that in many CDs of contemporary heavy metal groups, the inserts do not always include the texts of the songs, but only sinister-looking images of the rock stars. It is often difficult to understand the lyrics from the singing itself. These facts raise questions of the relevance of the 'explicit lyrics' to the listeners' reactions to certain kinds of music. Recently, though, I was introduced to the music of Marilyn Manson (the American group mentioned in Michael Moore's movie *Bowling for Columbine*). Some of my clients, young immigrants from Russia, identify with this music, and know enough English to understand the texts of the songs, which deal with issues such as drug abuse, violence, the Antichrist and hopelessness. We are now at the early stages of dealing with the meanings of this music to their lives, their drug habits and their rehabilitation.

MEDITERRANEAN MUSIC

Let us move on to another genre of popular music that can be dangerous to addicts. Israeli Mediterranean music is a hybrid genre created in Israel by Jews from Arabic speaking countries (Horowitz 1999). The music was, in the 1970s, thought to be culturally inferior by the mainstream, European-orientated culture and media. The music developed as an 'underground' alternative, giving voice to the themes and musical heritage of the lower-middle and working classes. The music is essentially either Western music overlaid with Middle-Eastern 'colours', and the Arabic melismatic form of singing, or authentic Turkish, Yemenite or Iraqi music with Hebrew texts.

The strongest connection the addicts have is with the sub-genre nicknamed 'crying songs'. The lyrics and music of these songs evoke feelings of melancholy and despair. My clients relate that in times of depression, they are drawn to choose music that mirrors their mood, and while identifying with the words, and the memories the song evokes, sink into feelings of self-pity and worthlessness. One man told the group that in the past, when feeling down, during periods of abstinence, he would listen to such songs alone in his room. His mother recognized such behaviour as a sign that he was on his way to a relapse.

Another client related his own repetitive pattern. He would choose a song that reminded him of his former girlfriend to evoke pleasant memories of their time together. While listening to the song he would identify with the lyrics, which usually spoke of abandonment and lost love. He would recall that, actually, his girlfriend left him for someone else. He would then become overwhelmed with emotions of despair and hopelessness. His only way of dealing with these emotions was to block them out with drugs.

Another client would turn the volume up high when listening to such music – so that his family and neighbours would know that he was depressed. It was the only way he knew to ask for help.

These are some examples of the ways addicts use – or abuse – music.

Music as a component of the culture of addiction

Looking back on our discussion of environmental cues and high-risk factors, we can begin to understand the role music has as a component in the culture of addiction, and the so-called 'danger' it presents in the transition to the culture of recovery.

The music stimuli evoke emotional and physical responses not just because of the music's properties, but because music recreates a mental and emotional representation of the essence of the moment when it was first heard (Ortiz 1997). The memory evoked can be of negative experiences or emotions, or of actual drug use. The established links between certain types of music and the euphoric recall of drug intoxication, reinforced through thousands of repetitions, serve as powerful connections to the culture of addiction (White 1996).

Treatment issues

How can we understand the addicts' susceptibility to the Sirens' call? Why are they drawn to listen to music that they know can endanger them? And, how is music different from other high-risk relapse factors?

Addicts may choose to listen to certain kinds of music as an attempt at self-healing, as a quest for integration of past pains and experiences with their present life, or as a search for emotional and spiritual catharsis. From a psychodynamic outlook, music can be seen as transitional phenomena – something that comes from the outside world but is experienced as part of the self. Music can offer consolation and at the same time evoke feelings of pain and longing (Franck-Schwebel 2002). Addicts are used to turning to external factors to manipulate their mood and emotional state, using drugs and music for this purpose interchangeably. The drugs they use block out almost all emotional activity, bringing them to a state of what they call 'living dead'. Listening to music, they feel alive, connected to their past and present emotional repertoire. But something goes wrong during what could have been a positive experience. The addicts' weak ego structure cannot deal with the overwhelming flood of emotional memories of pain, abuse and rejection. They figuratively 'drown' in the oceanic feeling of regression, and reach out to the kind of acting they know best – substance abuse or risk-seeking behaviour.

Relating to the issue of dangerous music, in our music therapy groups the first stage involves assessing the existence and intensity of musical cues from the culture of addiction. We explore the links between the clients' musical preferences and their drug-using identity and experiences.

The ancient Greeks had ways to deal with the sirens' dangerous music. Circe, the sorceress, advised Odysseus on how to deal with the danger when sailing by the sirens' island. She told him to order his sailors to plug their ears with bees' wax, thus preventing them from hearing the music. This is equivalent to the isolation techniques that involve protecting the client from exposure to the kinds of music that are so integrally bound to drug use that it is impossible to diminish its power as a conditioned stimulus. I believe that this technique is appropriate in the beginning stages of treatment, when the clients are just overcoming the physical stages of detoxification, and are experiencing withdrawal symptoms, among them an overwhelming flood of negative emotions. At this stage, clients are usually not fully committed to their recovery and can be easily dissuaded by exposure to drug-related music.

In many inpatient treatment centres, this method seems to be the only technique in dealing with dangerous music. The music the clients are allowed to listen to is monitored by the staff, whose policy is usually to censor rave music and Mediterranean 'crying songs', because of their strong connection to drug abuse. No attempt is made to deal with the threat this music presents to the addicts. When the clients finish the treatment programme, they are left to deal on their own with the sometimes critical effects such music may have on their emotional well-being.

Odysseus himself, feeling more privileged than his sailors, didn't want to plug his ears. He wanted to hear the sirens' music but knew that he was not strong enough to hold back while listening to it. Circe suggested that he have himself tied to the mast, and instruct his sailors not to heed his pleas to untie him, when he lost his sense of danger under the influence of the music. On the contrary, they were to see his pleas as a sign that they must lash him even tighter to the mast. Odysseus was willing to face the danger but both he and the sorceress knew that he needed external boundaries to contain his self-destructive tendencies.

By listening to each client's dangerous music, in the safe, containing environment of the music therapy group, we provide the figurative 'ropes', tying the addict to reality, holding him from drowning in the music's emotional ocean. The client is encouraged to share with the group his memories and associations evoked by the music. Often people will disclose personal stories that they had not previously revealed in therapy. But in order to enable the client to develop his own holding and containing powers, we turn to Orpheus for inspiration.

Orpheus, known for his creative, musical powers, found a way to deal with the sirens' music, saving his men and himself. Sailing by their island, he tuned his lyre and began to sing and his persuasive voice overcame the allure of the sirens. Thus vanquished, the sirens lost all powers to do harm and were changed to rocks from that moment on. One of them threw herself into the sea in vexation. Her body was tossed on to the shore by the waves and a tomb was erected for her on the very spot where later the city of Naples stands.

Group therapy

In one of my group meetings, we attempted Orpheus' 'method' in dealing with the danger the Israeli Mediterranean 'crying songs' posed for the group members. I proposed that, after listening to the song, we would improvise music that expressed the emotions evoked by the song. They chose to listen to one of the singers most identified with this genre – Ofer Levi, singing 'The Road of Temptation'. The song has a Turkish melody and is characteristically accompanied by a Middle-Eastern string orchestra. The lyrics are sung as a personal rendition – a plea to God from one who is no longer in control of his life. From a fulfilled existence he has slipped into ruin, tempted by drugs, and is alone and unrecognizable even to himself.

There is no hope in the lyrics of this song, and the style of singing – typical of this genre – reflects the feelings of despair and bleakness.

Listening

While listening to the song, I could see from their body language that my clients were very moved, some of them showing signs of distress. When the song was over, I asked them to close their eyes, to stay with the emotions the music aroused, and to notice what memories it evoked. After a few minutes, I invited them to choose instruments. The transition from listening to the song, to choosing instruments and playing themselves, was not easy. There were feelings of unrest that led to talking and fooling around. I had to assert gentle authority and help them settle down, without losing the feel of the song. The instruments they chose were: guitar, garmoshka (a small Russian accordion), two Darbukas (Egyptian drums), wave ring, domino, double cowbell. The guitar player had played professionally in the past; the rest of the group members had no musical experience, apart from two former improvisation group sessions. The improvisation lasted seven minutes.

Beginning

The beginning was tentative, even though the guitar played a constant rhythmic and harmonious base. The drummers had difficulty in staying with the slow, flowing rhythm of the guitar. I joined in with a hand drum in order to stabilize the rhythm, feeling that it was important to guide them towards a stable rhythmic container. The eventual result was an almost hypnotizing, repetitive flow of sound. I directed the entrances and exits of the players. The domino kept a stable rhythm; the garmoshka played long, poignant notes.

Group discussion

In the discussion that followed, I asked the group members to relate to the emotions evoked by the song, and to their feelings during the improvisation. The atmosphere was tense; some people spoke about their painful memories, while others chatted with their neighbours, laughed or fiddled with their instruments. Feelings of doubt, that maybe the song took them so deep that there was no safe way out – began to creep up on me. Soon there were outbursts of anger, insults and what seemed to be a regression to behaviour reminiscent of the culture of addiction. This was not their usual behaviour. The clients, having been in treatment for seven to eight months, had, for the most part, internalized the behavioural codes of the recovery culture. It seemed clear that the music we heard was responsible for this regression.

When I asked what was going on, and shared my feelings with them, they calmed down. One man said that this is how he behaves when over-whelmed by negative emotions. I pointed out how easy it was to revert to the addictive behaviour, to the aggressive, disrespectful ways of relating to each other, when exposed to music that reminded them of their past.

It's interesting to note that the improvisation itself was not sufficient to purge the negative emotions evoked by the song. The aggressive behaviour began after the improvisation, and escalated while group members were trying to share their difficult memories. The moment of recognition – that this music not only affects their emotions but also controls their behaviour – was a moment of revelation.

The domino player, who had been the main aggressor minutes ago, said that he hated Ofer Levi's music, and tried to avoid hearing it. It brought up feelings of pain and anger that had been part of his life since childhood. 'I feel angry, but I'm not angry at any of you. There's no one person that I'm angry at,' he said. He apologized for his behaviour and said that his rhythmic manipulation of the domino, accompanying the melodic music of the guitar and garmoshka, enabled him to express and release some his anger.

The guitar player said that during the song he could smell the rice his mother used to cook for him when he lived at home. He felt a wave of warm feelings for his mother, which surprised him. He said that he harboured a lot of anger towards his parents and felt ashamed of them. He had, during the past few days, even been debating whether or not to invite them to the family therapy sessions, which were going to take place soon. The positive memories of his mother challenged his conflict and ambivalence.

Regarding the aggressive atmosphere in the group, he said that if they had been active drug abusers, hearing that song, and if there had been a packet of heroin in the room – the result would have been fist fights and stabbing. It was a miracle that they could channel such negative energy into improvising music.

The garmoshka player was a young man, whom I will call Tommy. He was known among his friends as a 'clown', his behaviour characterized by much adolescent-like acting out. He said that the song took him back to the neighbourhood he grew up in. He described a closely knit society, where the people all knew each other. Ofer Levi's music in the air, the women cleaning and cooking inside, the guys sitting outside, eating sunflower seeds and smoking hash. The atmosphere was one of potential violence and reckless behaviour. The memory was nostalgic but tinged with pain and fear, bringing up traumatic events from his past. He told us that the main emotion he felt was stress and unrest. In the past, when feeling this way, he would take a friend's car and drive it, recklessly. That was the only way he could calm down.

It seems that by merging with the guitar music, Tommy could connect with and express the sadness that was under the unrest and aggression he usually felt and acted on.

The song evoked a totally reminiscent mode of being (smell, pictures, sounds, memories and emotions), and threatened to drown the people in an overwhelming emotional ocean. They responded by acting out their anxiety and negative emotions. Only after interpreting the connection between the song and their behaviour could they really look into the underlying emotions, and appreciate the purging and organizing effect the improvisation had on them.

Conclusion

In creating their own music, the group members had to adhere to the musical elements of time, rhythm, structure and dynamics, which required them to activate their ego capacities for focusing, relating to exterior boundaries and the behaviour of others, decision making and concentration on the here and now (Ansdell 1995). Into this structured container they each brought their own personal pain, fear, love and anger. Joining with their friends, they created together a total musical experience, loud and strong enough to at least partially, they hoped, drown out the dangerous music of the sirens, as Orpheus did so many years ago.

My role in the process was similar to that of Circe, the ancient sorceress who advised Odysseus on how to deal with the sirens. Circe symbolizes one who knows the secrets and dangers of the unconscious. I, myself, am not endangered by the music we listen to, and am aware of the perils it holds for my clients. My duty is to initiate the encounter between the addicts and their dangerous music; to supply a safe musical/emotional container within which they can 'face the music' and the emotional turmoil it evokes, and to guide them through the difficult encounter to a safe shore, to an ability to control their musical experience, rather than to be controlled by it.

Two of my clients, of their own initiative, have been working on finding an alternative musical repertoire for themselves, choosing music that is not connected to their drug-abusing past. They feel empowered by this independent project and they hope the personal growth accomplished through the musical work, by way of mastering the experience of 'dangerous music', can be applied to other parts of their lives.

Music, for addicts, has powerful destructive and healing potential. It can be abused, as drugs are. It can be misused and lead one into a vicious circle of dependency and self-destructiveness. But music has the potential to heal. By assisting addicts in rehabilitating their music-listening habits, they can learn to face their dangerous music, and begin to incorporate music into their lives as a source of enjoyment and enrichment.

Chapter 11

On a Journey to Somatic Memory

Theoretical and Clinical Approaches for the Treatment of Traumatic Memories in Music Therapy-Based Drug Rehabilitation

Marko Punkanen

Introduction

Drug addiction is a complex phenomenon. In my previous research and in my clinical music therapy work with drug addicts I have seen that there are quite often traumatic experiences in their past and clients will get in touch with their traumatic history during the therapy process (Punkanen 2004). Therefore it is very important to know how to work with those memories so that clients don't get re-traumatized by them.

What does it mean when we say that our client has a traumatic history? To put it simply it means that a person has experienced one or more traumatic events in her life. What can be considered as a traumatic event, then? The official definition of trauma is that it is caused by a stressful occurrence 'that is outside the range of usual human experience, and that would be markedly distressing to almost anyone'. This definition encompasses the following unusual experiences: 'serious threat to one's life or physical integrity; serious threat or harm to one's children, spouse, or other close relatives or friends; sudden destruction of one's home or community; seeing another person who is or has recently been seriously injured or killed as the result of an accident or physical violence' (Levine 1997, p.24). This definition is a good starting point but we have to remember that every human being is unique in her reactions to stressful events and there are of course lots of other events that can be traumatic for us. According to Herman, traumatic events are extraordinary not because they occur rarely, but rather because they overwhelm the ordinary human adaptations to life (Herman 1997, p.33). Accidents, illnesses, divorces and bullying are not outside the range of usual human experiences but can be very traumatic. Especially when the stressful events happen in childhood, they can have a powerful effect on a person's life later on. Neglect, physical and sexual abuse, failure of the attachment bond, and individual traumatic incidents like hospitalization, death of a parent, parents' divorce and being bullied at school are common trauma experiences with the drug addict clients I have worked with. We also have to remember that the client's traumatic history can be short or long. Lenore Terr has distinguished two types of trauma victims, Type 1 and Type 2. Her distinction was originally made with regard to children. Type 1 refers to those who have experienced only a single traumatic event in their history and Type 2 refers to those who have been repeatedly traumatized (Terr 1994). If our client has only one traumatic event in her history it is often much easier to work with the trauma compared to a client who has multiple traumatic incidents in her history.

Case examples

Riikka

Riikka was a 19-year-old young woman when I started to work with her. She lived alone and her father and stepmother were in prison at that time. Riikka's mother and little brother lived in the neighbourhood and Riikka saw them regularly. Riikka had neither boyfriend nor children. She had finished at comprehensive school and she had started studying several professions, but had dropped them. At the time when I started the music therapy process with her she was unemployed. This was the first time that she had searched for professional help for her addiction.

When she came to the first interview she hadn't used drugs for two weeks. She had been using drugs since she was 15 years old. During the history-taking Riikka said that her parents had been divorced four years ago and she was still bitter about that. Her mother had a 'new man' and Riikka was very jealous of her mother. Riikka felt that her mother didn't understand her feelings about that. When I asked if there were any other traumatic events in her life she told me about her childhood. Her family had moved a lot during her childhood and every time she made friends she had to move to another place. She had felt that she didn't belong anywhere. She felt that her parents didn't love her and that she wasn't good enough for them. The emotional atmosphere had been very cold in her family and she started to think that it was her fault. Little by little she took on the role of caretaker and felt herself guilty about everything that happened in her family.

When we talked more about emotions Riikka acknowledged that she had big problems in expressing her feelings verbally to others. She expressed bad feelings by ranting and raving when she was alone. Riikka said that she didn't want to show her weakness to anyone. She had noticed that when she used drugs it was easier to express and tolerate all kinds of emotions. When I asked what her goals for the therapy process were she initially replied that she was afraid to set any goals for herself; however after a moment she said that music therapy could be some kind of focal point in her life because she didn't want to continue her life with drugs. She wanted to change her life.

Sari

Sari was a 23-year-old woman when she came to music therapy. She had been using drugs since she was 14 years old. When I did the history-taking with her and asked about the traumatic events in her life, she told me that there had been some traumatic events in her childhood. Her parents were divorced when she was in primary school. That was a big shock for her. At the same time she was being bullied at school and this continued for some years. A couple of years ago Sari's boyfriend attempted suicide and this was the most recent traumatic experience which included a lot of fear and anxiety for her.

When we talked about emotions Sari spoke of how she was very sensitive on an emotional level and when she used drugs it was easier to handle all kinds of emotions because then she was not so sensitive anymore. She felt that without drugs she became stressed with everything in her life and using drugs was a kind of escape from strong emotions. She had also noticed that getting angry was impossible for her even though she wanted to be angry sometimes. When we linked this statement to her history of being bullied she noticed that she was very selective about people, and that was connected to the strong emotions of being bullied. Sari felt that she should be stronger and harder and she took on a kind of protective role, which included being rude and unfriendly. Sari felt this role very contradictory to what she felt inside her. It had become a way to survive in life and cope with the threatening emotions. During the history-taking Sari noticed that experiences of being bullied have a straight link to starting to use drugs. It gave her relief on an emotional level and provided a social group where she felt herself accepted. Sari told me that expressing anger was so difficult for her that when she had a quarrel with her boyfriend she froze. She described those situations as follows: 'I become like a little helpless child. I can't do anything. And then I am totally hysterical. I feel that everything will fall apart until someone solves the situation.'

In these situations Sari cannot act at all. This reaction is one of the three basic reactions that happen in traumatic situations. We fight, flee or freeze. Probably this is the reaction model for stressful situations that she has learned in her traumatic childhood experiences. Sari wanted to meet those old memories and painful, strong emotions connected to them together with the therapist and music and learn to deal with them. That was the main goal of the therapy process for her.

My clients mostly have quite a long history with drugs. That means 10 to 15 years of substance abuse. Sari's case is quite a common one with the clients I work with. She started to smoke when she was 13. One year later she started to use cannabis and then two years later amphetamine. The main drug for her then was the amphetamine even though she has also tried ecstasy, cocaine and heroin. Almost 100 per cent of my clients have started with cannabis and about 90 per cent have used amphetamine, 30 per cent have had LSD and methamphetamine experiences, 60 per cent have had shorter or longer ecstasy, cocaine and heroin experiences and almost everyone has used alcohol.

Method of treatment

The method of treatment that I mostly use in drug rehabilitation consists of three different elements: the physioacoustic method, combined with listening to music, which is then followed by a therapeutic discussion. The physioacoustic method (low frequency sound therapy chair or mattress) produces a state of deepened relaxation, which can also be called an altered state of consciousness. In the altered state of consciousness the person becomes more receptive and allows unconscious material to flow into her consciousness. In the altered state of consciousness, the ego becomes receptive to both inner and outer stimulation. This way memories and emotions that have been unconscious for years can come to consciousness (Fromm 1977, pp.373–377). Listening to music in this way can assist in achieving the altered state of consciousness and it can awaken emotions and images. The combination of the physioacoustic method and the listening to music provides the client with a very holistic experience that awakens both physical and mental sensations, thoughts, images and memories. The sharing of the experience with the therapist and the integration of treatment into the client's own life situation can open totally new perspectives and views of the addictive behaviour (Punkanen 2004).

A client is most at risk of becoming overwhelmed or re-traumatized when the therapy process accelerates faster than she can contain it. This often happens when more memories are elicited into consciousness (images and thoughts from the music or body sensations from the physioacoustic method) than can be integrated at one time (Rothschild 2000). By adding some trauma psychotherapy approaches into my clinical work I have found it safer for me as a therapist and for my clients to work with traumatic memories.

The store of traumatic memories: somatic memory

When we work with drug addicts who have traumatic backgrounds we have to understand how the traumatic memories affect the person and how they differ from other memories. In the beginning of the 1990s the idea of multiple memory systems became more accepted. During that time there was an important discovery of two new types of memory, which are called explicit and implicit. Explicit memory, which is sometimes called also declarative memory, is composed of facts, concepts and ideas. Explicit memory enables us to tell our life story, narrate events, put experiences into words, construct a chronology and extract a meaning (Rothschild 2000, pp.28–29).

Explicit memory depends on language but implicit memory bypasses it. Explicit memory involves facts, descriptions, and operations that are based on thought. Implicit memory involves procedures and internal states that are automatic. Implicit emotional or sensational memories stay unconscious until we are able to connect them to explicit memory, which will construct a narration about them. Implicit memory is sometimes also called procedural or non-declarative memory (Rothschild 2000, p.30).

What is meant by somatic memory? The implicit memory system is at the core of somatic memory. Drug addicts with traumatic history suffer inundation of images, sensations and behavioural impulses (implicit memory) disconnected from context, concepts and understanding (explicit memory) (Rothschild 2000, p.37). Traumatic memories lack verbal narrative and context. According to Herman (1997) 'they are encoded in the form of vivid sensations and images' and 'in their predominance of imagery and bodily sensation and in their absence of verbal narrative, traumatic memories resemble the memories of young children'. Traumatized people relive the moment of trauma in their thoughts and dreams and also in their actions (Herman 1997, pp.38–39).

Traumatic memories are often re-experienced as fragmented sensory perceptions: images, smells, sounds, tastes and bodily sensations, frequently accompanied by unregulated affect. Traumatized people 'remember' the trauma as disjointed somatosensory experiences rather than as narrative account (Van der Kolk, Van der Hart and Marmar 1996). It can be said that traumatic memories are stored in the body (somatic memory) and can be awakened with different sensory stimulus, for example with the physio-acoustic method, which sends low frequency sound waves to the client's body. Listening to music is another way to get in touch with traumatic memories. With Riikka and Sari the physioacoustic method proved to be an important producer of sensation. It brought up some painful memories but also very positive and strong bodily experiences and sensations of pleasure. As a consequence of the emotions wakened up by the bodily sensations, their feelings about their own lives started to come into their consciousness while the process was progressing. The music listened to during the physioacoustic treatment was also an important producer of sensations in addition to the physioacoustic method. This also activated feelings, as well as images and old forgotten somatic memories, which took them closer to emotions connected to their own lives (Punkanen 2004).

On braking and accelerating: how can one help the client control the traumatic memories?

Rothschild compares the treatment of traumatic memories to driving a car. If we want to drive safely we have to learn the good combination of braking and accelerating. It is the same thing with traumatic memories. According to Rothschild it is inadvisable for a therapist to accelerate trauma processes in clients or for a client to accelerate toward his own trauma, until each first knows how to hit the brakes. We have to learn first how to slow down or stop the traumatic memories reliably, thoroughly, and confidently (Rothschild 2000, p.79).

Caldwell talks about the addiction spiral that begins with an intolerable experience. Traumatic experience is always intolerable and even though the original experience is past and gone there are lots of triggers in the present that make us live it again. Sari's freezing reaction in quarrels and also the deep sorrow that she brought up during the therapy process were intolerable experiences for her. It is typical that this kind of experience is felt to threaten one's physical, mental or emotional survival. An intolerable experience stimulates a fight, flight or freeze reaction that makes us search for relief to the situation (Caldwell 1996, pp.29–30).

It is important to know how to bring the client back to the here and now, if she goes to the states of hyperarousal or hypoarousal which could happen easily while listening to music when images and memories start to awake. If the client is hyperaroused or hypoaroused it is impossible to work with traumatic memories so that she can integrate them into an explicit, narrative memory. As we see in Figure 11.1, if the client goes beyond the framework of the window of tolerance, which means the optimal arousal zone for work with traumatic memories, she will start to dissociate. That means that she is not here with us anymore. She feels that the traumatic event is happening right now and then we need to slow down the process and bring her back to the window of tolerance. For that we can use different clinical methods.

Anchors

The concept of anchors has came to trauma therapies from Neuro-Linguistic Programming. Basically, an anchor is a concrete, observable resource. It is advisable to choose the anchor from the client's life so that the positive

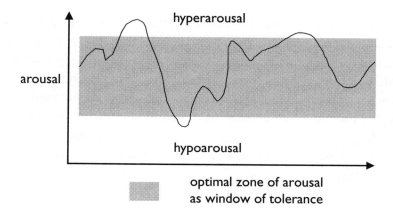

Figure 11.1 Arousal and the window of tolerance around optimal arousal. Adapted from Ogden and Minton (2000)

memories from her body and mind can be utilized. According to Rothschild (2000) an anchor can be a person (grandmother), an animal (favourite pet), a place (home, a site in nature), an object (a tree, a boat, a stone), an activity (swimming, hiking, gardening), and of course music itself and music which reminds the client of the person, animal, place, object or activity that is important and meaningful. A good anchor enables the client to feel herself relieved and relaxed, both bodily and emotionally (Rothschild 2000, p.93). When working with drug addicts with traumatic history it is useful in the beginning of the therapy process to establish at least one anchor to use as a braking tool at any time when the therapy gets too rough. One good way to do that is to ask the client to bring with her a song or piece of music which includes positive emotions and memories. Then you can establish the anchor by listening to that piece of music with the client and guiding her to the positive emotions, memories and images of that music.

The established anchor music can be applied quite easily during the therapy session. When I notice that my client's hyperarousal gets too high, I stop the process for a while and change the subject. I might ask the client to tell me about her anchor music and memories connected to it. And at the same time I change the music for the anchor music. The connection can be deepened by giving sensory cues that are associated to the anchor. One of the biggest difficulties of applying anchors is getting used to interrupting the client's memories and images while listening to music. When it becomes clear how much the use of anchors actually assists the processing of traumatic memories, the therapist and client will both gain greater tolerance for such interruptions. Anchors help you to keep clients in the window of tolerance and lower the base level of hyperarousal. After using an anchor you can guide your client back to her traumatic memories, but from a lower level of arousal than before the anchor was employed. According to Rothschild, in this way a traumatic memory can be fully addressed without the hyperarousal getting out of control (Rothschild 2000, p.94).

The safe place

The safe place is a specialized anchor, a current or remembered site of protection. The idea of the safe place was first used in hypnosis for reducing the stress of working with traumatic memories. The safe place should be a physical location that is familiar to the client. The memory of the chosen safe place should evoke somatic resonances with the client. These can be sights, smells, sounds or pieces of music, which are connected to that site. When the safe place includes lots of recorded sensory memory traces it can be used very successfully during the therapy process (Rothschild 2000, p.95). I always try to find suitable music with the client for her safe place and very often the client has it already. Quite often I also use slow, low frequencies (30–40 Hz) from the physioacoustic chair to help the client calm down and relax in her safe place image. The safe place image can be used during times of stress and anxiety, or as other anchors, to reduce hyperarousal during a therapy session (Rothschild 2000, p.95).

Body/somatic awareness

What is body/somatic awareness? One definition is that 'Body awareness implies the precise, subjective consciousness of body sensations arising from stimuli that originate both outside of and inside the body' (Rothschild 2000, p.101).

According to Rothschild, employing the client's own awareness of the state of her body, her perception of the precise, coexisting sensations that arise from external and internal stimuli, is a most practical tool in the treatment of traumatic memories. Consciousness of present sensory stimuli works as the primary link to the here and now. It can also be used as a direct link to all our emotions. However, it is important to notice the difference between body awareness and emotion. Body awareness is not an emotion, such as feeling fear or being afraid, but when we are aware of different body sensations or manifestations such as shallow breathing, elevated heart rate and cold sweat we can identify our emotional state as being afraid. Emotions are therefore combinations of different body sensations, which we can learn to recognize through body awareness. The use of body awareness is a good therapeutic tool. It helps us to gauge, slow down and even halt traumatic hyperarousal and most of all it helps the client to separate past from present. Later in the therapy process it can also be used for interpreting the client's somatic memory (Rothschild 2000, pp. 100–102).

Some clients have quite a good sense of their bodies and will be able to describe their bodily sensations to others. However, quite often with drug addicts, when you ask, 'What are you aware of in your body right now?', they simply don't know. They may be unable to feel their body sensations at all, or they may feel something but not have the words to describe their sensations. Some substance misusers have such little contact with their bodies that when asked about their physical sensations they start to talk about their thoughts.

There are several ways to help increase awareness of sensation: therapist's observations about client's bodily changes, establishing a vocabulary for sensation, asking accessing questions and the use of physioacoustic methods and music as external stimuli.

Therapist's observations about client's bodily changes

Therapists can help their clients to develop body awareness by observing the physical changes in the client's body: posture, gesture, facial expression, movements, self-touch, etc. The skill of observing both subtle and obvious shifts and changes as they are occurring in the client's body must be learned (Ogden 2003, p.10; Rothschild 2003). According to Ogden bodily changes can be 'as delicate as a slight skin colour change, the dilation of the nostrils or the pupils, or a change in the pulse noticed in the artery in the neck' or they can be 'as obvious as a collapse through the whole spine, a full gesture with the arm, or a kick of the leg' (Ogden 2003, p.10).

According to Ogden (2003) an effective intervention that naturally follows the observing is making verbal contact with the observed changes. Simple statements such as, 'I notice the collapse of your spine,' or, 'Your breathing is getting deeper,' or, 'You're getting warmer' (indicated by skin colour change), or, 'There's tension around your eyes right now,' direct the client's awareness to her body. The above statements may feel too simplified to the therapist, but according to Ogden they hold tremendous benefit in a therapy session where you want to help your client to a greater awareness of her bodily sensations and their connection to the traumatic memories (Ogden 2003, p.10; Rothschild 2003).

Inner body sensation vocabulary

As music therapists we are familiar with a variety of words to describe different emotions like sad, angry, hurt, disappointed, irritated, fearful, depressed and so on. However, we are not so familiarized with a vocabulary that describes inner body sensations. According to Ogden, when a client is describing physical pain, she can simply say, 'It hurts', although there are many kinds of pain. By providing a menu of sensation vocabulary, a therapist can help his client to refine and elaborate her description about her body sensations. That will provide verbal options for clients to choose from, and will spark their own acuity for the language of physical sensations. According to Ogden the following words are examples of sensation vocabulary: twitch, frozen, vibration, dull, airy, itchy, sharp, thick, intense, achy, tremble, mild, smooth, shivery, numb, jagged, chills, flaccid, and so on (Ogden 2003, pp.10–11).

Accessing questions

Accessing questions is a term which refers to questions that the therapist can use to help the client to sense her body better and to concentrate more on her physical experiences in the here and now. Accessing questions according to Ogden (2003) falls into the following categories:

1   *General questions:* These questions are general, non-specific queries into sensation. They are useful at the beginning stages of exploration to help clients sense their bodies in a diffuse, undifferentiated way. *What do you feel in your body? Notice your inner body sensations. Where is the feeling in your body? What is your experience on the level of sensation?*

2   *Specific accessing questions:* Specific questions help a client to discover the details of sensation. Describing the exact particulars about the sensation helps fine-tune the awareness and language of sensation. *What are the qualities of that sensation? Where exactly do you feel it in your body? What are the parameters? Do you notice a central point to that sensation? Where does it begin and end? Does that sensation have a direction – does it go from inward to outward or outward to inward? What else do you notice about this sensation?*

3   *Comparison:* Accessing questions that teach a client to compare various areas of the body may also help clients become more aware of their body sensations

(Ogden 2003, p.11)

The use of the physioacoustic method and music as external stimuli

In my clinical work I use the physioacoustic method and music as external stimuli to awaken the client's senses, images, emotions and memories. The physioacoustic device uses low frequency sinusoidal sound. This low frequency sound comes from a specially designated computer. In the physioacoustic method the frequency range varies from 27 Hz to 113 Hz. According to Lehikoinen the efficiency of this method is based on the exact ability of controlling the device and the body's sensitive ability to react to low sounds. The penetration of the low sounds in solids and in fluids used in the physioacoustic method is very good. Because of this the physioacoustic stimulation stays regular and therefore the tissue has enough time to react to the sound waves (Lehikoinen 1996, p.32).

Listening to music in music therapy can be realized in many different ways. In my clinical work I combine music with the physioacoustic method. The aim of listening to music in this case is to evoke sensations, images, emotions and memories and therefore activates symbolic work that is based on the primary process. The function of the music is also to help clients to get into the altered state of consciousness in which the connection to one's own unconscious and somatic memory would become possible.

In my previous research I found that the combination of the physio-acoustic method and the listening to music awakened the participants' senses in a very holistic way from the first treatment session on (Punkanen

2004). According to Caldwell (1996), when we treat addictions and talk about them, we often forget about the fact that our body with our senses forms the most important part of the addiction behaviour. Withdrawing from our bodies is the beginning of addictive behaviour (Caldwell 1996, pp.19–32). With this Caldwell refers to the neurologically proven fact that the bodily sensations function as awakeners of our emotions (for example, Damasio 2000). Therefore when we become estranged from our bodily sensations we also become estranged from our emotions.

The combination of the physioacoustic method and the listening to music seemed in the light of my research and clinical work a very useful method for the drug addicts to get in touch with their body sensations, emotions and traumatic memories.

Body/somatic awareness as a road to emotions: the cases of Riikka and Sari

During the therapy process Riikka and Sari revealed that there were lots of hidden and denied emotions in their lives, the emotions with which they got in touch through body awareness work with the physioacoustic method and listening to music. Trying to control situations and experience through denial is the second phase of the addictive spiral according to Caldwell (1996). We avoid feelings and body sensations that may prolong the upset but we cannot hide them because they are in our bodies. Riikka and Sari felt that during the treatment they could process things that they had left unprocessed. Riikka said that she has always tried to reject all the negative feelings and that can be seen as the third phase of addictive spiral. If as a child our anger threatens the working of the family system, as was the case with Riikka, the only solution is to get rid of it; but along with the feeling goes part of our self also. However, denial of feelings requires an amazing amount of energy and finally makes us hate ourselves because of the feelings that are not accepted by our environment (Caldwell 1996, pp.29–30). In Riikka's case this came up very clearly. She blamed herself for everything that had happened in her family. The denial of feelings caused psychosomatic reactions in both Riikka and Sari. Riikka said that she had often thrown up when something unprocessed started getting out from the inside of her body. She felt that the unprocessed things and the negative feelings connected to them never left her in peace even though she tried to escape from them. According to McDougall psychosomatic symptoms are sometimes connected to drug addiction problems. It is probable that psychosomatic vulnerability increases with people who use action as protection against psychic pain when in fact recalling the emotion or reflection would be a more suitable way to deal with it (McDougall 1999, pp.81–93). Using action instead of reflection is a typical reaction for people with traumatic history.

Caldwell writes that using drugs can be seen as the fourth and final phase of the addictive spiral. The last phase of the addictive spiral has to do with the domino effect brought on by marginal experiencing. Because we exert so much energy on controlling and rejecting our 'wrong', traumatic experiences, we have fewer resources available that enable us to tolerate any experience. A lot of our time and energy goes into maintaining a defensive wall against unacceptable and forbidden feelings, sensations, memories and thoughts. Drugs are a relief to this kind of situation. When using drugs the control loosens and we feel freer for a while. Through this, a feeling of illusion is also created in which we feel that we are taken care of (Caldwell 1996, pp.30–36). However, when the use of narcotics increases, fears and anxiety seem to be the chief experience of a drug addict.

At the end of the music therapy process Sari felt that trust of the therapist and of the whole treatment had made it possible for her to let her mind travel to the past with the music and experience those painful memories again and feel herself secure at the same time. Feeling herself secure was a very significant experience for Sari because she had felt herself insecure for so long.

Riikka felt that the music therapy process had above all brought up to consciousness things that she had not remembered for a long time. By this she referred to some childhood memories that she got in touch with during therapy. Riikka also felt that during the therapy process she became more curious and interested in self-examination. She was also positively surprised that she had committed to the therapy. Both Riikka and Sari thought that even surprising and unexpected things came out during the therapy process. Riikka described these as follows.

I've sometimes sort of felt like I don't wanna mess with my childhood or anything today when I've come here, but then I suddenly realize that it just drifts to that sort of thing. Well, it's been easy and so. It hasn't been sort of, that I'm gonna talk about this and this. It's somehow surprising that I've had those strong feelings in the physio-acoustic chair and those old, forgotten memories through music, so it just drifts to those old memories and then we just talk about them.

Conclusion

Drug addicts often have traumatic experiences in their history and we have to be aware of that when we begin therapy process. The physioacoustic method and listening to music will help our clients to get in touch with forgotten, unconscious, traumatic memories, which are stored through the amygdala in the somatic memory system. Those memories are loaded with strong and painful emotions and therapists have to have tools to make it safe for the client to face those memories.

Trauma-psychotherapy techniques such as anchors, safety places and body awareness can be easily added to the music therapy practice and it will give to our clients and to us as music therapists more control in dealing with traumatic memories.

Chapter 12

Music Therapy and Spirituality
A Transcendental Understanding of Suffering

David Aldridge

Introduction

There has been an emerging interest in spirituality in the field of music therapy, particularly for those working in the ecology of palliative care (Aldridge 1995, 2000b; Bailey 1997; Lowis and Hughes 1997; Magill and Luzzato 2002; Marr 1999; West 1994). In *Music Therapy in Palliative Care: New Voices* (Aldridge 1999), several authors reflect the need for spiritual considerations when working with the dying (Hartley 1999; Hogan 1999). Nigel Hartley has developed this work particularly in hospice settings (Hartley 2001) and with Gary Ansdell ensured that the theme was prominent at the 2002 Music Therapy World Congress in Oxford. In the world of music therapy, the importance of spiritual considerations is evident in the early work of Helen Bonny as a central plank of her approach (Bonny and Pahnke 1972) and in Susan Munro's pioneering work in palliative care (Munro and Mount 1978).

In the next chapter of this book, Lucanne Magill reflects on what she believes is really the heart of what we do, music therapy in spirituality. As she says, 'So much of what we do is beyond words and it is really because of this transcendental nature of music that important healing in music therapy can and does occur'. In her four themes in music therapy, she proposes that music builds relationship, enhances remembrance, gives a voice to prayer and instils peace. In the presence of music, when transformations begin to occur and healing begins, it is in the lived moments of music therapy that the essence of our work – music therapy, spirituality and healing – is experienced and known.

Her response was made from a long career of experiences with cancer sufferers and their families (Bailey 1983, 1984; Magill 1993, 2001; Magill, Chung and Kennedy 2000). Both of us emphasize the importance of the immediate family and the people working in the hospital ward. We refer to this as the 'ecology of singing in a hospital setting' (Aldridge and Magill 2002) as this fits into both our career experiences in clinical practice and community work (Aldridge 1986). This ecology will include the palliative care culture, as a broader team, but also the ethos of the working situation as a whole. Anyone who has had the opportunity to visit and work with Lucanne at Memorial Sloan Kettering Cancer Center in New York will have seen that there are possibilities of making music with the staff from the head physician to members of the ancillary staff. Music-making is not solely for the patients in this setting; healing lies in the whole healing culture of the hospital. Culture here is not simply the artefacts and the beliefs resident in the hospital, it is an actively maintained dynamic – culture is performed, and thereby is maintained both in activity and changes. In such a way we participate fully in culture; it is not something we have separately, we literally 'do' culture.

The World Health Organisation has a comprehensive picture of what palliative care is, emphasizing a total care of patients where the disease is not responsive to curative treatment and acknowledges that both psychological and spiritual problems may occur (WHO 1990). We could add here that psychological and spiritual opportunities also occur, the goal of palliative care being to achieve the best quality of life for patients and their families. From a holistic perspective, palliative care:

> affirms life and regards dying as a normal process; neither hastens nor postpones death; provides relief from pain and distressing symptoms; integrates the psychological and spiritual aspects of patients' care; offers a support system to help patients as actively as possible until death; offers a support system to help the family cope during the illness and in their own bereavement. (WHO 1990, p.11)

In clinical practice, I am pursuing this work further with Lucanne Magill at Memorial Sloane Kettering Cancer Center. As a former community worker, promoting the arts with different people and their communities, music therapy was no strange practice to me when I first came across it. From my work with people who were the dying in the community, I understood that we must implement an ecological approach to understanding these phenomena (Aldridge 1987a, 1987c, 1991a, 1991b; Aldridge and Magill 2002). Indeed, the reason why modern medicine sometimes fails to meet the needs of the dying is because it lacks such a perspective, or way of implementing such practice. What was formerly complementary and holistic medicine, and is now integrative medicine, has sought to bring various perspectives together and deliver them for and with the patient and his family (Aldridge 2004).

Considerations of spirituality then are not unique to music therapy; there is, and has been, over the last two decades, an increasingly vigorous debate over the need for spiritual considerations in health care delivery (Aldridge 1987a, 1987c, 1988, 1996; Bailey 1997). There is an overlap between music therapy and several other integrative medicine approaches particularly in the use of breath and how this is applied in altering consciousness (Aldridge 2002). My intention is to sponsor the discussion of spirituality as a legitimate topic in music therapy, just as I have tried to do in the field of medicine (Aldridge 1987c; Aldridge 1991a; Aldridge 1991b, 2000b).

My doctoral thesis in 1985 was concerned with an ecosystemic approach to understanding suicidal behaviour from a personal perspective embedded in a familial milieu located in cultural and social contexts (published in Aldridge 1998). Taking a spiritual perspective did not remove from this ecological approach but added another dimension. For those of us involved in the Family Therapy movement, the books of Gregory Bateson (Bateson 1972, 1978) were core texts. Everything became process, system and ecology with the intention of stamping out nouns. We see this perspective in Christopher Small's book *Musicking* (Small 1998) where he also references the same discourse as I have done in my earlier work. Indeed, I use culture as an ecological activity binding the meanings of individuals in relationships together, what Gregory Bateson refers to as an 'ecology of mind' (Bateson 1972). What we do as individuals is understood in the setting of our social activities and those settings are informed by the individuals that comprise them. Here too, the body, and the presentation of symptoms, is seen as an important non-verbal communication that has meaning within specific personal relationships, which are located themselves within a social context. Symptoms are interpreted within relationships. Meanings are embodied and expressed as performances that have a repertoire of expression possibilities.

Much of my thinking has been influenced by Sufi writings (Marsham 1990; Shah 1964, 1968, 1983; Tweedie 1995). One of the authors often cited in relation to music therapy and spirituality is Hazrat Inayat Khan (Khan 1974, 1983, 1996). What has to be remembered is that Inayat Khan gave up his music to concentrate on his spiritual teaching. Giving up music was seen as an important step in his spiritual life of detachment from the world. Similarly, Irina Tweedie also refers to music as being a worldly attachment (Tweedie 1995). Indeed, music is prohibited in some spiritual traditions and only allowed in special places at special times. The Afghan mystic and teacher, Rumi, is often seen as the prime example of a teacher who uses music and dance to inspire his disciples and promote their spiritual development. Shah (1983) reminds us that this may only have been so because Rumi's disciples, at that time and in that place, were so fixed in thinking as an activity, and so physically lethargic, that it was necessary to get them moving and thereby into activity. For those who developed a musical tradition from Rumis' teaching, the musicians and dancers were part of a ritual of healing but it did not necessarily mean that the identified patient participated in the music making. There were specific musicians for the job in hand and such traditions involved the whole community. Some recent writers have used Sufi movements as part of their own attempts to break from their own rigidity of thinking but this has been accompanied by a teacher as part of a particular guided activity at a particular time on their spiritual journey, not as a regular and fixed activity. To get people thinking in certain ways, we have to get them moving. Particular movements will correspond to particular elements of musical activity; this knowledge has been the basis of religious activities where the liturgical form of music and texts, oratory style, stylized and ritual movements, priestly vestments and architecture are coherent in promoting spiritual experience. While we often talk of symbolic imagery and music that has interpretive meaning, we forget that these activities work directly as symbols without a verbal interface. There is a direct effect without interpretation at a different level of consciousness.

For some people who are too active and too imaginative, then music may be proscribed. Thus, some teachers will recommend their students not to become involved with music for a time.

Health as performed: a praxis aesthetic in an immanent context

Health, like music (Aldridge 2002), is performed. Indeed, the process of 'healthing' can be understood as a dynamic improvised process like that of Small's 'musicking' (Small 1998). How health is performed depends upon a variety of negotiated meanings, and how those meanings are transcended. As human beings we continue to develop. Body and self are narrative constructions, stories that are related to intimates at chosen moments. These meanings are concerned with body, mind and spirit. My intention is to set about the task of reviving a set of meanings given to the understanding of human behaviour that is termed spiritual. It is legitimate to talk about spirituality in a culture of health care delivery. Human beings perform their lives together in meaningful contexts of significant others that are nested within broader social contexts. The different contexts of performance are related to an ecological understanding of what it is to be a human being amongst other human beings and will argue for a return to a sacred understanding of human beings and nature. In these instances, 'God', 'the divine', 'the cosmos' or 'nature' may be the name given to a meaningful immanent context in which life is performed.

Spiritual meanings are linked to actions, and those actions have consequences that are performed as prayer, meditation, worship, healing and, in our approaches, music. What patients think about the causes of their illnesses influences what they do in terms of health care treatment and to whom they turn for the resolution of distress. For some people, rather than consider illness alone, they relate their personal identities to being healthy, one factor of which is spirituality. The maintenance and promotion of health, or becoming healthy, is an activity. As such it will be expressed bodily, a praxis aesthetic. Thus we would expect to see people not only having sets of beliefs about health but also actions related to those beliefs.

Some of these may be dietary, some involve exercise and some prayer or meditation. Some will be musical.

Religion and spirituality

There is a link between religion and spirituality, which I argue extensively in my book *Spirituality, Healing and Medicine* (Aldridge 2000b), although the two are often confused. The same difficulty has prevailed in the medical and nursing literature where spirituality and religion are confounded.

All major religions recognize a spiritual dimension and that is the relationship between the human being and the divine. We see this reflected in the Yin and Yang symbol of traditional Chinese medicine which emphasizes the vertical relationship between the human and the divine, each in their manifestation containing a seed of the other and uniting together to form a whole. Similarly, the Christian cross reflects both the realms of horizontal earthly existence and vertical divine relationship. The difficulty lies in the explanations that are used for understanding when either a sacred ecology or the divine relationship is used; one is assumed to supersede the other according to the interpreter of events. Both are partial. Indeed, what many spiritual authors seek is to take us beyond the dualisms of the material and spiritual, beyond body and mind, to realize that in understanding the relations between the two we leap to another realm of knowledge. Indeed, the Buddhist concept of the 'middle way' is not to find some mid-point between the two, but to transcend the two ideas, unifying them in a balanced understanding. This leap that goes beyond dualism is the process of transcendence. In its simplest form, there is a change of consciousness to another level of knowledge; in short, the purpose of spirituality is achieved. Neither pole is denied but accepted, subsumed and reconciled by a higher order of understanding.

Spirituality in a late modern sense is used consistently throughout the literature related to medical practice as an ineffable dimension that is separate from religion itself. A person may regard herself as having a spiritual dimension but this may not be explored in any religious practice. Central to these arguments is the concept that spirituality lends a unity and purpose to life (see Table 12.1).

Table 12.1 Definitions of spirituality from journal articles

Author(s)	Definition
Reed 1987	'Spirituality is defined in terms of personal views and behaviors that express a sense of relatedness to a transcendent dimension or to something greater than the self… Spirituality is a broader concept than religion or religiosity… Indicators of spirituality include prayer, sense of meaning in life, reading and contemplation, sense of closeness to a higher being, interactions with others and other experiences which reflect spiritual interaction or awareness. Spirituality may vary according to developmental level and life events' (p.336).
Kuhn 1988	'Spiritual elements are those capacities that enable a human being to rise above or transcend any experience at hand. They are characterized by the capacity to seek meaning and purpose, to have faith, to love, to forgive, to pray, to meditate, to worship, and to seek beyond present circumstances' (p.91).
Highfield 1992	'The spiritual dimension of persons can be uniquely defined as the human capacity to transcend self, which is phenomenologically reflected in three basic spiritual needs: (a) the need for self-acceptance, a trusting relationship with self based on a sense of meaning and purpose in life; (b) the need for relationship with others and/or a supreme other (e.g., God) characterized by nonconditional love, trust, and forgiveness; and (c) the need for hope, which is the need to imagine and participate in the enhancement of a positive future. All persons experience these spiritual needs, whether or not they are part of a formal religious organization' (p.3).
Chandler, Holden, and Kolander 1992	'Spiritual: pertaining to the innate capacity to, and tendency to seek to, transcend one's current locus of centricity, which transcendence involves increased love and knowledge' (p.169).
Lapierre 1994	'Six clear factors…appear to be fundamental aspects of spirituality…those of the journey, transcendence, community, religion, "the mystery of creation", and transformation' (p.154).

Table 12.1 cont.

Author(s)	Definition
Borman and Dixon 1998	'Spirituality…pertains to one's relationship with others, with oneself and with one's higher power, which is defined by the individual and need not be associated with a formal religion' (p.287).
Lukoff, Provenzano, Lu *et al.* 1999	'Spirituality refers to the degree of involvement or state of awareness or devotion to a higher being or life philosophy. Not always related to conventional beliefs' (p.65).
Narayanasamy 1999	'Spirituality is rooted in an awareness which is part of the biological make-up of the human species. Spirituality is present in all individuals and it may manifest as inner peace and strength derived from perceived relationship with a transcendent God or an ultimate reality or whatever an individual values as supreme' (p.124).
Reed 1987	'The term religiousness has been used in operationalizing spirituality' (p.336).
Doyle 1992	'By religious we mean practices carried out by those who profess a faith' (p.303).
Decker 1993	'The term religious will be used to denote the part of the process when spiritual impulses are formally organized into a social/political structure designed to facilitate and interpret the spiritual search' (p.34).
Idler 1995	'Religion has a beneficial effect on human social life and individual well-being because it regulates behavior and integrates individuals in caring social circles' (p.684).
Long 1997	'Religion is considered by some to be of divine origin with a set of revealed truths and a form of worship' (p.500).
Walter and Davie 1998	'Religion is or has been a response to socially induced vulnerability; it is and always has been a response to the physical vulnerability of the body that has been the human condition' (p.648).
Ganzevoort 1998	'Religion will not be defined in strict terms, but will be used to denote experiences, cognitions and actions seen (by the individual or the community) as significant in relation to the sacred' (p.260).

Author(s)	Definition
Lukoff *et al.* 1999	'Religiosity is associated with religious organizations and religious personnel.' Religion involves subscribing to a set of beliefs or doctrines that are institutionalized.' 'People…can be religious without being spiritual by perfunctorily performing the necessary rituals. However, in many cases, spiritual experiences do accompany religious practices' (p.65).
King and Dein 1998	'Religion is the outward practice of a spiritual system of beliefs, values, codes of conduct and rituals' (p.1259).
Park 1998	'Religion encompasses that which is designated by the social group as nonroutine and uncontrollable and that which inspires fear, awe, and reverence, that is, the sacred. Through ritual, one gains carefully prescribed access to the sacred, which is carefully protected from the mundane, routine, instrumentally oriented beliefs and actions of the profane realm. Because sacredness is socially confirmed, stemming from the attitude of believers…political ideologies, value systems and even leisure activities such as sports and art (are viewed) as sacred activities' (p.407).

My position is that if spirituality is about the individual, ineffable and implicit, religion is about the social, spoken and explicit. Such definitions are an attempt to explicate the practices whereby spirituality is achieved. Spirituality lends meaning and purpose to our lives; these purposes help us transcend what we are. We are processes of individual development in relational contexts, that are embedded within a cultural matrix. We are also developing understandings of truth; indeed, each one of us is an aspect of truth. These understandings are predicated on changes in consciousness achieved through transcending one state of consciousness to another. This dynamic process of transcendence is animated by forces or subtle energies, and music is a primary example, in some contexts, of such subtlety.

To remain authentic to both traditional sacred texts and to the earlier part of this commentary, I would suggest the use of 'truthing' rather than truth, in the way that I have used 'healthing' rather than health, truth(ing) being a cosmic activity related to the breathing out and breathing in of the creator (Aldridge 2004), thus my previous remarks about life being analogous to music: 'living as jazz', where we are constantly being performed as living beings (Aldridge 2000b). Thus, truth is an activity; truthing is constantly in performance, and we are its examples. This separates us from the objective–subjective truth argument where either there is an objective universal truth 'out there', or a subjective truth 'in here' and places us into an interactive truthing that we live with others, of which we are part as we perform. In some way, this also resolves the argument often made by qualitative researchers against quantitative research that there is no objective Truth claim. If we see the activity of discerning the truth as being performed then we have the external laws of the Universe, that is, science and another aspect of truthing which is internal, which also connects us all. Performing the reconciliation of both internal and external realities, as we can in music, is a realization of truth brought into consciousness.

'Religious' is used as an operationalization, or outward manifestation of 'spirituality' (see Table 12.2). Spiritual practices that people engage in often take place in groups and are guided by culture. As a cultural system, religion is a meaning-seeking activity that offers the individual and others both purpose and an ability to perceive meaning. We have not only a set of offered meanings but also the resources and practices by which meanings can be realized. However, as Idries Shah reminds us, we must be wary of confusing 'spirituality' with what is manifested outwardly.

'The poetry and the teaching to which you have referred is an outward manifestation. You feed on outward manifestation. Do not, please, give that the name of spirituality' quoted in the story of 'The Cook's Assistant' by Idries Shah (1969, p.115).

The social is what is common to all religions; it offers forms for experiencing nature and the divine, for transforming the self that is the goal of human development. Consciousness, achieving truth, is a social activity dependent upon its embodiment in individuals. Culture is the specific manifestation of such social forms in symbols, language and ritual localized for temporal and geographical contexts, and thus specific cults and cultures. These are the containers for the content as it were. In globalization, we have the dissemination of culture but without social forms related to human contact. Therefore we may spread the idea of spirituality but offer no forms for the achievement of spiritual understanding. Achieving spiritual understanding, in terms of changing consciousness, is the traditional role of religious forms in everyday life. Religions provide the containers and the means to achieve the spiritual content.

Table 12.2 Definitions of religion from journal articles

Author(s)	Definition
Sims 1994	'In fact, re-ligio, from its roots, implies that "foundation wall" to which one is bound for one's survival, the basis of one's being' (p.444).
Cupitt 1997	'Religious life is an expressive, world-building activity through which we get ourselves together and find a kind of posthumous, or retrospective, happiness' (p.xiv).
Gillespie 1998	'A religion is a shared view into the heart of the world, a perspective into the truth, but a perspective that is always also a veil. It is, moreover, not just a view or a perspective; it is a perspective that faces up to the fundamental mystery of the world more or less well' (p.550).
Joseph 1998	'Religion is a comprehensive picturing and ordering of human existence in nature and the cosmos' (p.220).
Hanegraaff 1999	'Religion = any symbolic system which influences human action by providing possibilities for ritually maintaining contact between the everyday world and a more general met-empirical framework' (p.147).
Emblen 1992	'Religion refers to faith, beliefs, and practices that nurture a relationship with a superior being, force or power' (p.43).
Riis 1998	'One definition…regards religion as a source of shared norms and values. This approach stresses the motive of belonging and the role of integrating the community system. Another definition…regards religion as the relationship between human beings and a postulated supranatural sphere of power. This approach stresses the motive of empowerment and the role of religion in legitimating societal authority. Religion may be part of the political system or a resource of power for the social agents' (p.250).

We can speak of spiritual states, which are altered states of consciousness where we have access to other forms of knowledge about who we are, from where we come and to where we are going.

The same goes for the idea of music therapy; the idea of musicking as a performative health practice is useless unless we find cultural forms (as in perFORMance) such that healthing may be achieved. Through making and listening to music we can achieve altered states of consciousness that offer us other forms of knowledge, not only about ourselves but also about ourselves with others, the wider performed ecology.

The process of truthing behind the spirit of music therapy will be expressed socially in its forms and the names that they are given. These forms will be inevitably corrupted, like religions, as they appear at specific times, in specific places for particular peoples (even though the time may be centuries, the places inter-continental and the peoples varied). Expressive forms become corrupted simply because they are temporal and local. Eventually, they no longer 'fit' in an ecological sense. That is why it is also difficult to import traditional therapy forms into modern cultures: the musical styles and performances do not fit local modern culture. But the underlying influence of healing through music is still present.

Only spirit remains

We have the same situation about the naming of music therapy currently where forms have to be recognized – some will see music therapy as a psychotherapy, some will see it as a purely musical activity, others will see it as a social and communal activity – re-cognized in the sense that forms are being brought into cognition again and acknowledged (Aldridge 2000a). Forms have to come into being; the process of forming is at the heart of perFORMance. Through performance we become aware. This process of awareness, calling a religion by a name, and its associated divinity, is a political activity. So too is the naming of the performance of therapy. In the same sense, the experiences that we have in music therapy have form, sometimes as emotion, sometimes as emotions and imagery, and we give them names too. How we re-cognize experience and its varying forms, and interpret those expressive forms emotionally, is a cultural activity.

MUSIC THERAPY AND SPIRITUALITY   167

Beyond meaning: transcendence and suffering

Medicine, from the Latin root *medicus*, is the measure of illness and injury, and shares the Latin *metiri*, to measure. Yet this measurement was based on natural cycles and measures. To attend medically, Latin *mederi*, also supports the Latin word *meditari* from which we have the modern meditation, which is the measuring of an idea in thought. The task of the healer in this sense is to direct the attention of the patient through the value of suffering to a solution, which is beyond the problem itself. In this sense, the healer encourages a change in the sign of the patient's suffering from negative to positive. We are encouraged to see the benefit of suffering in bringing us beyond our present understandings, which is also an understanding of the transcendental. This, I argue, is what happens in music therapy, particularly in the context of palliative care and working with people who are dying.

Transcendence is a 'going beyond' a current awareness to another level of understanding, that is, a shift in consciousness. This does not necessarily imply a conventional set of beliefs, it is based upon an innate capacity that we have as human beings to rise above the situation. Boyd (1995) makes his argument for a consideration of the term 'soul' as separate from 'spirit'. 'Soul' is the subjective or inner person as a whole in the natural state, including the body as an inseparable part, and relates to the word 'psyche' (p.151). 'Spirit', however, refers to that which could be both inside and outside a person. Soul focuses on the secular self, spirit refers to that which brings the soul to transcend itself, from without or within. Changing from a personal, self-orientated consciousness, we move to another level of consciousness that takes us beyond ourselves.

The process of spiritual development can be seen as a 'quest' or a journey. In medieval times, the quest for the Holy Grail was not for a material chalice but symbolized the search for knowledge as a vessel in which the divine may be contained. However, what confounds this issue today is that we consider questioning to be an activity rather like the chatter of infants. Many spiritual traditions emphasize the importance of silence and non-activity where the appropriate question may be framed, and as importantly, the answer may be heard. Meditation, prayer and music have both been used to fulfil these functions. Silence is the core of music and was the reason that I gave my first music therapy book the subtitle 'From Out of the Silence' (Aldridge 1996). Listening is as important an activity as playing, and as musicians know, is an integral part of musical performance.

Techniques of questioning, embarking upon a quest, are the heart of both science and spirituality in the search for knowledge. However, both demand a discipline if answers are to be found. These appropriate methods of questioning have to be learned and the approaches taught. The answers, however, cannot be learned as prescriptions for they appear new to each generation and to the appropriate contexts.

Religious practice

While the spiritual dimension may be separate from the religious, religious practices are said to provide a bridge to the spiritual, thus assuming that the spiritual is a realm beyond the religious (Lukoff *et al.* 1999). This spiritual dimension is seen as a relationship with a higher power experienced as internal and intensely personal that need not be associated with the formal external aspects of religion: transcending sense phenomena, rationality and feelings and leading to a heightened state of consciousness or awareness. The danger is that what may be seen as 'spiritual illuminations' in the raw condition of altered states of consciousness are imagined to be spiritual experiences. These can become addictive (Shah 1983; Shah 1990) preventing any developmental change, hence the need for a spiritual guide, emphasized in the great traditions, and reflected too in secular psychotherapy as a wise counsellor, to prevent the interpretation of emotions as spirituality. The same confounding of emotion and spirituality may also occur in the use of music, hence the prohibition of musical experiences in some religions and at some stages of spiritual teaching.

The ability to rise above suffering, to go beyond the present situation to a realm where life takes on another, perhaps deeper, significance is an important factor in palliative care, in the long-term management of chronic illness and as the central plank of psychotherapy. In the treatment of alcoholism, it is the recognition of personal suffering and the need to transcend the limitations of the self, to understand that we are 'Not-God' (Kurtz 1979), as a process of spiritual awakening that brings about one of the vital steps in recovery. Deborah Salmon (Salmon 2001) refers to music therapy as a containing or sacred space that facilitates the process of connecting to that which is psychologically and spiritually significant for the patient, thereby transforming experiences of suffering into those of meaning. This is a useful definition as we can then separate the contained from the content. Music therapy is the container for experiences that are healing.

Transcending the current situation

From the literature it is possible to piece together a process of spiritual change that emphasizes the need to transcend the current situation. To achieve this there has to be a change both in thought and feeling accompanied by appropriate actions. This is expressed as a process of questioning, as a search for meaning. Such meanings take the searcher beyond what she is to a higher consciousness, or state of awareness, that is connected to the truth, which people refer to as 'God', 'the divine', 'the supreme power', or simply 'that'. This is a upwardly spiralling process of development based on revealed personal understandings achieved through transcendence, which lead to further understandings. Idries Shah refers to this process as a removal of veils to the Truth (Shah 1978). These veils that obscure the truth are formed either through indoctrination, that blinds us, or through the base aspirations of our subjective selves preventing subtle perceptions and higher visions. Religion itself may be a veil that hides the truth, although it claims to offer a public perspective into the truth. The task we face is how to make those veils transparent, or remove them. A further task is how to cope with the truth thus revealed – veils may be there as much to protect as to conceal. Knowing when to conceal and when to reveal is based on spiritual discernment and again is a reason for a spiritual teacher or guide.

The whole concept of pluralism, often invoked for justifying differing positions within the world of music therapy, is itself a term borrowed from theology. The basis of the concept of pluralism is that no one of us as human beings can begin to claim a full understanding of the divine (or what ever you may choose to call him or her); thus, in all modesty, we have to recognize that we have only parts of the whole picture. A challenge is for us all to come together and merge those various understandings. This is recognized in the Christian perspective of 'Though we are many, we are one body' (Aldridge 1987b). It also brings a necessary balance either to those who say that a scientific perspective alone can reveal the Truth, or those who say that a spiritual perspective alone can bring the Truth. It is both external and internal realities, the polar arcs of spirit and cosmos in combination that complete the circle of understanding.

Suffering and the loss of a coherent self

We suffer when we fail to make sense of our experience. One of the difficulties faced by people in the advanced stages of cancer, or neurodegenerative disease, is that they lose their sense of dignity. Pullman argues that this is an aesthetic perspective on suffering (Pullman 2002) and proposes that maintaining a meaningful life is an aesthetic project.

The spiritual elements of experience help us to rise above the matters at hand such that in the face of suffering we can find purpose, meaning and hope. It is in the understanding of suffering, the universality of suffering, and the need for deliverance from suffering, that varying traditions of music therapy and religion meet. Suffering is embodied as pain. While we may temporarily relieve pain with analgesics, our task is also to understand, and thereby relieve, suffering. In this way the ecology of ideas, that some call knowledge, is explicated within the body as a correspondence between mental representations and the material world.

While we may strive for the eradication of major diseases, the presence of suffering will be a part of the human narrative. So too, then, the relief of that suffering. How that relief is achieved will not be dependent solely upon a medical narrative but, as the major religions have offered throughout the ages, also upon spiritual understanding. We are all asked the ultimate question of what meaning and purpose our lives would have had if we were to die now. Most of our activities cut us off from this brutal confrontation, or are an attempt to shield us from this realization. While the management of pain is often a scientific and technical task, the relief of suffering is an existential task. According to the major spiritual traditions suffering has always had the potential to transform the individual. As Tournier (1981) reminds us, it is love that has the power to change the sign of suffering from negative to positive.

Coda: therapist heal thyself

There are different methods to approach truth and the performance of truthing. If we accept that in a modern vibrant culture there is a pluralism of truth claims, then a major task will be for us to reconcile what may appear to be disparate ideas. The argument here is not for some kind of homogeneity of thought but for an acceptance of the tension between ideas as a creative arena that pushes us beyond what we know. Thomas Merton writes in his journal for the 28th of April 1957:

> If I can unite in myself, in my own spiritual life, the thought of the East and West of the Greek and Latin fathers, I will create in myself a reunion of the divided Church and from that unity in myself can come the exterior and visible unity of the Church. For if we want to bring together East and West we cannot do it by imposing one upon the other. We must contain both within ourselves and transcend both. (Merton 1996, p.87)

My hope is that we can go some way to uniting the 'East' and 'West' of thinking in music therapy such that there is a reunion of thought about healing and the possibility of transcendence. This perhaps is the basis of healing and the core of hope. As Merton suggests, one cannot be imposed upon the other, it is the containment within ourselves that brings the change. This is simply an argument for diversity in the culture of music therapy that includes the many facets of its performance. In the same vein, I am not arguing against modern health care delivery, nor scientific methods, but for the development of an applied knowledge that relieves suffering and promotes tolerance and includes the creative arts therapies.

If each one of us is a living performed truth in itself, then other truths are made possible through relationship as encounter. Through this encounter with a living universe, we expand into an ecology of knowledge. Through music we have the possibility of performing this encounter; we literally bring truth into a temporal, albeit ephemeral, form. This is the unity of consciousness, becoming whole and the basis of the healing endeavour. As each person progresses, wholeness is achieved at a different level of understanding. These understandings may be horizontal in a natural ecology, vertical in a divine ecology, or both. In an horizontal ecology of ideas we have an expanded consciousness; in a vertical ecology of ideas we have a concept of higher consciousness. Spirituality enables the transcendence from one level to the next incorporating new perspectives and reconciling contradictions. Thus we become whole as a person; realizing that our relationships have to be healed, we become reconciled as a community; realizing that there is strife and discord, we search for political accord; realizing that there is imbalance and a lack of harmony, we search for a reconciliation with nature; realizing that we are alone we reach out to the cosmos.

Chapter 13

Music Therapy and Spirituality and the Challenges of End-Stage Illness

Lucanne Magill

Music is the mediator between the spiritual and sensual life. Although the spirit be not master of that which created through music, yet it is blessed in this creation, which, like every creation of art, is mightier than the artist.

Ludwig van Beethoven (cited in Bachelder 1975, p.36)

I am music. I make the world weep and laugh, wonder and worship.

Anonymous (cited in Bachelder 1975, p.19)

Spiritual issues are prominent in the care of patients and families facing the challenges of end-of-life stages of illness. As a result of advanced metastatic disease, there are usually losses of physicality and sociability and consequential losses of hope and community belonging. There may be pain, suffering, loss of self-identity, loss of sense of existential reasoning, and loss of control. Emotional suffering at the end-of-life stage can be profound. Patients and their caregivers are faced with situations that naturally call into question the meaning, purpose and value of their lives. The search for meaning and purpose is often of momentous importance for those facing the end-of-life (Pulchalski 2002).

Spirituality has been defined as an understanding that there are levels of reality not immediately apparent and that there is a quest for personal integration in the face of forces of fragmentation and depersonalization (Downey 1997). Spirituality refers to an individual's or a group's relationship with the transcendent, however that may be construed, and is the search for transcendent meaning (Sulmasy 2002). Spirituality is the concern with acquiring or maintaining an existential way to view and live one's life at a deeper and more meaningful level, and to search for an understanding of the purpose of their joys, trials and sufferings. Spirituality, then, is this search for meaning in times of distress; is the search for faith, hope and inspiration; is the human tendency to transcend to places, times and concepts that convey the magnitude of life and creation; and is the search for connectedness with self, others and that which lies beyond.

In palliative medicine, spiritual concerns are at the heart and centre of patient and caregiver issues. In recent years, there has been a growing interest in and recognition of the need to provide spiritual care to those enduring the difficult challenges of advanced illnesses (Joint Commission on Accreditation of Healthcare Organizations 1996). Medical professionals are being taught to listen 'to what is important to patients, respect their spiritual beliefs, and [be] able to communicate effectively about these spiritual beliefs, as well as about their preferences at the end-of-life' (Pulchalski 2002, p.800). Likewise, it has become recognized that the primary function of medicine and allied health care professions is essentially to minister to the suffering occasioned by the necessary physical finitude of humans, in their living and their dying (Sulmasy 1999). Palliative Medicine professionals are recognizing their obligation to respond to and relieve physical and psychological suffering, and help patients and caregivers access spiritual resources.

Music therapy offers meaningful benefits to those facing end-of-life. In music therapy, the healing attributes of music reach beyond words to soothe, restore, refresh and create a sense of unity. It is well known that music therapy treats a multitude of symptoms simultaneously and can ease pain, promote relaxation and feelings of comfort, diminish feelings of fatigue and other debilitating symptoms (Cassileth, Vickers and Magill 2003; Dileo and Bradt 1999; Magill 2001; Magill and Luzzato 2002; O'Callaghan 2001; Salmon 2001; Standley 1996). In addition to helping improve symptoms, music therapy helps restore a sense of order and congruency. In music therapy, the compassionate presence of the music therapist plays a key role in helping foster a sense of personhood and spirituality in those faced with existential losses (Magill 2005).

Music therapy enhances spirituality in those contending with the advanced illness through facilitating four primary aspects of spirituality: transcendence, faith and hope, sense of meaning and purpose and search for connectedness.

Transcendence

Music gives soul to the universe, wings to the mind, flight to the imagination, a charm to sadness and life to everything. Fine music is the essence of order and leads to all that is just and good, of which it is the invisible, but nevertheless dazzling, passionate and eternal form. (Plato, in Leventhal 2003, p.57)

Transcendence is the process in which humans move beyond the immediate time, place, circumstance and transport to places and concepts of meaning, enlightenment and inspiration. Aldridge states that 'as a process, transcendence is seen as taking us beyond our small selves, outside the everyday limitations of personality...[to] take an enlightened interest in others and the world through which we are led to a greater knowledge and capacity to love' (Aldridge, 2000b, p.38). In times of loss, there is often a need to move beyond the current situation as a means for coping, obtaining a sense of peace and comfort, feeling love and for gaining deeper understanding.

Music facilitates transcendence. This most likely is a result of the multi-dimensional nature of music and its tendency to reach a multitude of domains simultaneously (Magill 2005). This intrinsic power of music to lift and inspire the human psyche is significant in palliative care. In music therapy with those facing end-of-life, patients often report being 'transported' to other places, times, images and ideas (Magill 2001). This process of transcendence through music inspires patients in that they report 'being in touch with' nature and/or become more aware of their inner spiritual essence. As a result of hearing the aesthetic qualities of music, patients report feeling a sense of calm and serenity. The music therapist works closely with patients and caregivers in ways that support the patients' needs while offering music, careful attention being made in the selection of rhythms, melodies, harmonies, tones and lyrics. The aim is to help instil peace and comfort, and facilitate the emergence of meaningful insight.

Faith and hope

> Music is well said to be the language of angels. (Thomas Carlyle, cited in Bachelder 1975, p.14)

Faith and hope are predominant aspects of spirituality in palliative care. While they are often termed in tandem, they have unique applications and meanings to patients and caregivers. Faith is 'the confident belief in a Supreme Being' (Koenig 1999, p.26). Faith is a conviction, or is said to be a 'belief system' (Koenig 1999, p.297). Faith conveys a belief in a construct or a belief in the assurance of being cared for by a divine principle or being. Hope has a future directedness in that it is an anticipation, a wish or a looking forward to something. Hope in palliative medicine is seen as going beyond hope for cure, and is that which is anticipation for the possibility 'to rise above the situation at hand' (Aldridge 2000b, p.196). According to Aldridge, the psychological importance of hope may be 'in the act of hoping...[since] it is not that a definite goal will be reached for the dying, but the possibility for transcendence' (Aldridge 2000b, p.196). The processes of faith and hope are commonly interrelated in that if one has faith, one usually has a sense of hope and vice versa. For example, having faith in a construct, idea, or a Supreme Being brings hope, the sense that there is peace and comfort in that in which one has faith. Faith and hope ease suffering in patients and caregivers and are means for coping with loss, demise and personal demoralization.

The universal qualities of music elicit awareness of that which lies beyond physical existence and brings forward inspirations about infinity, boundlessness and timelessness. Throughout time, music has been associated with the Divine, with the heavens and with creation. Music can bring these contemplations to mind and can enhance patients' and caregivers' sense of faith, providing the means for petition, prayer and praise. Music can help people remember their connection with creativity and ultimately with the creative life force. Music also motivates a looking forward and beyond. Through the aesthetic nature of the predictable yet transcendent characteristics of music, patients and caregivers may conjure images of nature or places of restitution that may bring feelings of hope. The power of music to evoke these feelings of faith and hope is significant, bringing eternal and timeless dimensions into the moment, and calling to mind universalism.

Sense of meaning and purpose

> Music reveals us to ourselves…it feeds that deep ineradicable instinct within us of which all art is only the reverberated echo, that craving to express, through the medium of the senses, the spiritual and eternal realities which underlie them. (Hugh R. Haweis, in Bachelder 1975, pp.61–62)

The search for meaning and purpose plays a vital role in the lives of those facing the end of their life. During times of loss, people often feel out of touch with themselves, others, and with that which has been their source of identity to date, for example a profession or a significant role. There often are existential questions, such as 'Who am I?', 'What am I here for?', 'What am I worth now?' Such ruminations sometimes elicit feelings of failure, doubt and uncertainty that can lead to difficult suffering and feelings of discouragement, failure and hopelessness. When people are faced with loss and end-of-life, these questions are predominant and there is commonly an attempt to seek meaning and a sense of purpose. All individuals seek meaning and purpose in life, and when facing death this search is intensi-fied (Pulchalski 2002). According to Doyle, spirituality means 'searching for existential meaning' (Doyle 1992, p.303). It is this quest to regain a sense of understanding of the real purpose for living and being that looms within the hearts and minds of those undergoing the challenges of loss.

There are many characteristics of music that facilitate this search for meaning and purpose. Music evokes memory and enhances life review, the looking back over one's life to view the path one has taken. As patients and families partake in this process, there may be a range of thoughts and feelings that emerge, and there is often renewed insight. Unresolved issues and feelings may bring grieving, feelings of anger and sadness. Compas-sion is essential in this work so as to assist the patient and caregivers in finding resolution and meaning. Through music and with the accompani-ment of the music therapist, patients may regain inner peace as they, through the process of life review, gain perspectives on their inner values, strengths and life accomplishments. In music therapy, the music therapist offers techniques, such as making audio recordings for family members, writing songs of dedication, biographical songs, or songs of hopes and wishes for loved ones, or techniques focusing on songs that nurture the patient's sense of personal significance. The support of the music therapist may assist the patient in gaining new perspectives that may reframe and re-view the situation at hand, a process that helps diminish suffering. Music can also foster meaningful communication between patients and caregivers and can bring forth tenderness and feelings of love. The expressive nature of music plays an important role in the music therapy process in facilitating a sense of meaning and purpose.

Search for connectedness

> When I hear music, I fear no danger. I am invulnerable. I see no foe. I am related to the earliest times and the latest. (Henry David Thoreau, in Leventhal 2003, p.5)

Advanced metastatic illness often results in loss of self-esteem, self-identity, and loss of sense of connectedness with self and others. Patients often report feeling out of touch with who they are as individuals. Illness has been said to disturb relationships both inside and outside the body, i.e. bio-chemical imbalances, disturbing mind–body synchrony, disturbing relationships between people, others and the transcendent (Sulmasy 2002). Spirituality has been identified as 'that aspect of human beings that seeks to heal or be whole' (Pulchalski 2002, p.799). Healing is considered to be the restoration of wholeness (Foglio and Brody 1988). According to Aldridge, 'healing arises from within a patient as a search for wholeness [and] this wholeness refers not just to a physical integrity but also to a broader unity' (Aldridge 2000b, p.36). The fragmentation that can occur as a result of disfigurement, loss of energy, isolation, loss of sense of goal directedness, and overall loss of well-being can lead to this loss of identity. Patients often search for their sense of belonging, and the ability to reconnect with self and others and all that is meaningful. Seeking connectedness can lead to an awareness of a higher self that is connected to a higher unity (Aldridge 2000b). The search for relationship and connectedness needs to be addressed so as to relieve the suffering, and is a process that can lead to spiritual awakening and the gaining of new perspectives.

Music can help restore a sense of self-identity and a sense of relatedness. The evocative and expressive attributes of music facilitate communication between patients and caregivers. Music also enhances a sense of person-hood. The process of life review in music therapy restores a sense of self-identity and patients generally are reminded of and feel reconnected with who they are as human beings beyond the illness. Patients often report feeling 'human again' as a result of choosing, hearing and participating in songs. The act of singing fosters a sense of community and belonging, since there is a natural and universal association between singing and human relationships (Bailey 1984). Likewise, the transcendent nature of music 'lifts' patients into higher realms and can elicit intuitive realizations of one's sense of belonging to a greater whole. As Michael Mayne says: 'Music can...expose us to a kind of beauty and hopefulness about the human race that cannot be expressed in any other terms' (Mayne 2002, p.136). Music can thus play an important role in helping patients renew their sense of self-identity, and in helping restore unity with others and with the universe.

Four recurring spiritual themes in music therapy

As discussed, the impact of metastatic illness can have devastating effects. There may be pain, numerous psychosocial losses, loss of control and overall diminished quality of life. The losses may bring feelings of suffering, characterized by loss of sense of faith and hope, sense of meaning and purpose, and loss of connectedness. Music can help restore, refresh and create union.

In music therapy, there are four main recurring spiritual themes that emerge in sessions. These themes have been gathered through a review of many years of music therapy work with patients and caregivers facing the challenges of end-of-life metastatic illness, and are themes that naturally carry spiritual significance for those taking part in the sessions.

Relationship

A first theme in music therapy is relationship. As explained above, patients and their caregivers faced with the prospects of dying often feel out of touch with self and others. They may feel depressed, withdrawn, isolated and may be separated for long periods of time. Music reaches beyond words and touch, builds bridges of communication and helps restore unity.

Example: Emanuella, aged 78, was an Afro-American woman with an advanced brain tumour. She was depressed and withdrawn and was observed to be sitting in a chair in her room, staring at the wall for long periods of time, not speaking to staff. A nurse asked the music therapist to make contact with her. The music therapist sat near her and sang the song 'He's got the Whole World'. During this song, Emanuella sat up and began to sing all the words of the song with energy and expression. She looked at the music therapist and spoke in fragments about her life.

After this session, Emanuella burst into this song whenever anyone, for example, nurses, doctors, housekeepers, the music therapist, walked into her room. Two weeks later, she had deteriorated and was described as being in a semi-comatose state. She was for the most part unresponsive. The music therapist sat near her and sang the same song again. After a few measures, Emanuella began to sing along, using all the words she had sung before. At the completion of the song, she stated, 'I may not be here the next time you sing this song, but you can sing it anyway.'

This example demonstrates the use of a simple familiar song, one that inherently depicts contact with others and with a higher power, to build bridges of communication, reduce isolation and re-establish relationship.

Remembrance

A second theme in music therapy is remembrance. During time of pain and loss, people are often driven back to times of comfort, security, predictability, or even times of hardship. As described, there is a natural tendency to review one's life. The link between music and memory is strong and enhances this process.

Example: Janet, aged 65, had a brain tumour that was progressing rapidly. She had disease-related aphasia and was very agitated due to her lack of ability to communicate. Her son, who was with her most of the time, was very sad and frustrated. He told the music therapist stories about her favourite times in Ireland where she lived and worked for some years. The music therapist showed Janet the songbook. After several minutes, she slowly pointed to the song 'Danny Boy'. The music therapist sat down next to her and encouraged her to sing along. The music therapist kept a gently firm rhythm to help engage her. The music therapist also paused between verses to offer her the choice as to whether to sing the second verse that talked about dying. Janet joined the music therapist in singing all the words and also began singing the second verse on her own. Her son sat nearby and wept a little as he listened to his mother sing one of her favourite songs. Janet smiled at the end of the song, and seemed relaxed and content.

This is an example of the use of a familiar song to support remembrance. Janet chose a song that was important to her in her life and one that most likely conjured thoughts and memories of comfort, meaning and importance. She remembered the words and was able to sing them at a time when she was otherwise expressively compromised. She also had the opportunity to say words about dying within the context of song. She seemed to be in touch with times of closeness with her son, who stated that they used to sing this song together. Her son seemed to feel relief in hearing her communicate in the music and see her reminisce about her time in Ireland. Music was an important medium that enhanced remembrance for the patient and her son.

Prayer

A third theme in music therapy is prayer. Patients and caregivers often have a need and desire to call out for relief from anguish, pain or sorrow. Prayer is meant in a broader sense of the word, since it may or may not be in a religious context, and is a *calling* from the deeper corners of heart, mind and spirit. Sometimes this need is repressed. Music reaches and is a voice.

Example. Wendell, aged 45, was from the West Indies. He had been in the hospital for one month prior to referral to music therapy. He was not responding to his rigorous chemotherapy treatments for his acute leukaemia. He knew he was getting sicker, not better. He was immersed in his TV, communicating very little. He was referred by his nurse, with her hope that music therapy would help him begin to express his feelings.

The music therapist went into his room and sat with him as he watched TV, to begin a dialogue. He initially stayed focused on the TV as he talked a little about his homeland. After three sessions of dialogue and three songs, Wendell gradually began to focus more and more on the topic of music. In the fourth session, the music therapist asked if she could lower the volume of the TV. Wendell agreed, and asked, for the first time, for the reggae song 'Fly Away Home'. As the music therapist sang this song, Wendell sang with expression all of the words to the song that speaks poignantly about the heavenly home and the hoping to be taken there. Following this, Wendell began to engage himself more with other staff, and also talked about his faith at length. Wendell requested to sing this song repeatedly during his last month before dying.

This example exemplifies the use of song as a voice to prayer. There are times when patients may not know if, how or what they desire to call for, as the need may be repressed. In this case, the patient used a favourite song to talk about his finality and to express deeper thoughts. The song afforded him the opportunity to express his faith and his hope to ultimately 'fly away home'.

Peace

A fourth theme in music therapy is peace. As described earlier, patients often long for comfort, relief from pain, peace of mind, relief from interruptions, uncertainties and relief from lack of control.

Example. Lois, aged 68, had metastatic cervical cancer and was receiving palliative care for her difficult-to-manage pain. She was agitated and angry. She was referred by a doctor who requested music therapy to help her with her pain and agitation. She was reported by staff to be a 'difficult patient' due to her incessant demands. When the music therapist and her colleague went to her room, the patient's son and friend were in far corners of the room. As the music therapist and colleague entered the room, they ran up and requested 'Flamenco' music, stating that this was Lois's favourite music. The music therapist and her colleague sat near the patient and asked her, 'What music would help you today?' Lois answered, 'I want to be in peace.'

The music therapist and her colleague sang a chant, the lyrics of which stated: 'Peace is flowing over you, you are waiting. Peace is flowing over me. I am waiting. Peace is flowing over us. We are waiting.' Other words were improvised in the song to echo Lois's needs and hopes. At the end of the music, Lois said: 'I am in beauty, I am in peace' (Sound 14.1).

This example demonstrates the use of the aesthetic characteristics of music to reach, help calm agitation and help instil feelings of peace. The music had reached her and also had a calming effect on the family. During the music, the son moved closer to Lois and faced her, appearing calm and relaxed. In time, the son became more involved in the singing of this chant for his mother, and healing of many years' worth of dissension between them began to take place. The lyrics of the song met the patient's needs and the tempo and dynamics conveyed the state of peace, the state for which she had hoped.

In these four themes, the power of music to build relationship, enhance remembrance, be a voice to prayer and instil peace is evident. In music therapy sessions, the music therapist offers the less threatening medium of music to mobilize, express and to meet the spiritual needs and issues presented by patients and caregivers.

The presence of the music therapist

The presence of the music therapist plays a key role in music therapy sessions. The caring and compassionate characteristics that the music therapist brings into sessions, along with the intangible gift of music, creates a sacred space within which patients and caregivers may safely be where they need to be and experience their feelings, wishes, hopes, images, memories and prayers. In this space, also, patients and caregivers may renew their awareness of the essence of the meaning and purpose of their lives (Magill 2005).

In working with those facing end-of-life, it is helpful and important for the music therapist to bring three qualities to sessions, qualities that play a vital role in the flow that develops in music therapy. These three qualities are: empathy (compassionate understanding and open heart), acceptance (respect, support and affirmation) and reflective listening (restating and paraphrasing expressed thoughts and feelings as a way to convey support and understanding) (Magill 2005). These qualities offer the support that patients and family members need during the very difficult times of loss that they are facing. Compassion is essential in the care of all patients, especially those facing life-threatening illness and dying. Compassionate care is vital and is the offering of presence with an open and caring heart, offering empathy, acceptance and listening. The presence of the music therapist can be an important source of support to patients and caregivers. The music therapist can be and usually is a healing partner in their spiritual quest for transcendence, faith and hope, meaning and purpose and sense of connectedness.

Conclusion

Patients and caregivers faced with the challenges of end-of-life due to advanced illness often experience suffering as a result of the difficult losses involved. Spirituality plays an important role in helping patients and caregivers cope with the losses and gain healing perspectives. Music therapy is helpful in allowing individuals to experience four key aspects of spirituality – the need for: transcendence, gaining a sense of meaning and purpose, having faith and hope and searching for connectedness. In music therapy sessions, four common themes emerge, relationship, remembrance, prayer and peace. Music therapy offers the means through which and in which patients and caregivers can find solace, comfort, support and spiritual healing. The grace of music speaks beyond words, and with the compassionate, caring presence of the music therapist can provide for moments of enlightenment and inspiration.

Music therapists are presented with the challenge and the opportunity to define, describe and verify what is done. In addition to the need to document and research, it is important for us to remember the real, indescribable essence of music therapy. It is in the lived moments of music therapy when the essence of the work – music therapy, spirituality and healing – is experienced and known. It is in the lived moments in music therapy, when as Michael Mayne says, the whole being, body, mind and spirit, are in the presence of music, that transformations begin to occur and healing begins (Mayne 2002). It is these lived moments that are the heart of what music therapy can do to help patients and caregivers experience renewal and spiritual healing.

In the words of a dying leukaemia patient:

When I am in the presence of music, I hear the voice of God;

When I am in the presence of music, I fly like a bird;

When I am in the presence of music, my spirit is free and I am in peace.

References

Abdelkader, N. (1994) 'Tanz im Underground oder Wo tanzt das Volk heute.' *Tanz Affiche 52*, 20–22.

Adlaf, E. M. and Smart, R. G. (1997) 'Party subculture or dens of doom? An epidemiological study of rave attendance and drug use patterns among adolescent students.' *Journal of Psychoactive Drugs 29*, 2, 193–198.

Agawu, V. K. (2001) 'An African understanding of African music.' *Research in African Literatures 32*, 2 (Summer), 187–194 (Indiana University Press).

Agmon, E. (1989) 'A mathematical model of the diatonic system.' *Journal of Music Theory 33*, 1–25.

Aldrich, C.K. (1944) 'The effect of synthetic marihuana-like compound on musical talent.' *Public Health Report 59*, 431–435.

Aldridge, D. (1986) 'Licence to heal.' *Crucible April–June*, 58–66.

Aldridge, D. (1987a) 'Families, cancer and dying.' *Family Practice 4*, 212–218.

Aldridge, D. (1987b) *One body: A Guide to Healing in the Church*. London: S.P.C.K.

Aldridge, D. (1987c) 'A team approach to terminal care: personal implications for patients and practitioners.' *Journal of the Royal College of General Practitioners 37*, 364.

Aldridge, D. (1988) 'Families, cancer and dying.' *Journal of the Institute of Religion and Medicine 3*, 312–322.

Aldridge, D. (1991a) 'Healing and medicine.' *Journal of the Royal Society of Medicine 84*, 516–518.

Aldridge, D. (1991b) 'Spirituality, healing and medicine.' *British Journal of General Practice 41*, 351, 425–7.

Aldridge, D. (1995) 'Spirituality, hope and music therapy in palliative care.' *The Arts in Psychotherapy 22*, 2, 103–109.

Aldridge, D. (1996) *Music Therapy and Research in Medicine – From Out of the Silence*. London: Jessica Kingsley Publishers.

Aldridge, D. (1998) *Suicide: The Tragedy of Hopelessness*. London: Jessica Kingsley Publishers.

Aldridge, D. (1999) *Music Therapy in Palliative Care: New Voices*. London: Jessica Kingsley Publishers.

Aldridge, D. (2000a) *Music Therapy in Dementia Care*. London: Jessica Kingsley Publishers.

Aldridge, D. (2000b) *Spirituality, Healing and Medicine*. London: Jessica Kingsley Publishers.

Aldridge, D. (2002) 'Philosophical speculations on two therapeutic applications of breath.' *Subtle Energies and Energy Medicine 12*, 2, 107–124.

Aldridge, D. (2004) *The Individual, Health and Integrated Medicine: In Search of an Health Care Aesthetic*. London: Jessica Kingsley Publishers.

Aldridge, D. and Magill, L. (2002) 'The ecology of singing in an hospital setting.' Memorial Sloan Kettering Cancer Center, October 10th, Palliative Care and Pain Group Meeting.

Aldridge, D., Gustorff, D. and Hannich, H. J. (1990) 'Where am I? Music therapy applied to coma patients.' *Journal of the Royal Society of Medicine 83*, 6, 345–346.

Ansdell, G. (1995) *Music for Life*. London: Jessica Kingsley Publishers.

Arnett, J. (1996) *Metal Heads*. Colorado: Westview Press.

Atwater, F. H. (1995) 'The Monroe Institute's Hemi-Synch Process (Online Document).' The Monroe Institute. Retrieved 16.11.2003 2003 from www.monroeinstitute.org/programs/ hemi-sync.html

Bachelder, L. (ed.) (1975) *The Gift of Music*. Mount Vernon, NY: The Peter Pauper Press.

Bailey, L. (1983) 'The effects of live music versus tape-recorded music on hospitalised cancer patients.' *Music Therapy 3*, 1, 17–28.

Bailey, L. (1984) 'The use of songs with cancer patients and their families.' *Music Therapy 4*, 1, 5–17.

Bailey, S. (1997) 'The arts in spiritual care.' *Seminars on Oncology Nursing 13*, 4, 242–7.

Baklanoff, J.D. (1987) 'The celebration of a feast: music, dance, and possession trance in the black primitive baptist footwashing ritual.' *Ethnomusicology 31*, 381–394.

Balzano, G. J. (1980) 'The group-theoretic description of 12-fold and microtonal pitch systems.' *Computer Music Journal 4*, 4, 66–84.

Barber-Kersovan, A. (1991) 'Turn on, Tune in, Drop out: Rockmusik zwischen Drogen und Kreativität.' In H. Rösing (ed.), *Musik als Droge? Zu Theorie und Praxis bewußtseinsverändernder Wirkungen von Musik*, 89–104. Mainz: Villa Musica.

Basar, E., Schurmann, M., BasarEroglu, C. and Karakas, S. (1997) 'Alpha oscillations in brain functioning: an integrative theory.' *International Journal of Psychophysiology 26*, 1–3, 5–29.

Basar, E. and Schürmann, M. (1996) 'Alpha Rhythms in the Brain: functional correlates.' *News of Physiological Science 11*, April, 90–96.

Bateson, G. (1972) *Steps to an Ecology of Mind*. New York: Ballantine.

Bateson, G. (1978) *Mind and Nature*. Glasgow: Fontana.

Baudelaire, C. (1966) 'An exerpt from the seraphic theatre.' In D. Solomon (ed.) *The Marihuana Papers*, 179–190. New York: New American Library.

Baumeister, R. F. (1984) 'Acid rock: a critical reappraisal and psychological commentary.' *Journal of Psychoactive Drugs 16*, 4, 339–345.

Becker, H.S. (1963) *Outsiders: Studies in the Sociology of Deviance*. New York: Free Press.

Becker, H.S. (1967) 'History, culture and subjective experience: an exploration of the social basis of drug-induced experiences.' *Journal of Health and Social Behavior 8*, 163–176.

Becker-Carus, C. (1971) 'Relationships between EEG, Personality and vigilance.' *Electroencephalography and Clinical Neurophysiology 30*, 519–526.

Behr, H.G. (1982) *Von Hanf ist die Rede*. Basel: Sphinx Verlag.

Behrendt, J.E. (1956) *Variationen über Jazz*. München: Nymphenburger Verlagsanstalt.

Benedict, R. (1934) 'Anthropology and the abnormal.' *Journal of General Psychology 10*, 77.

Berger, H. (1991) *Das Elektroenkephalogram des Menschen – Kommentierter Reprint des Erstdruckes aus dem Jahre 1938*. Frankfurt am Main: PMI Verlag.

Berthier, J. (1978) *Music from Taizé*. Chicago, IL: G.I.A. Publications, Inc.

Bertz, W. (1995) 'Working memory in music: a theoretical model.' *Music Perception 12*, 3, 353–364.

Bessler, J. and Opgenoorth, N. (2000) *Anekdoten aus der Musikwelt*. Bonn: Voggenreither.

Biasutti, M. (1990) 'Music ability and altered states of consciousness: an experimental study.' *International Journal of Psychosomatics 37*, 1–4, 82–85.

Blätter, A. (1990) *Kulturelle Ausprägungen und die Funktion des Drogengebrauchs*. Hamburg: Wayasbah Verlag.

Blätter, A. (1992) 'Das Vergnügen, die Sucht und das Bewußtsein – Einstellungen zum Cannabis Konsum.' In C. Rätsch (ed.) *Yearbook for Ethnomedicine and the Study of Consciousness*, 117–132. Berlin: VWB-Verlag.

Blätter, A. (1995) 'Die Funktionen des Drogengebrauchs und ihre kulturspezifische Nutzung.' *Curare – Journal for Ethnomedicine 18*, 2, 279–290.

Blood, A. J. and Zatorre, R. J. (2001) 'Intensely pleasurable responses to music correlate with activity in brain regions implicated in reward and emotion.' *Proceedings of the National Academy of Sciences of the United States of America 98*, 20, 11818–11823.

Böhm, T. (1997) *Beatles und LSD. Zum Einfluß von Drogen auf den musikalischen Kompositionsprozeß*. Unpublished MA Thesis (Magisterarbeit), Universität Gießen.

Böhm, T. (1999) 'Was ist Psychedelic Rock? Zum Einfluß von Drogen auf die Musik am Beispiel der Beatles und LSD.' In H. Rösing and T. Phleps (eds.) *Erkenntniszuwachs durch Analyse – Populäre Musik auf dem Prüfstand*, 7–25. Karben: Coda.

Boltz, M. (1991) 'Some structural determinants of melody recall.' *Memory and Cognition 19*, 239–251.

Bonde, L. O. (1999) 'Introduction to Helen L. Bonny's article "Music and Consciousness".' *Nordic Journal of Music Therapy 8*, 2, 168–170.

Bonny, H.L. (1975) 'Music and consciousness.' *Journal of Music Therapy 12*, 3, 121–135.

Bonny, H. and Pahnke, W. (1972) 'The use of music in psychedelic (LSD) psychotherapy.' *Journal of Music Therapy 9*, 2, 64–87.

Bonny, H.L. and Savary, L.M. (1973) *Music and Your Mind. Listening with a New Consciousness.* New York: Harper & Row.

Borman, P. and Dixon, D. (1998) 'Spirituality and the 12 steps of substance abuse recovery.' Journal of Psychology and Theology 26, 3, 287–291.

Bossinger, W. and Hess, P. (1993) 'Musik und außergewöhnliche Bewußtseinszustände.' *Musiktherapeutische Umschau 14*, 3, 239–254.

Bourguignon, E. (ed.) (1973) *Religion, Altered States of Consciousness, and Social Change.* Columbus: Ohio State University Press.

Bourguignon, E. (1976) 'Possession and trance in cross-cultural studies of mental health.' In William P. Lebra (ed.), *Culture-Bound Syndromes, Ethnopsychiatry, and Alternate Therapies.* Vol. IV of Mental Health Research in Asia and the Pacific. An East-West Center Book, pp.47–55. Honolulu: The University Press of Hawaii.

Bowers, K.S. (1983) *Hypnosis for the Seriously Curious.* New York: Norton.

Boyd, Jenny (1992) *Musicians in Tune.* New York: Fireside, a Simon & Schuster imprimateur.

Boyd, J. (1995) 'The soul as seen through evangelical eyes, Part I: mental health professionals and "the Soul".' *Journal of Psychology and Theology 25*, 3, 151–160.

Brady, B. and Stevens, L. (2000) 'Binaural-beat induced theta EEG activity and hypnotic susceptibility.' *The American Journal of Clinical Hypnosis 43*, 1, 53–69.

Brandl, R. M. (1993) 'Musik und veränderte Bewußtseinszustände.' In H. Bruhn, R. Oerter and H. Rösing (eds.) *Musikpsychologie. Ein Handbuch.* 599–610. Reinbek: Rowohlt.

Bulfinch, T. (1959) *Mythology.* New York: Dell Publishers.

Bush, C.A. (1988) 'Dreams, mandalas, and music imagery: therapeutic uses in a case study.' *Arts in Psychotherapy 15*, 3, 219–225.

Caldwell, C. (1996) *Getting Our Bodies Back.* USA: Shambhala Publications, Inc.

Cambor, C. G., Lisowitz, G. M. and Miller, M. D. (1962) 'Creative jazz musicians: a clinical study.' *Psychiatry 25*, 1, 1–15.

Carey, J.T. (1968) *The College Drug Scene.* Englewood Cliffs, NJ: Prentice-Hall.

Cassileth B., Vickers, A. and Magill, L. (2003) 'Music therapy for mood disturbance during hospitalization for autologous stem cell transplantation.' *CANCER 98*, 12, 2723–2729.

Chaffin, R. and Imreh, B. (1997) 'Pulling teeth and torture: musical memory and problem solving.' *Thinking and Reasoning 3*, 4, 315–336.

Chandler, C., Holden, J. and Kolander, C. (1992) 'Counseling for spiritual wellness: theory and practice.' Journal of Counseling and Development 71, 168–175.

Chashba, M. (1998) 'The Abkhaz musical folklore.' In B. Kagazezhev (ed.) *The Problems of Art and Ethnography*, Vol. 2, pp.30–39. Maikop: Adyghea State University.

Clottes, J. and Lewis-Williams, D. (1998) *The Shamans of Prehistory: Trance and Magic in the Painted Caves.* New York, NY: Harry N. Abrams Inc. Publishers.

Cohen, D. (1994) 'Directionality and complexity in music.' *Musikometrica 6*, 27–77.

Cohen, D. and Dubnov, S. (1997) 'Gestalt phenomena in musical texture.' In M. Leman (ed.), *Music, Gestalt and Computing*, 386–405. Berlin: Springer.

Cohen, D. and Granot, R. (1995) 'Constant and variable influences on stages of musical activities: research based on experiments using behavioral and electrophysiological indices.' *Journal of New Music Research 24*, 197–229.

Cohen, D. and Wagner, N. (2000) 'Concurrence and nonconcurrence between learned and natural schemata: the case of Johann Sebastian Bach's saraband in C minor for cello solo.' *New Music Research 29*, 1, 23–36.

Corballis, M. C. (2003) 'From mouth to hand: gesture, speech, and the evolution of right-handedness.' *Behavour and Brain Sciences 26*, 2, 199–208; discussion 208–160.

Cousto, H. (1995) *Vom Urkult zur Kultur – Drogen und Techno.* Solothurn: Nachtschatten.

Crawford, H. J. (1994) 'Brain dynamics and hypnosis: attentional and disattentional processes.' *The International Journal of Clinical and Experimental Hypnosis 42*, 3, 204–232.

Cupitt, D. (1997) After God. The future of religion. New York: Basic Books.

Curry, A. (1968) 'Drugs in rock and jazz music.' *Clinical Toxicology 1*, 2, 235–244.

Cytowic, R.E. (1993) *The Man who Tasted Shapes*. London: Abacus.

Czadek, H. (1986) 'Jazzmusik und Drogen – Eine Wechselbeziehung?' In J. Mayr-Kern (ed.) *Musik – Eine Droge?*, 69–74. Eisenstadt/Austria: E. Rötzer.

d'Aquili, E.G. and Newberg, A.B. (1999) *The Mystical Mind: Proving the Biology of Religious Experience*. Minneapolis, MN: Fortress Press.

Damasio, A. (2000) *The Feeling of What Happens: Body, Emotion and the Making of Consciousness*. London: Vintage.

David, E., Berlin, J. and Klement, W. (1983) 'Physiologie des Musikerlebens und seine Beziehung zur trophotropen Umschaltung im Organismus.' In R. Spintge and R. Droh (eds.) *Musik in der Medizin – Neurophysiologische Grundlagen, Klinische Applikationen, Geisteswissenschaftliche Einordnung*, 33–48. Berlin: Springer-Verlag.

Davis, A. and Pieper, W. (1993) *Die psychedelischen Beatles*. Löhrbach: Werner Piepers MedienXperimente.

Decker, L. (1993) 'The role of trauma in spiritual development.' Journal of Humanistic Psychology 33, 4, 33–46.

DeNora, T. (2000) *Music in Everyday Life*. Cambridge: Cambridge University Press.

de Rios, M. D. (1972) *Visionary Vine: Hallucinogenic Healing in the Peruvian Amazon*. San Francisco: Chandler.

de Rios, M. D. (1984) *Hallucinogens: Cross-cultural Perspectives*. Albuquerque, NM: University of New Mexico Press.

de Rios, M. D. (2003) *LSD, Spirituality and the Creative Process*. Rochester, Vermont: Park Street Press.

de Rios, M. D. and Grob, C. S. (1994) 'Hallucinogens, Suggestibility and Adolescence in Cross-cultural Perspective.' In *Yearbook for Ethnomedicine and the Study of Consciousness*, Vol. 3. Berlin: Verlag für Wissenschaft und Bildung.

de Rios, M. D. and Katz, F. (1975) 'Some Relationships between Music and Hallucinogenic Ritual: the Jungle Gym in Consciousness.' *Ethos 3*, 74–76.

de Souza, M. R., Karniol, I. G. and Ventura, D. F. (1974) 'Human tonal preferences as a function of frequency under delta8-tetrahydrocannabinol.' *Pharmacology, Biochemistry and Behavior 2*, 5, 607–611.

Diaz de Chumaceiro, C. (1996) 'Unconsciously induced song recall: the process of unintentional rather than so called spontaneous evocations of music.' *The American Journal of Psychoanalysis 56*, 1, 83–89.

Dileo, C. and Bradt, J. (1999) 'Entrainment, resonance and pain-related suffering.' In C. Dileo (ed.) *Music Therapy in Medicine: Theoretical and Clinical Applications*, 181–188. Silver Spring MD: American Music Therapy Association.

Dittrich, A. (1996) *Ätiologie-unabhängige Strukturen veränderter Wachbewusstseinszustände. Ergebnisse empirischer Untersuchungen über Halluzinogene I. und II. Ordnung, sensorische Deprivation, hypnagoge Zustände, hypnotische Verfahren sowie Reizüberflutung*. Berlin: Verlag für Wissenschaft und Bildung.

Dittrich, A. (1998) 'The standardized psychometric assessment of altered states of consciousness (ASCs) in humans.' *Pharmacopsychiatry 31 Suppl. 2*, 80–84.

Dittrich, A., Lamparter, D. and Maurer, M. (2002) *5D-ABZ – Fragebogen zur Erfassung außergewöhnlicher Bewusstseinszustände*. Zürich: PSIN PLUS.

Donchin, E. and Coles, M. G. (1988) 'Is the P300 component a manifestation of context updating?' *Behavioral and Brain Science 11*, 357–374.

Douse, M. (1973) 'Contempory music, drug attitudes and drug behaviour.' *Australian Journal of Social Issues 8*, 1, 74–80.

Dowling, W. J. (1978) 'Scale and contour: two components of a theory of memory for melodies.' *Psychological Review*, 341–354.

Downey, M. (1997) *Understanding Christian Spirituality*. New York: Paulist Press.

Doyle, D. (1992) 'Have we looked beyond the physical and psychosocial?' *Journal of Pain Symptom Management 7*, 5, 302–11.

Eagle, C.T. (1972) 'Music and LSD: an empirical study.' *Journal of Music Therapy 9*, Spring, 23–36.

Eckel, K. (1982) 'Der Anteil der Sinnesphysiologie an der menschlichen Hörwelt.' In G. Harrer (ed.) *Grundlagen der Musiktherapie und Musikpsychologie*, 55–85. Stuttgart: Gustav Fischer Verlag.

Eisner, B. (1997) 'Set, setting and matrix.' *Journal of Psychoactive Drugs 29*, 2, 213–216.

Eliade, M. (1954) *Schamanismus und archaische Ekstasetechnik.* Zürich Stuttgart: Rascher.

Emblen, J. (1992) 'Religion and spirituality defined according to current use in nursing literature.' Journal of Professional Nursing 8, 1, 41–47.

Empson, J. (1986) *Human Brainwaves – The Psychological Significance of the Electroencephalogram.* Houndmills: Macmillan Press.

Emrich, H. M. (1990) *Psychiatrische Anthropologie – Therapeutische Bedeutung von Phantasiesystemen.* München: Pfeiffer.

Emrich, H. M., Weber, M. M., Wendl, A., Zihl, J., Von Meyer, L. and Hanish, W. (1991) 'Reduced binocular depth inversion as an indicator of cannabis-induced censorship impairment.' *Pharmacology, Biochemistry & Behaviour 40*, 689–690.

Fachner, J. (2000a) 'Cannabis, Musik und ein veränderter metrischer Bezugsrahmen.' In H. Rösing and T. Phleps (eds.) *Populäre Musik im kulturwissenschaftlichen Diskurs – Beiträge zur Popularmusikforschung* 107–122. Karben: CODA.

Fachner, J. (2000b) 'Der musikalische Zeit-Raum, Cannabis, Synästhesie und das Gehirn.' In A. Erben, C. Gresser and A. Stollberg (ed.) *Grenzgänge – Übergänge: Musikwissenschaften im Dialog*, 171–198. Hamburg: von Bockel.

Fachner, J. (2001) 'Veränderte Musikwahrnehmung durch Tetra-Hydro-Cannabinol im Hirnstrombild. Info CD-ROM.' In D. Aldridge and J. Fachner (eds.) *Music Therapy Info CD-ROM III.* Witten: University Witten/Herdecke.

Fachner, J. (2002a) 'The space between the notes: research on cannabis and music perception.' In K. Kärki, R. Leydon and H. Terho (eds.) *Looking Back, Looking Ahead: Popular Music Studies 20 Years Later*, 308–319. Turku, Finland: IASPM-Norden.

Fachner, J. (2002b) 'Topographic EEG changes accompanying cannabis-induced alteration of music perception: cannabis as a hearing aid?' *Journal of Cannabis Therapeutics 2*, 2, 3–36.

Fachner, J. (2004a) 'Cannabis, brain physiology, changes in states of consciousness and music perception.' In D. Aldridge (ed.) *Case Study Designs in Music Therapy*, 211–233. London: Jessica Kingsley Publishers.

Fachner, J. (2004b) 'CLEAN UP! "Heimatschutz", Anti-Drogenpolitik und legislative Auswirkungen auf die Rave-Kultur nach dem 11 September 2001.' In D. Helms and T. Phleps (eds.) *9/11 – The World's All Out of Tune – Populäre Musik nach dem 11 September* 2001, 81–98. Bielefeld: Transkript Verlag.

Fachner, J. and Rittner, S. (2004) 'Sound and trance in a ritualistic setting visualised with EEG Brainmapping.' *Music Therapy Today 5*, 2, www.musictherapytoday.com.

Fernald, A. (1991) 'Prosody in speech to children: prelinguistic and linguistic functions.' *Annals of Child Development 8*, 43–80.

Fernandez, J. (1982) *Bwiti. An Ethnography of the Religious Imagination of Africa.* Princeton: University Press.

Fink, M., Volavka, J., Panaiyotopoulos, C. P. and Stefanis, C. (1976) 'Quantitative EEG-studies of marihuana, Delta-9-Tetrahydrocannabinol and hashish in man.' In M. C. Braude and S. Szara (eds.) *The Pharmacology of Marihuana*, 383–391. New York: Raven Press.

Fischer, R. (1971) 'A cartography of the ecstatic and meditative states.' *Science 174*, 897–904.

Fischer, R. (1976) 'Transformations of consciousness. A cartography, II. The perception– meditation continuum.' *Confinia Psychiatrica 19*, 1, 1–23.

Fischer, R. (1998) 'Über die Vielfalt von Wissen und Sein im Bewusstsein. Eine Kartographie außergewöhnlicher Bewusstseinszustände.' In R. Verres, H. C. Leuner and A. Dittrich (eds.) *Welten des Bewußtseins*, 43–70. Berlin: Verlag für Wissenschaft und Bildung (VWB).

Flynn, C. P. (1984) 'Meanings and implications of near-death experiencer transformations.' In B. Greyson and C. P. Flynn (eds.) *The Near-Death Experience*, 278–289. Springfield: Charles C. Thomas.

Foglio, J. P. and Brody, H. (1988) 'Religion, faith and family medicine.' *Journal of Family Practice 27*, 473–474.

Franck-Schwebel, A. (2002) 'Developmental trauma and its relation to sound and music.' In J. P. Sutton (ed.) *Music, Music Therapy and Trauma*. London: Jessica Kingsley Publishers.

Freeman, W. (2000) 'A neurobiological role of music in social bonding.' In N. L. Wallin, B. Merker and S. Brown (eds.) *The Origins of Music*, 411–424. Cambridge, MA: MIT Press.

Freud, S. (1904) *Zur Psychopathologie des Alltagslebens: (Über Vergessen, Versprechen, Vergreifen, Aberglaube und Irrtum)*. Berlin: S. Karger.

Fromm, E. (1977) 'An ego-psychological theory of altered states of consciousness.' *The International Journal of Clinical and Experimental Hypnosis 25*, 4, 372–387.

Gabrielsson, A. (2001) 'Emotions in strong experiences with music.' In L. Sloboda and P. Juslin (eds.) *Music and Emotion*, 431–449. Oxford: Oxford University Press.

Ganzevoort, R. (1998) 'Religious coping considered, Part One: An integrated approach.' Journal of Psychology and Theology 26, 3, 260–275.

Gardner, H. (1982) *Art, Mind and Brain*. New York: Basic Books.

Gautier, T. (1877) 'Le Hachich.' In *Œuvres complètes*, 47–56. Paris.

Gelineau, J. (1962) *30 Psalms and Two Canticles*. Chicago, IL: G.I.A. Publications.

Gillespie, M. (1998) 'Nietzsche and the premodernist critque of postmodernity.' Critical Review 11, 4, 537–554.

Glicksohn, J. (1993) 'Altered sensory environments, altered states of consciousness and altered-state cognition.' *The Journal of Mind and Behaviour 14*, 1, 1–12.

Globus, G. G., Cohen, H. B., Kramer, J. C., Elliot, H. W. and Sharp, R. (1978) 'Effects of marihuana induced altered state of consciousness on auditory perception.' *Journal of Psychedelic Drugs 10*, 1, 71–76.

Goldstein, L., Murphree, H. B., Sugerman, A. A., Pfeiffer, C. C. and Jenney, E. H. (1963) 'Quantitative electroencephalographic analysis of naturally occurring (schizophrenic) and drug-induced psychotic states in human males.' *Clinical Pharmacology and Therapeutics 4*, 10–21.

Gollnhofer, O. and Sillans, R. (1997) *La mémoire d'un peuple. Ethno-histoire des Mitsogho, ethnie du Gabon central*. Paris: Présence africaine.

Goodman, F.D. (1990) *Where the Spirits Ride the Wind*. Indianapolis, IN: Indiana University Press.

Goodman, F. (2000) 'Ritual body postures and ecstatic trance: implicit myths and healing.' In H. Kalweit and S. Krippner (ed.) *Mythology and Healing: Cross-Cultural Perspectives. Yearbook of Cross-Cultural Medicine and Psychotherapy 1998/99*, 43–50. Berlin: Verlag für Wissenschaft und Bildung.

Goutarel, R. (2000) 'Pharmacodynamics and therapeutic applications of Iboga and Ibogaine.' Retrieved March 7, 2000 from www.ibogaine.desk.nl/ bwiti1.html

Graffin, N. F., Ray, W. J. and Lundy, R. (1995) 'EEG concomitants of hypnosis and hypnotic susceptibility.' *Journal of Abnormal Psychology 104*, 1, 123–131.

Green, E., Green, A. and Walters, E. (1970) 'Transpersonal potentialities of deep hypnosis.' *Journal of Transpersonal Psychology 2*, 1, 1ff.

Gregory, A. (1997) 'The roles of music in society: the ethnomusicological perspective.' In David J. Hargreaves and Adrian C. North (eds.) *The Social Psychology of Music*, 123–140. Oxford, UK: Oxford University Press.

Greyson, B. (1984) 'The near-death experience scale: construction, reliability and validity.' In B. Greyson and C. P. Flynn (eds.) *The Near-Death Experience*, 45–60. Springfield: Charles C. Thomas.

Grob, C. S. and de Rios, M. D. (1996) 'Hallucinogens, suggestibility and adolescence in cross-cultural perspective.' *Journal of Drug Issues 22*, 1,121–138.

Grocke, D. (2005) 'A case study in the Bonny method of guided imagery and music (BMGIM).' In D. Aldridge *Case Study Designs in Music Therapy*, 97–117. London. Jessica Kingsley Publishers.

Grof, S. (1993) *Topographie des Unbewußten. Konzepte der Humanwissenschaften – LSD im Dienste der tiefenpsychologischen Forschung*. Stuttgart: Klett-Cotta.

Grof, S. (1994) *LSD Psychotherapy* (2nd edn.) Alameda, CA: Hunter House.

Groth-Marnat, G. and Summers, R. (1998) 'Altered beliefs, attitudes and behaviors following near-death experiences.' *Journal of Humanistic Psychology 38*, 3,110–125.

Gustorff, D. and Hannich, H.-J. (2000) *Jenseits des Wortes: Musiktherapie mit komatösen Patienten auf der Intensivstation*. Bern: Hans Huber.

Guttmann, G. (1990) 'Zur Psychophysiologie der Bewusstseinssteuerung. Meditation – Trance – Hypnose: Wurzeln und biologische Korrelate.' In J. Bandion (ed.) *Einheit der Vielfalt*. Wien: Gerold.

Haerlin, P. (1998) 'The use of music instruments in psychotherapy in order to alter states of consciousness.' *Psychotherapeut 43*, 4, 238–242.

Hagemann, D., Naumann, E., Lurken, A., Becker, G., Maier, S. and Bartussek, D. (1999) 'EEG asymmetry, dispositional mood and personality.' *Personality and Individual Differences 27*, 3, 541–568.

Hanegraaff, W. (1999) 'New Age spiritualities as secular religion:. a historian's perspective.' Social Compass 46, 2, 145–160.

Harner, M. (1990) *The Way Of The Shaman: A Guide to Power and Healing*. New York: Harper & Row.

Harrer, G. (1991) 'Zur Bedeutung psychischer und somatischer Reaktionen beim Erleben von Musik.' In H. Rösing (ed.) *Musik als Droge? Zu Theorie und Praxis bewußtseinsverändernder Wirkungen von Musik*, 9–21. Mainz: Villa Musica.

Hartley, N. (1999) 'Music therapist's personal reflections on working with those who are living with HIV/AIDS.' In D. Aldridge (ed.) *Music Therapy in Palliative Care: New Voices*, 105–124. London: Jessica Kingsley Publishers.

Hartley, N. (2001) 'On a personal note: a music therapist's reflections on working with those who are living with a terminal illness.' *Journal of Palliative Care 17*, 3, 135–141.

Herkenrath, A. (2002) 'Musiktherapie und Wahrnehmung: Ein Beitrag der Musiktherapie zur Evaluierung der Wahrnehmungsfähigkeit von Patienten mit schweren Hirnverletzungen.' In D. Aldridge and M. Dembski (eds.) *Musiktherapie: Diagnostik und Wahrnehmung*, 122–132. Witten: Universität Witten-Herdecke.

Herman, J. (1997) *Trauma and Recovery. The Aftermath of Violence: From Domestic Abuse to Political Terror*. New York: Basic Books.

Hess, P. (1973) *Experimentelle Untersuchung akuter Haschischeinwirkung auf den Menschen*. Doctoral Thesis (MD), Medical Faculty, Ruprecht-Karl-University Heidelberg.

Hess, P. (1992) 'Die Bedeutung der Musik für Set und Setting in veränderten Bewußtseinszuständen.' In H. C. Leuner and M. Schlichting (eds.) *Jahrbuch des Europäischen Collegiums für Bewußtseinsstudien 1992*, 133–140. Berlin: Verlag für Wissenschaft und Bildung (VWB).

Hess, P. (1995) 'Licht und Schatten: Hanf aus medizinisch-psychiatrischer Sicht.' In R. Cosack and R. Wenzel (eds.) *Das Hanf-Tage-Buch: Neue Beiträge zur Diskussion über Hanf, Cannabis, Marihuana*. 25–44. Hamburg: Wendepunkt.

Hess, P. and Rittner, S. (1996a) 'Trance.' In H. H. Decker-Voigt, P. Knill and E. Weymann (eds.) *Lexikon Musiktherapie*, 395–398. Göttingen: Hogrefe.

Hess, P. and Rittner, S. (1996b) 'Verändertes Wachbewusstsein.' In H. H. Decker-Voigt, P. Knill and E. Weymann (eds.) *Lexikon Musiktherapie*, 398–403. Göttingen: Hogrefe.

Highfield, M. (1992) 'Spiritual health of oncology patients. Nurse and patient perspectives.' Cancer Nursing 15, 1, 1–8.

Hilgard, J. R. (1974) 'Imaginative involvement: some characteristics of the highly hypnotizable and the non-hypnotizable.' *The International Journal of Clinical and Experimental Hypnosis 22*, 2, 138–156.

Hogan, B. (1999) 'Music therapy at the end of life: searching for the rite of passage.' In D. Aldridge (ed.) *Music Therapy in Palliative Care: New Voices*, 68–81. London: Jessica Kingsley Publishers.

Horowitz, A. (1999) 'Israeli Mediterranean Music.' *Journal of American Folklore 112*, 445, 450–463.

Huron, D. (1997) 'The melodic arch in Western folksongs.' *Computing in Musicology 10*, 3–23.

Idler, E. (1995) 'Religion, health and the nonphysical senses of self.' Social Forces 74, 22, 683–704.

Insinger, M. (1991) 'The impact of a near-death experience on family relationships.' *Journal of Near-Death Studies 9*, 3, 141–181.

Ivry, R. (1997) 'Cerebellar timing systems.' *International Review of Neurobiology 41*, 555–573.

Jaffe, J. R. and Toon, J. H. (1980) 'EEG and polygraphic changes during hypnotic suggestibility.' *Journal of Electrophysiological Technology 6*, 2, 75–92.

James, W. (1902) *The Variety of Religious Experience*. New York: Modern Library.

Jausovec, N. (1997) 'Differences in EEG alpha activity between gifted and non-identified individuals: insights into problem solving.' *Gifted Child Quarterly 41*, 1, 26–32.

Joint Commission on Accreditation of Healthcare Organizations (JCAHO) (1996) *Implementation Section of the 1996 Standards for Hospitals by JCAHO*. Oakbrook Terrace, IL: Joint Commission on Accreditation of Healthcare Organizations.

Jones, R. T. and Stone, G. C. (1970) 'Psychological studies of marijuana and alcohol in man.' *Psychopharmacologia 18*, 1, 108–117.

Jones, R., Hux, K., Morton-Anderson, K. A. and Knepper, L. (1994) 'Auditory stimulation effect on a comatose survivor of traumatic brain injury.' *Archives of Physical Medicine and Rehabilitation 75*, 2, 164–171.

Jonnes, J. (1999) *Hep-Cats, Narcs and Pipe Dreams*. Baltimore: John Hopkins University Press.

Joseph, M. (1998) 'The effect of strong religious beliefs on coping with stress.' Stress Medicine 14, 219–224.

Joy, J.E., Watson, S.J. and Benson, J.A. (eds.) (1999) *Marijuana and Medicine: Assessing the Science Base*. Washington, DC: National Academy Press.

Julien, R. M. (1997) *Drogen und Psychopharmaka*. Heidelberg: Spektrum Akademischer Verlag.

Kartomi, M.J. (1973) 'Music and trance in central Java.' *Ethnomusicology 17*, 163–208.

Katz, F. and de Rios, M. D. (1971) 'Hallucinogenic music: an analysis of the role of whistling in Peruvian Ayahuasca healing sessions.' *American Journal of Folklore 84*, 320–327.

Katz, M. M., Waskow, I. E. and Olsson, J. (1968) 'Characterizing the psychological state produced by LSD.' *Journal of Abnormal Psychology 73*, 1, 1–14.

Kaufman, E. (1994) *Psychotherapy of Addicted Persons*. New York: The Guilford Press.

Keidel, W. D. (1975) *Kurzgefaßtes Lehrbuch der Physiologie*. Stuttgart: Georg Thieme Verlag.

Kelly, S. F. (1993) 'The use of music as a hypnotic suggestion.' *The American Journal of Clinical Hypnosis 36*, 2, 83–90.

Kerr, B. (1992) 'Substance abuse of creatively talented adults.' *Journal of Creative Behaviour 25*, 2, 145–153.

Khan, I. (1974) *The Development of Spiritual Healing*. Claremont, CA: Hunter House.

Khan, I. (1983) *The Music of Life*. Santa Fe: Omega Press.

Khan, I. (1996) *The Mysticism of Sound and Music*. Boston, MA: Shambala.

Kharaeva-Gvasheva, F. F. (1999) 'The mysticism of the timbre (on the mythology of musical instruments).' In A. Sokolova and R. Unarokova (eds.) *Etudes on Adygh history and culture*, Vol. 2, 43–52. Maikop: The Adygh Republic Institute of the Humanity Researches.

Khorram-Sefat, D. (1997) 'fMRI correlates of music listening.' *Psychiatry Research 68*, 2–3, 167–168.

Kimmens, A. (ed.) (1977) *Tales of Hashish: A Literary Look at the Hashish Experience*. New York: William Morrow.

King, M. and Dein, S. (1998) 'The spiritual variable in psychiatric research.' Psychological Medicine 28, 1259–1262.

Kirsch, I. (1997) 'Hypnotic suggestion: a musical metaphor.' *The American Journal of Clinical Hypnosis 39*, 4, 271–277; discussion 277–281.

Kleinman, A. (1988) *Rethinking Psychiatry*. New York and London: Free Press and Collier Macmillan Publishers.

Klimesch, W. (1999) 'EEG alpha and theta oscillations reflect cognitive and memory performance: a review and analysis.' *Brain Research. Brain Research Reviews 29*, 2–3, 169–195.

Koenig, H. G. (1999) *The Healing Power of Faith*. New York: Simon & Schuster, Inc.

Kohlmetz, C., Kopiez, R. and Altenmüller, E. (2003) 'Stability of motor programs during a state of meditation: electrocortical activity in a pianist playing *Vexations* by Erik Satie continuously for 28 hours.' *Psychology of Music 31*, 2, 173–186.

Kolb, B. and Whishaw, I.Q. (1996) *Neuropsychologie*. Heidelberg: Spektrum Verlag.

Kopiez, R., Bangert, M., Goebl, W. and Altenmüller, E. (2003) 'Tempo and Loudness Analysis of a Continuous 28-Hour Performance of Erik Satie's Composition *Vexations*.' *Journal of New Music Research 32*, 3, 243–258.

Koukkou, M. and Lehmann, D. (1976) 'Human EEG spectra before and during cannabis hallucinations.' *Biological Psychiatry 11*, 6, 663–677.

Koukkou, M. and Lehmann, D. (1978) 'Correlations between cannabis-induced psychopathology and EEG before and after drug ingestion.' *Pharmakopsychiatry Neuropsychopharmakol 11*, 5, 220–227.

Krause, C. M., Porn, B., Lang, A. H. and Laine, M. (1999) 'Relative alpha desynchronization and synchronization during perception of music.' *Scandinavian Journal of Psychology 40*, 3, 209–215.

Krippner, S. (1977) 'Research in creativity and psychedelic drugs.' *The International Journal of Clinical and Experimental Hypnosis 25*, 4, 274–290.

Krippner, S. (1985) 'Psychedelic drugs and creativity.' *Journal of Psychoactive Drugs 17*, 4, 235–245.

Kuhn, C. (1988) 'A spiritual inventory of the medically ill patient.' Psychiatric Medicine 6, 2, 87–100.

Kupfer, A. (1996a) *Die künstlichen Paradiese: Rausch und Realität seit der Romantik.* Stuttgart: J. B. Metzler.

Kupfer, A. (1996b) *Göttliche Gifte: Kleine Kulturgeschichte des Rausches seit dem Garten Eden.* Stuttgart Weimar: J. B. Metzler.

Kurtz, E. (1979) *Not-God. A history of Alcoholics Anonymous.* Center City, Minnesota: Hazelden Pittman Archives Press.

Laing, R. D. (1967) *The Politics of Experience.* New York: Pantheon Books.

Lapierre, L. (1994) 'A model for describing spirituality.' Journal of Religion and Health 33, 2, 153–161.

Leary, T.F. (1990) *Flashbacks: A Personal and Cultural History of an Era. An Autobiography.* Los Angeles; New York: J. P. Tarcher; Distributed by St Martin's Press.

Lee, M. M. and Shalin, B. (1992) *Acid Dreams.* New York: Grove Press.

Lehikoinen, P. (1996) 'Matalataajuuksinen värähtelyenergia ja musiikkiterapian neurofysiologinen perusta.' In H. Ahonen-Eerikäinen (ed.) *Taide psykososiaalisen työn välineenä.* 26–34. Joensuu: Pohjois-Karjalan ammattikorkeakoulu.

Lehmann, D., Faber, P. L., Achermann, P., Jeanmonod, D., Gianotti, L. R. and Pizzagalli, D. (2001) 'Brain sources of EEG gamma frequency during volitionally meditation-induced, altered states of consciousness, and experience of the self.' *Psychiatry Research 108*, 2, 111–121.

Leman, M. (1995) *Music and Schema Theory: Cognitive Foundations of Systematic Musicology.* Berlin and Heidelberg: Springer.

Lenton, S., Boys, A. and Norcross, K. (1997) 'Raves, drugs and experience: drug use by a sample of people who attend raves in Western Australia.' *Addiction 92*, 10, 1327–1337.

Leuner, H. C. (1974) 'Die Bedeutung der Musik in imaginativen Techniken der Psychotherapie.' In W. J. Revers, G. Harrer and W. C. M. Simon (eds.) *Neue Wege der Musiktherapie.* 178–200. Düsseldorf, Wien: Econ Verlag.

Leuner, H. and Richards, W.A. (1984) *Guided Affective Imagery – The Basic Course: Mental Imagery in Short-term Psychotherapy.* Stuttgart and New York: Thieme-Stratton and G. Thieme Verlag.

Leventhal, S. (ed.) (2003) *Notations: Quotations on Music.* New York: Barnes and Nobles Books.

Levine, P. A. (1997) *Waking the Tiger.* Berkeley, CA: North Atlantic.

Lommel, van P., Wees, van R., Meyers, V. and Elfferich, I. (2001) 'Near-death experience in survivors of cardiac arrest: a prospective study in the Netherlands.' *Lancet 358*, 2039–2015.

Long, A. (1997) 'Nursing: A spiritual perspective.' Nursing Ethics 4, 6, 496–510.

Lowis, M. J. and Hughes, J. (1997) 'A comparison of the effects of sacred and secular music on elderly people.' *The Journal of Psychology 131*, 1, 45–55.

Ludwig, A. M. (1966) 'Altered states of consciousness.' *Archives of General Psychiatry 15*, 3, 225 –234.

Ludwig, A. (1969) 'Altered states of consciousness.' In Charles T. Tart (ed.) *Altered States of Consciousness,* 9–22. New York: John Wiley.

Lukoff, D., Provenzano, R., Lu, F. and Turner, R. (1999) 'Religious and spiritual case reports on medline: a systematic analysis of records from 1980 to 1996.' *Alternative Therapies 5*, 1, 64–70.

Lull, J. (ed.) (1987) *Popular Music and Communication.* Beverly Hills: Sage Publishers.

Lyttle, T. and Montagne, M. (1992) 'Drugs, music, and ideology: a social pharmacological interpretation of the Acid House Movement.' *The International Journal of the Addictions 27*, 10, 1159–1177.

McDougall, J. (1999) *Ruumiin näyttämöt. Psykoanalyyttinen näkökulma psykosomaattiseen sairastamiseen.* Suomentajat Maarit Arppo ja Ritva Levä. Helsinki: Therapeia-säätiö.

McKenna, T.K. (1992) *Food of the Gods. The Search for the Original Tree of Knowledge: A Radical History of Plants, Drugs, and Human Evolution.* New York: Bantam Books.

Magill, L. (1993) 'Music therapy in pain and symptom management.' *Journal of Palliative Care 9*, 4, 42–48.

Magill, L. (2001) 'The use of music therapy to address the suffering in advanced cancer pain.' *Journal of Palliative Care 17*, 3, 167–172.

Magill, L. (2005). 'Music therapy: Enhancing spirituality at the end-of-life.' In C. Dileo and J. Loewy (eds.) *Music Therapy at the End of Life.* Cherry Hill, NJ: Jeffrey Books.

Magill, L. and Luzzato, P. (2002) 'Music therapy and art therapy.' In A. Berger, R. Portenoy and D. Weissman (eds.) *Principles and Practice of Palliative Care and Supportive Oncology*, 993–1006. New York: Lippincott, Williams and Wilkins.

Magill, L., Chung, M. and Kennedy, F. (2000) 'Music therapy in palliative care: Regaining control.' *Journal of Palliative Care 16*, 3, 92.

Markert, J. (2001) 'Sing a song of drug use-abuse: four decades of drug lyrics in popular music – from the sixties through the nineties.' *Sociological Inquiry 71*, 2, 194–220.

Marr, J. (1999) 'GIM at the End of Life: Case Studies in Palliative Care.' *Journal of The Association for Music and Imagery 6*, 1998–99, 34–54.

Marsham, R. (1990) 'Sufi orders.' In I. Shah (ed.) *Sufi Thought and Action*, 112–122. London: Octagon Press.

Martin, G. and Pearson, W. (1995) *Summer of Love – The Making of Sgt. Pepper.* London: Pan Books-Macmillan.

Mary, A. (1983) 'L'alternative de la vision et de la possession dans les sociétés religieuses et thérapeutiques du Gabon.' *Cahier d'etudes africaines 91*, 13, 281–310.

Mathew, R.J., Wilson, W.H., Turkington, T.G. and Coleman, R.E. (1998) 'Cerebellar activity and disturbed time sense after THC.' *Brain Research 797*, 2, 183–189.

Masters, R.E. and Houston, J. (1968) *Psychedelic Art.* London: Weidenfeld & Nicolson.

Maurer, R. L., Sr., Kumar, V. K., Woodside, L. and Pekala, R. J. (1997) 'Phenomenological experience in response to monotonous drumming and hypnotizability.' *The American Journal of Clinical Hypnosis 40*, 2, 130–145.

Maxfield, M. (1992) *The Journey of the Drum. Effects of Rhythmic Drumming on EEG and Subjective Experience.* Unpublished Ph.D. Thesis, Institute of Transpersonal Psychology, Menlo Park, California, US.

Mayne, M. (2002) *Learning to Dance.* London: Darton, Longman and Todd Ltd.

Mayr-Kern, J. (ed.) (1985) *Musik – eine Droge?* Gemunden: Rötzer Verlag in Eisenstadt.

Melechi, A. (ed.) (1997) *Psychedelia Britannica.* London: Turnaround.

Mellgren, A. (1979) 'Hypnotherapy and art (vocalists and musicians).' *The Journal of the American Society of Psychosomatic Dentistry and Medicine 26*, 4, 152–155.

Merton, T. (1996) *A Search for Solitude: Pursuing the Monk's True Life.* New York: HarperCollins.

Meszaros, I., Szabó, C. and Csako, R. I. (2002) 'Hypnotic susceptibility and alterations in subjective experiences.' *Acta Biologica Hungarica 53*, 4, 499–514.

Metzner, R. (1992) 'Molekulare Mystik: Die Rolle psychoaktiver Substanzen bei der Transformation des Bewußtseins.' In C. Rätsch (ed.) *Das Tor zu den inneren Räumen.* 63–78. Südergelleresen: Verlag Bruno Martin.

Meyer, L.B. (1967) *Music, the Arts, and Ideas: Patterns and Predictions in Twentieth Century Culture.* Chicago, IL: The University of Chicago Press.

Mezzrow, M. (1946) *Really the Blues* (Reprint 1993). A Flamingo Modern Classic. London: Flamingo/HarperCollins Publishers.

Mitterlehner, F. (1996) 'Let's Fly Together, zur Untersuchung veränderter Bewußtseinszustände während einer Techno-Party.' In H. C. Leuner and M. Schlichting (eds.) *Jahrbuch des Europäischen Collegiums für Bewußtseinsstudien*, 49–62. Berlin: Verlag für Wissenschaft und Bildung.

Moreau de Tours, J. J. (1845) *Du haschisch et de l'aliénation mentale. Etudes psychologiques.* (Réédition Genève, Slatkine, 1980 edn.) Paris: Fortin et Masson.

Munro, S. and Mount, B. (1978) Music therapy in palliative care. *Canadian Medical Association Journal 119,* 9, 1029–34.

Nagy, K. and Szabó, C. (2003) 'The influence of intensity of musical involvement and type of music on musical experiences.' In R.Kopiez, A.C. Lehmann, I. Wolther, I. and C.Wolf, (eds.) *5th Triennial ESCOM Conference,* 429–432. Hanover: European Society for the Cognition of Music.

Narayanasamy, A. (1999) 'A review of spirituality as applied to nursing.' International Journal of Nursing Studies 36, 117–125.

Neher, A. (1962) 'A physiological explanation of unusual behavior in ceremonies involving drums.' *Human Biology: An International Record of Research 34,* 151–160.

Newberg, A.E., d'Aquili E. and Rause, V. (2001) *Why God Won't Go Away.* New York: Ballantine Books.

Niedermeyer, E. and Lopes de Silva, F. (1993) *Electroencephalogralography.* Baltimore: Williams and Wilkins.

Nixon, G. M. (1999) 'Whatever happened to heightened consciousness?' *Journal of Curriculum Studies 31,* 6, 625–633.

O'Callaghan, C. (2001) 'Bringing music to life: a study of music therapy and palliative care experiences within a cancer hospital.' *Journal of Palliative Care 17,* 3, 155–160.

Ogden, P. (2003) *Somatic Awareness: The Role of Body Sensation in Psychotherapy with Traumatized Clients,* Unpublished Paper.

Ogden, P. and Minton, K. (2000) 'Sensorimotor Psychotherapy: One method for processing traumatic memory.' *Traumatology 6,* 3, Article 3.

Oohashi, T., Kawai, N., Honda, M., Nakamura, S., Morimoto, M., Nishina, E. and Maekawa, T. (2002) 'Electroencephalographic measurement of possession trance in the field.' *Clinical Neurophysiology 113,* 3, 435–445.

Ornstein, R (1996) *The Mind Field.* Cambridge: Malor Books ISHK.

Ortiz, J. M. (1997) *The Tao of Music.* York Beach: Samuel Weiser Books.

Park, J. R., Yagyu, T., Saito, N., Kinoshita, T. and Hirai, T. (2002) 'Dynamics of brain electric field during recall of Salpuri dance performance.' *Perceptual and Motor Skills 95,* 3, Pt 1, 955–962.

Park, K. (1998) 'The religious construction of sanctuary provision in two congregations.' Sociological Spectrum 18, 393–421.

Pekala, R. J. (1985) 'A phenomenological approach to mapping and diagramming states of consciousness.' *The Journal of Religion and Psychical Research 8,* 4, 199–214.

Pekala, R. J. (1991) *Phenomenology of Consciousness Inventory (PCI) Form I.* West Chester PA: MID-Atlantic Educational Institute.

Pekala, R. J. and Kumar, V. K. (2000) 'Operationalizing "trance" I: Rationale and research using a psychophenomenological approach.' *The American Journal of Clinical Hypnosis 43,* 2, 107–135.

Pekala, R. J. and Pekala, C. E. (2000) 'Methodological issues in the study of altered states of consciousness and anomalous experiences.' In E. Cardena, S. J. Lynn and S. Krippner (eds.) *Varieties of Anomalous Experience: Examining the Scientific Evidence,* 47–82. Washington DC: American Psychological Association.

Petsche, H. (1994) 'The EEG while listening to music.' *EEG–EMG–Zeitschrift für Elektroenzephalographie, Elektromyographie und verwandte Gebiete 25,* 2, 130–137.

Pilch, J.J. (2000) *Healing in the New Testament: Insights from Medical and Mediterranean Anthropology.* Minneapolis, MN: Fortress Press.

Pilch, J.J. (2004) *Visions and Healing in Acts of the Apostles: How the Earlier Believers Experienced God.* Collegeville, MN: The Liturgical Press.

Plant, S. (1999) *Writing on Drugs.* London: Faber and Faber.

Plucker, J.A. and Dana, R.Q. (1998) 'Creativity of undergraduates with and without family history of alcohol and other drug problems.' *Addictive Behaviours 23,* 5, 711–714.

Pressing, J., Magill, J. and Summers, J. (1996) 'Cognitive multiplicity in polyrhythmic pattern performance.' *Journal of Experimental Psychology, Human Perception and Performance 22,* 5, 1127–1148.

Price-Williams, D.R. (1975) *Explorations in Cross-Cultural Psychology.* San Francisco: Chandler & Sharp Publishers, Inc.

Pulchalski C. M. (2002) 'Spirituality.' In A. Berger, R. Portenoy and D. Weissman (eds.) *Principles and Practice of Palliative Care and Supportive Oncology* (2nd edn.), 799–812. New York: Lippincott, Williams and Wilkins.

Pullman, D. (2002) 'Human dignity and the ethics and aesthetics of pain and suffering.' *Theoretical Medicine 23,* 75–94.

Punkanen, M. (2004) 'On a journey to mind and emotions: the physioacoustic method and music therapy in drug rehabilitation.' In J. Fachner and D. Aldridge (eds.) *Dialogue and Debate: Conference Proceedings of the 10th World Congress on Music Therapy.* 1333–1357. (D. Aldridge and J. Fachner (eds.) *Music Therapy Info CD-ROM, V.*) Witten: MusicTherapyWorld.net

Rätsch, C (1986) 'Musique Fantastique.' In S. Höhle, C. Müller-Ebeling, C. Rätsch and O. Urchs (eds.) *Rausch und Erkenntnis: Das Wilde in der Kultur.* München: Knaur-Verlag.

Rätsch, C. (ed.) (1992a) *Das Tor zu inneren Räumen.* Südergellsen: Verlag Bruno Martin.

Rätsch, C. (1992b) 'Setting: Der Ort der psychedelischen Erfahrung im ethnographischen Kontext.' In H. C. Leuner and M. Schlichting (eds) *Jahrbuch des Europäischen Collegiums für Bewußtseinsstudien 1992,* 123–132. Berlin: Verlag für Wissenschaft und Bildung (VWB).

Rätsch, C (1995a) *Heilkräuter der Antike in Ägypten, Griechenland und Rom: Mytologie und Anwendung.* München: Eugen Diederichs Verlag.

Rätsch, C (1995b) 'Ritueller Gebrauch psychoaktiver Substanzen im modernen Mitteleuropa.' *Curare: Journal for Ethnomedicine 18,* 2, 297–324.

Reed, P. (1987) 'Spirituality and well-being in terminally ill hospitalized adults.' Research in Nursing and Health 10, 5, 335–344.

Riis, O. (1998) 'Religion re-emerging. The role of religion in legitimating integration and power in modern societies.' International Sociology 13, 2, 249–272.

Risch, M., Scherg, H. and Verres, R. (2001) 'Music therapy for chronic headaches. Evaluation of music therapeutic groups for patients suffering from chronic headaches.' *Schmerz 15,* 2, 116–125.

Rittner, S. (1994) 'Die menschliche Stimme als Medium zur Induktion veränderter Wachbewußtseinszustände.' In A. Dittrich, A. Hoffmann and H. C. Leuner (eds) *Welten des Bewußtseins.* Berlin: VWB.

Rittner, S. (1996) 'Stimme.' In H. H. Decker-Voigt, P. Knill and E. Weymann (eds) *Lexikon Musiktherapie,* 359–368. Göttingen: Hogrefe.

Roberts, D.F., Henriksen, L. and Christenson, P.G. (1999) *Substance Use in Popular Movies and Music.* Washington: White House Office of National Drug Control Policy; US Department of Health and Human Services' Substance Abuse and Mental Health Services Administration.

Robinson, J. P., Pilskaln, R. and Hirsch, P. (1976) 'Protest rock and drugs.' *Journal of Communication Disorders 26,* 4, 125–136.

Rösing, H. (1991a) 'Heavy Metal, Hard Rock, Punk: Geheime Botschaften an das Unbewusste?' In H. Rösing (ed.) *Musik als Droge? Zu Theorie und Praxis bewußtseinsverändernder Wirkungen von Musik,* 73–89. Mainz: Villa Musica.

Rösing, H. (1991b) 'Musik als Droge?' In H. Rösing (ed.) *Musik als Droge? Zu Theorie und Praxis bewußtseinsverändernder Wirkungen von Musik,* 7–8. Mainz: Villa Musica.

Roth, G. (1994) *Das Gehirn und seine Wirklichkeit: kognitive Neurobiologie und ihre philosophischen Konsequenzen.* Frankfurt am Main: Suhrkamp.

Rothschild, B. (2000) *The Body Remembers: The Psychophysiology of Trauma and Trauma Treatment.* New York: W. W. Norton & Company.

Rothschild, B. (2003) *The Body Remembers Casebook: Unifying Methods and Models in the Treatment of Trauma and PTSD.* New York: W. W. Norton & Company.

Rouget, G. (1977) 'Music and possession trance.' In J. Blaching (ed.) *The Anthropology of the Body,* 232–239. London: Academic Press.

Rouget, G. (1985) *Music and Trance: A Theory of the Relations between Music and Possession.* Chicago: University of Chicago Press.

Rouget, G. (1990) *La musique et la transe.* Paris: Edition Gallimard.

Rubin, V. and Comitas, L. (1975) *Ganja in Jamaica.* The Hague: Mouton.

Sabourin, M. E., Cutcomb, S. D., Crawford, H. J. and Pribram, K. (1990) 'EEG correlates of hypnotic susceptibility and hypnotic trance: spectral analysis and coherence.' *International Journal of Psychophysiology 10,* 2, 125–142.

Salmon, D. (2001) 'Music therapy as psychospiritual process in palliative care.' *Journal of Palliative Care 17,* 3, 142–6.

Samorini, G. (2000) 'The initiation rite in the Bwiti religion.' In C. Müller-Ebeling (ed.) *Yearbook for Ethnomedicine and the Study of Consciousness – Special: Psychoactivity,* Vol. 6–7, 1997/1998, 39–56. Berlin: Verlag für Wissenschaft und Bildung.

Satoh, M. (2001) 'Activated brain regions in musicians during an ensemble.' *Cognitive Brain Research 12,* 1, 101–108.

Schacter, D. L. (1977) 'EEG Theta-Waves and psychological phenomena: a review.' *Biological Psychology 5,* 47–82.

Scharfetter, C. (1995) 'Welten des Bewußtseins und ihre Kartographen.' *Curare – Journal for Ethnomedicine 18,* 1, 161–171.

Schröter-Kunhardt, M. (1999) 'Nah-Todeserfahrungen aus psychiatrisch-neurologischer Sicht.' In H. Knoblauch und H. Soeffner (eds.) *Todesnähe. Wissenschaftliche Zugänge zu einem außergewöhnlichen Phänomen,* 65–97. Konstanz: Universitätsverlag Konstanz.

Schwartz, E. and Feinglass, S. J. (1973) 'Popular music und drug lyrics: analysis of a scapegoat.' In *US National Commission on Marijuana and Drug Abuse,* 718–746. Washington: USGPO.

Shah, I. (1964) *The Sufis.* London: Octagon Press.

Shah, I. (1968) *The Way of the Sufi.* London: Octagon Press.

Shah, I. (1969) *Wisdom of the Idiots.* London: Octagon Press.

Shah, I. (1978) *A Veiled Gazelle.* London: The Octagon Press.

Shah, I. (1983) *Learning How to Learn.* London: Octagon Press.

Shah, I. (1990) *Sufi Thought and Action.* London: Octagon Press.

Shapiro, H. (1998) *Sky High: Drogenkultur im Musikbuisiness.* St Andrä-Wördern: Hannibal.

Shor, R. E. and Orne, E. C. (1962) *The Harvard Group Scale of Hypnotic Susceptibility.* Palo Alto: Consulting Psychologists Press.

Shor, R. E. and Orne, E. C. (1963) 'Norms on the Harvard group scale of hypnotic susceptibility, form A.' *The International Journal of Clinical and Experimental Hypnosis 11,* 39–47.

Short, A.E. (1997) 'Jungian archetypes in GIM therapy: approaching the client's fairytale.' *Journal of Music and Imagery 5,* 1996–97, 35–49.

Shu, S.S. (1997) *Musical Folklore of Adyghs in Notation of G. Mkontsevich.* (Chief Editor and Compiler S. S. Shu) Maikop.

Sims, A. (1994) '"Psyche"-spirit as well as mind?' British Journal of Psychiatry 165, 441–446.

Sloman, L. (1998) *Reefer Madness: The History of Marijuana in America.* New York: St Martin's Griffin.

Small, C. (1998) *Musicking: The Meanings of Performing and Listening.* Hanover, USA: Wesleyan University Press.

Snodgrass, M. and Lynn, S. J. (1989) 'Music absorption and hypnotizability.' *The International Journal of Clinical and Experimental Hypnosis 37,* 1, 41–54.

Sokolova, A. N. (1998) 'Sandrak.' In M. Sementsov (ed.) *The Results of Folk-ethnographic Studies on Ethnic Cultures of Kuban for 1997,* 79–82. Belorechensk: Kuban Kazak Chorus.

Sokolova, A. N. (1999) 'Mythological aspects of the traditional Adygh instrumental culture.' In Tatyana Rudichenko (ed.) *History and Culture of the Step Pre-Caucasus and North Caucasus Nationalities: Toward the Interethnic Relations,* 175–183. Rostov on Don: The Rachmaninov State Conservatoire Publishers.

Spintge, R. (1991) 'Die therapeutisch-funktionalen Wirkungen von Musik aus medizinischer und neurophysiologischer Sicht: Musik als therapeutische Droge.' In H. Rösing (ed.) *Musik als Droge? Zu Theorie und Praxis bewußtseinsverändernder Wirkungen von Musik,* 13–22. Mainz: Villa Musica.

Standley, J. (1996) 'Research in medical/dental treatment: an update of a prior meta-analysis.' In *Effectiveness of Music Therapy Procedures: Documentation of Research and Clinical Practices,* 1–60. Silver Spring MD: National Association for Music Therapy, Inc.

Strobel, W. (1988) 'Sound–Trance–Healing.' *Musiktherapeutische Umschau 9*, 119–139.

Struve, F. A. and Straumanis, J. J. (1990) 'Electroencephalographic and evoked potential methods in human marihuana research: historical review and future trends.' *Drug Development Research 20*, 369–388.

Sulmasy, D. P. (1999). 'Finitude, freedom, and suffering.' In R. Hanson and M. Mohrman (eds.) *Pain Seeking Understanding: Suffering, Medicine and Faith*, 83–102. Pilgrim Press: Cleveland, OH.

Sulmasy, D. (2002). A biopsychosocial-spiritual model for the care of patients at the end-of-life. *The Gerontologist 42*, 24–33.

Szasz, T.S. (2003) *Ceremonial Chemistry: The Ritual Persecution of Drugs, Addicts, and Pushers.* Syracuse, NY: Syracuse University Press.

Taeger, H.H. (1988) *Spiritualität und Drogen: Interpersonelle Zusammenhänge von Psychedelika und religiös-mystischen Aspekten in der Gegenkultur der 70er Jahre.* Markt Erlbach: Raymond Martin.

Taqi, S. (1969) 'Approbation of drug usage in rock and roll music.' *Bulletin on Narcotics 21*, 4, 29–35.

Taqi, S. (1972) 'The Drug Cinema.' *Bulletin on Narcotics 24*, 19–28.

Tart, C. (1971) *On Being Stoned, A Psychological Study of Marihuana Intoxication.* Palo Alto: Science and Behaviour Books.

Tart, C. T. (1975) *States of Consciousness.* New York: E. P. Dutton & Co.

Tassi, P. and Muzet, A. (2001) 'Defining the states of consciousness.' *Neuroscience and Biobehavioral Reviews 25*, 2, 175–191.

Tellegen, A. and Atkinson, G. (1974) 'Openness to absorbing and self-altering experiences ("absorption"), a trait related to hypnotic susceptibility.' *Journal of Abnormal Psychology 83*, 3, 268–277.

TenBerge, J. (1999) 'Breakdown or breakthrough? A history of European research into drugs and creativity.' *Journal of Creative Behavior 33*, 4, 257–276.

Terr, L. (1994) *Unchained Memories.* New York: Basic.

Thomas, W. I. (1927) 'Situational analysis: the behavior pattern and the situation.' *Publications of the American Sociological Society 22*, 1–13.

Timmermann, T. (1996) 'Ethnologische Aspekte in der Musiktherapie.' In H. H. Decker-Voigt, P. Knill and E. Weymann (eds.) *Lexikon Musiktherapie*, 87–90. Göttingen: Hogrefe.

Tournier, P. (1981) *Creative Suffering.* London: SCM Press.

Trehub, S.E. (2003) 'The developmental origins of musicality.' *Nature Neuroscience 6*, 669–673. www.nature.com/neuro/journal/v6/n7/full/nn1084.html

Trehub, S.E. and Trainor, L. J. (1998) 'Singing to infants: lullabies and play songs.' *Advanced Infant Research 12*, 43–77.

Tucek, G. K., Auer-Pekarsky, A. M. and Stepansky, R. (2001) 'Altorientalische Musiktherapie bei Schädel–Hirn–Trauma.' *Musik- Tanz- und Kunsttherapie 12*, 1,1–12.

Tversky, A. (1977) ' Features of similarity.' *Psychological Review 84*, 4, 327–352.

Tweedie, I. (1995) *Daughter of Fire: A Diary of a Spiritual Training with a Sufi Master.* San Fransisco: The Golden Sufi Centre.

Van der Kolk, B., Van der Hart, O. and Marmar, C. R. (1996) 'Dissociation and information processing in posttraumatic stress disorder.' In B. Van der Kolk, A. C. McFarlane and L. Weisaeth (eds.) *Traumatic Stress: The Effects of Overwhelming Experience on Mind, Body and Society*, 303–327. New York: Guilford Press.

Volavka, J., Crown, P., Dornbush, R., Feldstein, S. and Fink, M. (1973) 'EEG, heart rate and mood change ("high") after cannabis.' *Psychopharmacologia 32*, 1, 11–25.

Wackermann, J., Putz, P., Buchi, S., Strauch, I. and Lehmann, D. (2002) 'Brain electrical activity and subjective experience during altered states of consciousness: ganzfeld and hypnagogic states.' *International Journal of Psychophysiology 46*, 2, 123–146.

Walker, A. (1979) 'Music and the unconscious.' *British Medical Journal 2*, December, 1641–1643.

Walter, T. and Davie, G. (1998) 'The religiosity of women in the modern West.' British Journal of Sociology 49, 4, 640–660.

Waskow, I. E., Olsson, J. E., Salzman, C. and Katz, M. M. (1970) 'Psychological effects of tetrahydrocannabinol.' *Archives of General Psychiatry 22*, 2, 97–107.

Weber, K. (1974) 'Veränderungen des Musikerlebens in der experimentellen Psychose (Psylocibin) und ihre Bedeutung für die Musikpsychologie.' In G. H. Revers and W. C. Simon (eds.) *Neue Wege der Musiktherapie*, 201–225. Düsseldorf, Wien: Econ Verlag.

Webster, P. (2001) 'Marijuana and music: a speculative exploration.' *Journal of Cannabis Therapeutics 1*, 2, 105.

Weil, A. (1998) *The Natural Mind*. Boston: Houghton Mifflin.

Weil, G.M., Metzner, R. and Leary, T. (eds.) (1965) *The Psychedelic Reader*. New York: University Books.

Weir, D.R. (1991) *Trance: From Magic to Technology*. Ann Arbor, MI: Trans Media. (For a summary, see 'A Suggested Model for Trance.' www.trance.edu/theory.htm)

Weitzenhoffer, A.M. and Hilgard, E.R. (1959) *Stanford Hypnotic Susceptibility Scale, for Use in Research Investigations in the Field of Hypnotic Phenomena*. Palo Alto, CA: Consulting Psychologists Press.

Weitzenhoffer, A.M. and Hilgard, E.R. (1963) *Stanford Profile Scales of Hypnotic Susceptibility: Forms I and II, To Provide Measures of Differential Susceptibility to a Variety of Suggestions Within the Induced Hypnotic State*. Palo Alto, CA: Consulting Psychologists Press.

Welsh, J., Yuen, G., Placantonakis, D., Vu, T., Haiss, F., O'Hearn, E., Molliver, M. and Aicher, S. (2002) 'Why do Purkinje cells die so easily after global brain ischemia? Aldolase C, EAAT4, and the cerebellar contribution to posthypoxic myoclonus.' *Advances in Neurology 89*, 331–59.

West, M. A. (1980) 'Meditation and the EEG.' *Psychological Medicine 10*, 2, 369–375.

West, T.M. (1994) 'Psychological issues in hospice music therapy. Special Issue: Psychiatric music therapy.' *Music Therapy Perspectives 12*, 2, 117–124.

Westermann, G. and Reck Miranda, E. (2004) 'A new model of sensorimotor coupling in the development of speech.' *Brain and Language 89*, 2, 393–400.

Whinnery, J. (1997) 'Psychophysiologic correlates of unconsciousness and near-death experiences.' *Journal of Near-Death Studies 15*, 4, 231–258.

White, W. (1996) *Pathways from the Culture of Addiction to the Culture of Recovery*. Center City: Hazeldon Publishers.

Whiteley, S. (1992) *The Space Between the Notes: Rock and the Counter Culture*. London: Routledge.

Whiteley, S. (1997) 'Altered sounds.' In A. Melechi (ed.) *Psychedelia Britannica*, 120–142. London: Turnaround.

WHO (1990) 'Cancer pain relief and palliative care.' In W. E. Committee (eds) *WHO Technical Report Series 804*, 1–75. Geneva: World Health Organisation.

Winick, C. (1959) 'The Use of Drugs by Jazz Musicians.' *Social Problems 7*, 240–253.

Winick, C. (1961) 'How high the moon: jazz and drugs.' *Antioch Review* Spring, 53–68.

Winick, C. and Nyswander, M. (1961) 'Psychotherapy of successful musicians who are drug addicts.' *American Journal of Orthopsychiatry 31*, 622–636.

Winkelman, M. J. (1986) 'Trance states: a theoretical model and cross-cultural analysis.' *Ethos 14*, 174–203.

Zemtsovsky, I. I. (1986) 'The theory of perception and ethnomusicological practice.' *Sovetskaya Musyka 3*, 62–63.

Zinberg, N.E. (1984) *Drug, Set, and Setting: The Basis for Controlled Intoxicant Use*. New Haven: Yale University Press.

The Contributors

David Aldridge is Chair for qualitative research in Medicine at the Faculty of Medicine, University of Witten-Herdecke. He specializes in developing research methods for various therapeutic initiatives including creative arts therapies, complementary medicine and nursing. He teaches and supervises research in medicine, music therapy, creative arts and nursing.

He initially trained in Fine Arts, and his interests have since extended to photography and large format print media, with a focus on landscape photography. He is currently working on 'Stations of the Cross'; a series based on Australian landscapes.

With the aim of broadening the audience for creative arts therapies, David has created a website, www.musictherapyworld.net, which includes an electronic journal, free access to a variety of complementary medicine databases and information about music therapy worldwide.

Dalia Cohen is retired from the Hebrew University Department of Musicology and the Jerusalem Academy of Music. She graduated from the Academy of Music in Tel-Aviv in music theory and piano performance and gained a Ph.D. in musicology and an M.Sc. in physics and mathematics from the Hebrew University.

Her research interests are Arab music in theory and practice; music theory; learned and natural musical schemata; style (of different cultures, periods, etc.) as determined by both aesthetic ideals and cognitive constraints; ERP (event-related brain potential) responses to musical stimuli; the musical language of Bach; music and speech; expression of categories of emotions in music; birdcalls and musical rules; performance practice; and music education.

Marlene Dobkin de Rios is a medical anthropologist and specialist in Peruvian Amazonian healing, and is currently Associate Clinical Professor of Psychiatry & Human Behavior at the University of California, Irvine. She is a licensed psychotherapist specializing in Hispanic mental health issues. Dr. de Rios has authored several papers and book chapters on music and hallucinogenic healing.

Jörg Fachner is Senior Research Fellow at the Department for Qualitative Research in Medicine, University of Witten-Herdecke. He is Managing Editor of the music therapy research and service site www.musictherapyworld.net, and Editor of the eJournal www.musictherapytoday.com.

He studied social and educational sciences and formerly worked as a research assistant in physiology. He finished his doctoral thesis on cannabis and music perception in an EEG investigation at the Chair for Qualitative Research in Medicine in 2001. Jörg's research interests and publications focus on qualitative research aspects of music, therapy and medicine; music physiology and psychology; youth and pop culture; altered states of consciousness; transcultural psychiatry; and anthropology of the body.

Tsvia Horesh was born in the US and grew up in Israel. She qualified as a music therapist at the David Yellin College in Jerusalem in 1990, and has been working in the field of addiction treatment and rehabilitation with adolescent and adult substance abusers since 1995.

She has recently finished a research thesis on 'The many meanings of music in the lives of substance abusers undergoing treatment and rehabilitation', and has published and lectured on related subjects at music therapy congresses in Israel, Italy, England and Canada.

Uwe Maas has worked as a clinical pediatrician in Lübeck, Berlin, Moers and Witten since 1985, after training in systemic family therapy. Following his working visits to Bangladesh (1992) and the Albert Schweitzer Hospital in Gabon (1998), he developed friendships with traditional Mitsogho healers, and his interest in their practices led him to be initiated into the Missoko men's cult in 2001. Dr Maas is a classical and folk guitarist and violinist, and is the father of two sons.

Lucanne Magill is Manager of the music therapy program at the Integrative Medicine Service, Memorial Sloan-Kettering Cancer Center, where she provides clinical and educational services. She has been working closely with cancer patients and families since 1973 and developed MSKCC's music therapy program. She has conducted research, lectured internationally and has published numerous papers on topics relating to music therapy, cancer and palliative care. She is Workshop Leader for Cancer Care, NY and is a doctoral candidate at New York University. She is per diem music therapist at Cabrini Hospice NY, where she is also conducting research on music therapy and spirituality.

John J. Pilch is Professorial Lecturer in the Department of Theology, Georgetown University, Washington DC since 1993. He is the author of numerous articles, book reviews, and books including Visions and Healing in the Acts of the Apostles, How the Early Believers Experienced God and Healing in the New Testament: Insights from Medical and Mediterranean Anthropology. He studies voice with Mary Ruzicka Crook (Timonium, MD) and currently sings with the Baltimore Opera Company Chorus, the Baltimore Choral Arts Society and the Cathedral of Mary our Queen Choir.

Marko Punkanen is a social educator, music therapist, dance/movement therapist and Eye Movement Desensitization and Reprocessing (EMDR) therapist, working in a private practice in Lahti, Finland. He works mainly with children, youngsters and young adults with traumatic background and with different psychiatric problems. His special interest is how traumatic background affects and is related to addiction behavior.

He studied music therapy in Sibelius Academy and in Jyväskyla University. In addition to his therapy practice, he is also a music therapy and dance/movement therapy trainer and is currently undertaking doctoral studies in music therapy at the University of Jyväskyla, Finland. He is also currently training as a traumapsychotherapist.

Alla Sokolova is a specialist in ethnomusicology. She is Assistant Professor at the Institute of the Arts at Adyghea State University, a member of the Russian Union of Composers, and the author of more than 100 scholarly and 200 popular works. These works are devoted to an analysis of the Adygh and Cossack cultures, as well as to modern composition.

Alla graduated with honors from the Department of Theory and Composition at Alma-Ata State University. In 1994 she completed post-graduate courses at the Russian Institute of the History of the Arts in St. Petersburg. Since 1979 she has lived and worked in Maikop (Adyghea Republic, Russia).

Süster Strubelt wrote her MA thesis on Iboga healing ceremonies in Gabon, and was initiated into the Mabanji women's cult of the Mitsogho in 2003. After completing her initial studies in sociology and psychology, Süster worked as a journalist in Central America and for a radio station in Germany. She trained in systemic family therapy, before wokring as a psychologist in a children's hospital and facility for supervised living for children and youth.

Csaba Szabó is an associate professor at Debrecen University Institute of Psychology in Hungary, where he lectures on learning and memory, thinking, experimental psychology and altered states of consciousness. He is currently undertaking research in the field of hypnosis, EEG and laterality problems, and the effects of induction styles on subjective experiences. He trained in hypnosis, autogenic training and meditation, and also works as a psychotherapist at a private practice.

Subject Index

Page numbers in *italics* refer to figures, illustrations and tables.

Author Index